DIVINE EMBRACE

Cover Design by: Sean Osmond

Published by Mirror Word Publishing

Francois' ministry page is www.mirrorword.net

See also www.mirrorfriends.com

Highly recommended books by the same author: Mirror Bible, God Believes in You, Done!
The Eagle Story, by Lydia and Francois du Toit, beautifully illustrated by Carla Krige

Both The Mirror Bible and Divine Embrace are also abailable on Kindle

Subscribe to Francois facebook updates http://www.facebook.com/francois.toit

The Mirror Translation fb group http://www.facebook.com/groups/179109018883718/

ISBN 978-0-9921769-1-4

New Revised and Updated DIVINE EMBRACE
A Bouquet of Inspirational Mirror-thoughts
Chapters 3-6 are 4 messages I preached 21 years ago
these were transcribed from audiotapes
New chapters include the following:
There is nothing wrong with the human race
What about the sinful nature?
A new perspective on the New Birth
The great awakening. The Metanoia-moment!
The logic of God's economy of inclusion
How does this gospel translate into a transformed life?
Thoughts on hell

To my darling Lydia and our amazing children,
Renaldo, Tehilla, Christo and Stefan

TABLE OF CONTENTS

Introduction

Religion thrives on two lies: distance and delay.

This book celebrates the initiative that God undertook to cancel every possible definition of distance. Emmanuel is introduced to a hostile humanity as the lover of their lives. Their sins did not distract from his extravagant love.

Our calendar acknowledges the fact that 2000 years ago human history was divided into a before and after Christ.

While the vast expanse cannot even begin to measure or define him, the invisible God of creation has made his image and likeness known in the only possible space wherein his being can be fully and accurately unveiled: human life.

The mission of Jesus was not to begin the Christian religion but to reveal and redeem the image and likeness of God in human form. He did not come as an example for us but of us. Much of popular Christian doctrine reduces the life and teaching of Jesus to yet another 'display-window' message, while the very intent of God was to uncover the blueprint life of our design in Christ as in a mirror, where he is introduced to us not as Christ in history, or Christ in outer space, nor even as Christ in a future event, but as Christ in you! This alone completes your every expectation! Col 1:27. In John 14:20 Jesus announces the conclusion of his amazing mission: his brilliant act of salvation was not to reserve a place for a few in a distant heaven, but to redeem our oneness! He boldly declares, "I and the Father are one! If you have seen me you have seen the Father." Anything we thought that we knew about God that is unlike Jesus is not God. "In that day (the day that you hear the good news) you will know that I am in my Father and you in me and I in you!"

He is closer to you than your next breath! Now distance is replaced with oneness. Oneness is not the end result of our diligent striving to get closer to God; oneness is the fruit of his initiative in reconciling humanity to their Maker. The good news announces our moment by moment point of reference in this life. Intimate romance is ours now and for all eternity! "He is not far from each one of us!" says Paul to a group of idol worshiping philosophers in Athens. Acts 17:23-31. Every sacrifice ever brought in any religious context is an appeal to innocence; be it as fragile or momentarily as it may. In Jesus Christ God gave proof of mankind's redeemed innocence by raising him from the dead! Our sins resulted in his death; his resurrection is proof of our innocence. Rom 4:25. In the economy of God every single human life is equally represented and included in Christ. God is not more Emmanuel to some than what he is to others! In the light of the good news there can no longer remain an 'us and them'! Nothing that you can ever do can make you more God's, and nothing that God can ever do can make him more yours!

The thought of you intrigues your Maker with delight! Faith has nothing to do with our ability to concentrate on God for at least five uninterrupted minutes; faith is my glorious awakening to the fact that my Maker is mindful of me! He cannot get me out of his mind!

Jesus is what God believes about you! Jesus is God's mind made up about the human race! Awake to innocence, awake to oneness!

His words are kisses; his kisses words. Everything about him delights me, thrills me through and through! Song of Songs 5:14,15 (The Message)

The Mirror Message

People often ask me how we got started in this wonderful mirror message. There are many moments of reflection and impression that triggered our awareness and appreciation of God's love initiative. Our parents and others have laid such a sure foundation in demonstrating the simplicity of the love of God and his desire to bring about closeness and friendship; but I must mention four outstanding moments that are deeply impressed in my memory:

The first was in October 1978 during a devotional time. I remember how it dawned on me that we cannot even begin to understand the cross until we realize Genesis 1:26. Humankind was made in the image and likeness of God. It was not the pitiful state of mankind that moved God to pay such a ridiculous price for humanity's redemption; it was his love knowledge of our likeness that persuaded this act. My mother used to say, "The lost coin never lost its original value!" The man who redeemed the hidden treasure sold all that he had to buy that field! Math 13:44. I began to see that while we reduce the cross of Christ to a mere historic and sentimental reference, the amazing mystery of what actually happened there remains veiled from us.

I was reading systematically through the Bible at that time, doing two chapters daily from both the Old and the New Testaments. Part of my reading that morning was from 1 Kings 6. Verse 7 spoke powerfully to me, "When the house was built, it was with stone prepared at the quarry; so that neither hammer nor axe nor any tool of iron was heard in the temple, while it was being built." What struck me was the thought that enough happened to the stone in the quarry to cut it to such precision that no further chiseling was needed! How do we define the quarry in our theology? So much of our sincere Christian doctrine encourages us to believe that God has to daily employ the 'hammer and chisel' to continue to chip away little bit by little bit of our characters to hopefully eventually get us ready for heaven one day! God would use anything, like your wife, or your boss, or neighbor, even your neighbor's dog sometimes, we believed!

If our perfection and 'sanctification' depended on how many years we spend in some wilderness, whether domestic or financial or some human crisis we are facing, then sanctification would be reduced to the law of works and human experience again, and we would have to pray and play for time! We would need to grow as old as possible, because this is gonna take at least a lifetime!

In the light of the finished work of Christ I became convinced that any doctrine that distracts from the success of the cross was a waste of time to pursue. The only possible way we can delay the glory that follows the cross is by underestimating what happened there when Jesus died and cried: "It is finished!" If it did not happen in the death and resurrection of Jesus it is not going to happen anywhere else! In God's economy Jesus died humanity's death, once and for all! None of the rulers of the religious system of the day understood this mystery; if they did they would never have crucified the Lord of glory! 1 Corinthians 2:8, 1 Cor 1:30.

While the cross cannot be reversed, man's understanding of how included we were in his death and resurrection can be veiled; yet this 'veiling' can only happen with your permission! Paul says that the minds of the 'unbelievers' are veiled from seeing the light of the gospel. Unbelief simply means to believe a lie about yourself! Just like Israel did in Numbers 13:33. See also 2 Cor 4:4.

I was in a mission at that time where inner healing, spiritual warfare and deliverance were very popular teachings; I began to see how many of our pet doctrines and interpretations clashed with the simple message of the cross.

If we do not understand that the body on the cross was the document of humanity's guilt, we will never understand how God succeeded to disarm the devil and cancel his claim to blackmail human life, once and for all!

It has become fashion to preach a defeated devil back into business again, almost as if Pharaoh was not thoroughly beaten in the prophetic picture of Israel's deliverance! Israel did not die in the desert because of an inferior deliverance out of Pharaoh's hand! Ex 14:13 "And Moses said to the people, "Fear not, stand firm, and see the salvation of the LORD, which he will work for you today; for the Egyptians whom you see today, you shall never see again." Israel wasted forty years living a neutralized life in the wilderness and that entire generation except two died because they believed a lie about themselves and underestimated their salvation! Num 13:33, Josh 2:11, Hebrews 2:3. The supernatural is proof of God's mercy and not proof of faith; they died because of unbelief.

The next passage in my reading that day was from 1Peter 2, and I quote v 2-5 "Like newborn babies, long for the pure spiritual milk, that by it you may grow up to salvation; for you have tasted the kindness of the Lord. Come to him, to that living stone, rejected by men but in God's sight chosen and precious; and like living stones be yourselves built into a spiritual house." Jesus is the living stone and we are like him! Even as new born babies we share his perfection; no chiseling required, only nurturing! We grow up by our addiction to the undiluted pure milk of the gospel message that proclaims how Jesus fulfilled and perfected the prophetic word of our salvation. Peter says in the previous chapter that we were born anew when Jesus was raised from the dead! What God spoke prophetically about the sufferings of Christ and the subsequent glory is the living and incorruptible seed of the Word. This truth realized awakens us into newness of life! Col 1:6. In the calculation of God we died with him and were raised together with him! Hosea 6:2, Ephesians 2:5. Notice that Peter writes, "Be ye built into a spiritual house" he doesn't tell us to first get chiseled and shaped in order to eventually become something useful to God! The language of the Old Testament was, "Do in order to become", while the language of the New Testament is, "Be because of what was done!" We do not grow in completeness; we only grow in the knowledge of our completeness!

It is interesting to note that it is Mr Rock himself (Petros) who writes about us being living stones! When asked who he thought Jesus the son of man was, it was revealed to Simon that Jesus was the Messiah, the son of the living God. Immediately Jesus then introduced Simon to the fact that even he, the son of Jonah was

8

hewn from the same Rock! Deuteronomy 32:18 You were unmindful of the Rock that begot you, and you forgot the God who gave you birth. Isa 51:1 "Hearken to me, you who pursue deliverance, you who seek the LORD; look to the rock from which you were hewn, and to the quarry from which you were dug." It is upon this same Rock that God builds his ekklesia and the gates of hades (ignorance) shall not prevail against his ekklesia's claim! Jesus has come to introduce man to himself again, because we have forgotten what manner of man we are! "By the waters of reflection my soul remembers who I am by God's design" Ps 23:2,3

The second memorable encounter was during our honeymoon in January 1979 in the Bourke's Luck area in Mpumalanga. Lydia and I met a nature conservation officer who told us the remarkable story of how they released a Black eagle that was in the Pretoria zoo for ten years. This happened about a week prior to our visit. She told us how excited they were when the bird finally arrived from Pretoria in its wooden crate. They knew that this was the day for the eagle to return to the life and environment of its design. It would never need to waste another day in a cage.

Their excitement soon turned to frustration when, after opening the cage, the bird just sat there with blank eyes and refused to fly! This continued for several hours. The ten years of caged life must have trapped this poor bird's mind in an invisible enclosure! How could they get the eagle to realize that it was indeed free? Then suddenly she looked up, and in the distance they heard the call of another eagle; immediately the zoo-eagle took off in flight!

No flying lessons are required when truth is realized! This story gives such clarity and content to the fact that Jesus came to the planet not to upgrade the cage of Jewish or any other religion by starting a new brand called, 'the Christian religion'; but to be the incarnate voice of the likeness and image of God in human form! He came to reveal and redeem the image of God in us! His mission was to mirror the blueprint of our design, not as an example for us but of us! Col.1:15, 2:9,10. In God's faith mankind is associated in Christ even before the foundation of the world. Jesus died humanity's death and when the stone was rolled away, we were raised together with him! Every human life is fully represented in him! Hosea 6:2, Ephesians 1:4, and 2:5,6. "While we were still dead in our sins he made us alive together with him and raised us together with him!" If the gospel is not the voice of the free eagle it is not the gospel.

The third vivid memory that molded this message in me was a few years later. In 1983 I was asked to pastor a church in White River, Mpumalanga. Until that time I was preaching in the schools of Kangwane along the border of the Kruger National park and I would speak only once or perhaps twice a week to the same audience. I felt a bit worried at the prospect that I would now have to speak to the same group of people almost daily. One morning I was specifically praying about this when God reminded me of the five loaves and two fish miracle. I realized that Jesus just continued to multiply the same five loaves and two fish! He did not at some point run out and then had to ask for a few more fish or another loaf! Everyone enjoyed exactly the same miracle meal. The numbers two and five somehow prompted me to read 2 Corinthians 5. I already knew verse 17 off by heart but my eyes were drawn to verse 16. It felt like I was reading it for the first time in my life! When I read the first line, I started weeping as God began to open my understanding to what it was that caused Paul to say, "From now on therefore..." That morning became my personal, "From now on therefore" moment! "From now on therefore, I no longer know anyone after the flesh!" Wow, I mean Paul was so aware of people's natural pedigrees; even his own prominent lineage dwarfed into insignificance when he realized that whoever he was by natural birth, died when Jesus died. One has died for all can only mean that all have died!" I was totally overwhelmed with this thought and realized that this simple calculation was the only possible conclusion of the gospel according to God's point of view. I had always thought that verse 17 said, "If any man be in Christ he is a new creature!" I suddenly realized that Paul didn't say that! Instead he said, THEREFORE if any man be in Christ! The 'if' is not a condition but a conclusion! Mankind is associated in Christ to begin with! Eph 1:4

If in God's economy one has died for all then we were included in Jesus' death before anyone but God believed it! In Eph 2:5 Paul makes this astounding statement, "While we were still dead in our sins, God made us alive together with Christ!"

No wonder then that Paul could encourage Titus to speak evil of no man, to avoid quarreling and to show perfect courtesy towards all men; for we ourselves were once ignorant! Titus 3:2-5. The only difference in who we are now and who we were then is in what we now know to be true about us! What is true in him is equally true in us! 1John2:7,8. This message sets the stage for New Testament ministry! When Jesus motivated his own ministry nothing could better illustrate his mission but the three parables of Luke 15. The stories of the lost sheep, coin and son clearly confirm original ownership and the fact that their lost condition did not cancel their original value! From there Paul's urgency declares, "the love of Christ constrains me." 2 Cor. 5:14. In the most dramatic fashion God persuades Peter to no longer call any man unholy or unclean! Acts 10:28. The Lamb of God has taken away the sin of the world! It is about time that the good news of great joy is proclaimed with bold clarity! Mankind is the property of God, both by design and redemption! "The earth is fully the Lord's, the world and those who dwell in it!" Psalm 24:1 It is so important to ponder the Genesis of it all, where did we begin? What an amazing thought to consider that he knew us before he even formed us in our mother's womb. Our brief history on this planet did not introduce us to him! We are his love dream…how easy it becomes then to understand the gospel and why our Father paid a non-negotiable price to redeem his own! He bought the whole field because only he knew of the treasure it holds! Jer 1:5, 2 Cor 4:7, Mth 13:44.

Fourthly, the mirror message became a very prominent ingredient of our ministry focus in the next few years. It dawned on me that James, the younger brother of Jesus also once knew his brother merely from a human point of view; John 7:5 "For even his brothers did not believe in him!" But after the resurrection, Jesus specifically also appears to James. 1 Cor 15:7.

The enormous impact of this encounter prompted James to discover and write that God birthed us by the Word of truth, and to hear this word is to see the face of your birth as in a mirror! James understood that what was veiled from us in the law of Moses was now redeemed in us in the law of perfect liberty! We are no longer window'shopping. While the Old Testament represented a display window of promises, the New Testament unveils mankind's redeemed likeness and innocence as in a mirror. The one who gazes deeply into this law of our perfect liberty discovers the freedom of his redeemed identity!

James shows how contradiction would attempt to veil a person's mind in unbelief and give one a 'valid' excuse to walk away from the influence of the mirror word and thus immediately forget what manner of person you are. Jas 1:23 The difference between a mere spectator and a participator is that both of them hear the same voice and perceive in its message the face of their own genesis reflected as in a mirror. Jas 1:24 They realize that they are looking at themselves, but for the one it seems just too good to be true, he departs *(back to his old way of seeing himself)* never giving another thought to the man he saw there in the mirror. Jas 1:25 The other one is mesmerized by what he sees, he is captivated by the effect of a law that frees man from the obligation to the old written code that restricted him to his own efforts and willpower. No distraction or contradiction can dim the impact of what he sees in that mirror concerning the law of perfect liberty (the law of faith) that now frees him to get on with the act of living the life *(of his original design.)* He finds a new spontaneous lifestyle; the poetry of practical living. *(The law of perfect liberty is the image and likeness of God revealed in Christ, now redeemed in man as in a mirror. Look deep enough into that law of faith that you may see there in its perfection a portrait that so resembles the original that He becomes distinctly visible in the spirit of your mind and in the face of every man you behold Mesmerized, para-kupto, para, a preposition indicating close proximity, a thing proceeding from a sphere of influence, with a suggestion of union of place of residence, to sprung from its author and giver, originating from, denoting the point from which an action originates, intimate connection, and **kupto**, to bend, stoop down to view at close scrutiny, parameno, to remain under the influence. Freedom, eleutheria, without obligation.)* Mirror Bible

Man began in God

We are not the invention of our parents.

It is not our brief history on planet earth that introduces us to God; he knew us before he formed us in our mother's womb! Jer 1:5.

To consider that God imagined and knew me before time began is the most liberating thought! It immediately gives substance to faith and relevance to the gospel. I matter to my Maker! He is mindful of me!

The gospel beautifully frames the picture that God painted and exhibits it in the grand gallery of our own reflections.

When God imagined you, he thought of you on equal terms as he would of himself; a being whose intimate friendship would intrigue him for eternity. Man would be partner in God's triune oneness! His image and likeness would be unmasked in human life.

Every invention begins with an original thought; you are God's original thought; you are the greatest idea that God has ever had!

Human life was fashioned in the same mold; we are the expression of the same thought. Our Author's signature and invisible image is nowhere better preserved or displayed than in our inner consciousness. Our origin traces the very imagination of God.

God is head over heels in love with you! He cannot get you out of his mind! His thoughts are consumed with you from before time began!

He fashioned you in your mother's womb when he wrote the three billion-character script of your DNA, mirrored in everyone of your seventy five trillion cells!

The first Hebrew word in the Bible, *bereshet*, from *be*, in and *rosh*, head, literally means "in the head." You are his work of art; his inspired thought. We do not invent God; he invented us!

Eph 2:10 We are engineered by his design; he molded and manufactured us in Christ. We are his workmanship, his poetry. (God finds inspired expression of Christ in us. Greek, poeima,) We are fully fit to do good, equipped to give attractive evidence of his likeness in us in everything we do. (God has done everything possible to find spontaneous and effortless expression of his character in us in our everyday lifestyle.) Mirror Bible

Every human life is equally valued and represented in Christ. He gives context and reference to our being as in a mirror, not as an example for us, but of us.

We are not merely Christ-cloned; we are individually crafted to give display to the image and likeness of our Maker within our own person, our fingerprint, our touch, our smile, and the cadence of our voice.

The mandate of Jesus was not to begin the Christian religion but to reveal and redeem the image of the invisible God in human form.

Col 1:15 In him the invisible God is made visible again; in order that every one may recognize their true origin in him; he is the firstborn of every creature. *(What darkness veiled from us he unveiled. In him we clearly see the mirror reflection of our original image and likeness redeemed. The son of his love gives evidence of his image in human form.)* Mirror Bible

The Christian calendar celebrates the moment when human history was forever divided into a before and after Christ. The Creator God visited our planet camouflaged in a human body; his mother's womb was his passport. Had he arrived in a "superman suit" his life death and resurrection would be irrelevant. He came to prove that God did not make a mistake when he made you.

Heb 4:15 As High Priest he fully identifies with us in the context of our frail human lives. Having subjected it to close scrutiny, he proved that the human frame was master over sin. His sympathy with us is not to be seen as excusing weaknesses that are the result of a faulty design, but rather as a trophy to humanity. Mirror Bible

As head of the human race he represents every human life; he represents the original blueprint of the life of our design.

The most labeled sinners in society were irresistibly attracted to him; what the prostitutes and publicans witnessed in his life mirrored the redeemed integrity of their own; they knew that what they thought to be their life was a lie.

In all three parables that Jesus told in Luke 15, the word "lost" immediately implies ownership. You cannot be lost unless you belong! The lost coin never lost its original inscription and value! "Show me a coin, whose image and inscription does it bear? Return to Caesar what belongs to Caesar and to God what belongs to God." Luke 22:24,25.

Mankind is the property of God. A thief never takes ownership.

Psa 24:1 A Psalm of David. The earth is the LORD's and the fullness thereof, the world and those who dwell therein. RSV

Mat 13:44 "The kingdom of heaven is like treasure hidden in a field, which a man found and covered up; then in his joy he goes and sells all that he has and buys that field. RSV *(Greek, Agricultural field)* The field was defined for many years by its agricultural value. But there is so much more to the field than what meets the eye!

We have this treasure in earthen vessels, says Paul in 2 Cor 4:7, but in verse 4 he says that the religious systems of this world have blindfolded us with unbelief to keep us from seeing the light of the gospel! The gospel reveals the glory of God in the face of the man Jesus Christ. Every human life is an individual masterpiece; a selfportrait of God, hidden in the very DNA of their design! This is what Jesus came to reveal and redeem; the image of God in human form, not as in a display window, but as in a mirror!

13

He sold all he had and bought the field! Now the field is all he has. You are bought at the highest price.

The theme of prophetic scripture pointed to the sufferings of Christ and the subsequent glory. The glory of God is his image and likeness redeemed in human form.

The heavens declare his glory, night to night exhibits the giant solar testimony that is mathematically precise, revealing that God knew before time was the exact moment he would enter our history as a man, and the exact moment the Messiah would expire on the cross!

Seven hundred years BC the prophet Isaiah saw his slaughtered body on the cross as the redemptive love of God; Jesus is the Scapegoat of the human race:

1Pet 1:10 The prophets who prophesied of the grace that was to be yours searched and inquired about this salvation;

1Pet 1:11 they inquired what person or time was indicated by the Spirit of Christ within them when predicting the sufferings of Christ and the subsequent glory. RSV

Isa 53:3 He was despised and rejected by men; a man of sorrows, and acquainted with grief; and as one from whom men hide their faces he was despised, and we esteemed him not. Isa 53:4 Surely he has borne our agony and carried our sorrows; yet we esteemed him stricken, smitten by God, and afflicted. Isa 53:5 But he was wounded for our transgressions, he was bruised for our iniquities; upon him was the chastisement that made us whole, and with his stripes we are healed. Isa 53:6 The Shepherd never forsook the sheep! All we like sheep have gone astray; we have turned everyone to his own way; and the LORD has laid on him the iniquity of us all. RSV The horror of humanity's sin was laid upon him.

In Psalm 22 David dramatically prophesies detail of his death on the cross, and concludes in verse 27, "The ends of the earth shall remember and turn to the Lord".

2 Cor 3:16 The moment anyone [1]returns to the Lord the veil is gone! *(The word, [1]epistrepho means to return to where we've wandered from; "we all like sheep have gone astray." Jesus is God unveiled in human form. [Col 1:15] See also Hebrews 8:1, "The conclusion of all that has been said points us to an exceptional Person, who towers far above the rest in the highest office of heavenly greatness. He is the executive authority of the majesty of God. 8:2 The office he now occupies is the one which the Moses-model resembled prophetically. He ministers in the holiest place in God's true tabernacle of worship. Nothing of the old man-made structure can match its perfection. 8:10 Now, instead of documenting my laws on stone, I will chisel them into your mind and engrave them in your inner consciousness; it will no longer be a one-sided affair. I will be your God and you will be my people, not by compulsion but by mutual desire." See James 1:25, "Those who gaze into the mirror reflection of the face of their birth is captivated by the effect of a law that frees them from the obligation to the old written code that restricted them to their our own efforts and willpower. No distraction or contradiction can dim the impact of what they see in that mirror concerning the law of perfect liberty [the law of faith] that now frees them to get on with the act of living the life [of their original design]. They find a new*

14

spontaneous lifestyle; the poetry of practical living." [The law of perfect liberty is the image and likeness of God revealed in Christ, now redeemed in human life as in a mirror.])

2 Cor 3:17 The Lord and the Spirit are one; his Lordship sanctions our freedom. A freedom from rules chiseled in stone to the voice of our redeemed design echoing in our hearts!

2 Cor 3:18 The days of window-shopping are over! In him every face is [1]unveiled. In [2]gazing with wonder at the [5]blueprint likeness of God displayed in human form we suddenly realize that we are looking at ourselves! Every feature of his [3]image is [2]mirrored in us! This is the most radical [4]transformation engineered by the Spirit of the Lord; we are led [6]from an inferior [5]mind-set to the revealed [5]endorsement of our authentic identity. We are his [5]glory! *(The word, [1]anakekalumeno, is a perfect passive participle from anakalupto; ana, a preposition denoting upward, to return again, and kalupto, to uncover, unveil. The word, [2]katoptrizomenoi, is the present middle participle from katoptrizomai, meaning to gaze into a reflection, to mirror oneself. The word [4]metamorphumetha is a present passive indicative from metamorpho; meta, together with, and meros, form. [The word commonly translated for sin, hamartia, is the opposite of this as ha, means without, and meros, form.] The word, [3]eikon, translates as exact resemblance, image and likeness; eikon always assumes a prototype, that which it not merely resembles, but from that which it is drawn; [5]doxa, glory, translates as mind-set, opinion from dokeo, authentic thought. Changed 'from glory to glory', apo doxes eis doxan; eis, a point reached in conclusion; [6]apo, away from, meaning away from the glory that previously defined us, i.e. our own achievements or disappointments, to the glory of our original design that now defines us. [Paul writes in Romans 1:17 about the unveiling of God's righteousness and then says it is from faith to faith. Here he does not use the word apo, but the preposition, ek, which always denotes source or origin.] Two glories are mentioned in this chapter; the glory of the flesh, and the unfading glory of God's image and likeness redeemed in us. The fading glory represented in the dispensation of the law of Moses is immediately superseded by the unveiling of Christ in us! Some translations of this scripture reads, "we are being changed from glory to glory." This would suggest that change is gradual and will more than likely take a lifetime, which was the typical thinking that trapped Israel for forty years in the wilderness of unbelief! We cannot become more than what we already are in Christ. We do not grow more complete; we simply grow in the knowledge of our completeness! [See Col 3:10] We are not changed "from one degree of glory to another," or step by step. How long does it take the beautiful swan to awaken to the truth of its design? The ugly duckling was an illusion! Whatever it was that endorsed the 'ugly duckling' mindset, co-died together with Christ!)* Mirror Bible

The "ugly duckling" saw reflected in the water the truth that freed the swan!

Ps 23 says, "He leads me beside still waters, and restores my soul" or this can be translated as, "by the waters of reflection my soul remembers who I am".

James 1:17 Without exception God's gifts are only good, its perfection cannot be improved upon. They come [1]from above, *(where we originate from)* proceeding like light rays from its source, the Father of lights. With whom there is no distortion or even a shadow of shifting to obstruct or intercept the light; no hint of a hidden agenda. *(The word, [1]anouthen, means, from above [Jn 3:3, 13]. Man is not the product of his mother's womb; man began in God.)*

15

James 1:18 It was his delightful [1]resolve to give birth to us; we were conceived by the [2]unveiled logic of God. We lead the exhibition of his handiwork, like first fruits introducing the rest of the harvest he anticipates. *(The word, [1]boulomai, means the affectionate desire and deliberate resolve of God. Truth, [2]alethea, from a, negative + lanthano, meaning hidden; that which is unveiled; the word of truth.)*

John 1:1 To go back to the very [1]beginning is to find the [2]Word already [3]present there. The [2]Logic of God defines the only possible place where humankind can trace their [4]genesis. The Word is [3]I am; God's eternal [2]eloquence echoes and [5]concludes in him. The Word equals God. *([1]arche, to be first in order, time, place or rank. The Word, [2]logos, was [5]"with" God; here John uses the Greek preposition [5]pros, which indicates direction, forward to; that is toward the destination of the relation. Face-to-face. "For as the rain and the snow come down from heaven and return, having accomplished their purpose (canceling distance and saturating the earth and awakening the seed in the soil), so shall my word be that proceeds from my mouth." [Isa 55:10, 11]). The destiny of the word is always to return face to face. Three times in this sentence John uses the imperfect of [3]eimi, namely [3]en, to be, which conveys no idea of origin for God or for the Logos, but simply continuous existence. Quite a different verb egeneto, "became," appears in John 1:14 for the beginning of the Incarnation of the Logos. See the distinction sharply drawn in John 8:58, "before Abraham was born ([1]genesthai from egeneto) I am" (eimi, timeless existence.)*

John 1:2 The beginning mirrors the Word face to face with God. *(Nothing that is witnessed in the Word distracts from who God is. "If you have seen me, you have seen the Father." [John 14:9])*

John 1:3 The Logos is the source; everything commences in him. He remains the exclusive Parent reference to their genesis. There is nothing original, except the Word!

John 1:4 His life is the light that defines our lives. *(In his life man discovers the light of life.)*

John 1:5 The darkness was pierced and could not comprehend or diminish the-light. *(Darkness represents man's ignorance of his redeemed identity and innocence [Isa 9:2-4, Isa 60:1-3, Eph 3:18, Col 1:13-15].)*

John 1:6 Then there was this man John *(Jesus' cousin)* commissioned by God;

John 1:7 his mission was to draw attention to the light of their lives so that what they witnessed in him would cause them to believe *(in their original life redeemed again).*

John 1:8 His ministry was not to distract from the light, as if he himself was the light but rather to point out the light Source.

John 1:9 A new day for humanity has come. The authentic light of life that illuminates everyone was about to dawn in the world! *(This day would begin our calendar and record the fact that human history would forever be divided into before and after Christ. The incarnation would make the image of God visible in human form. In him who is the blueprint of our lives there is more than enough light to displace the darkness in every human life. He is the true light that enlightens every man! [Col 1:15; 2:9, 10; 2 Cor 4:6])*

John 1:10 Although no one took any notice of him, he was no stranger to the world; he always was there and is himself the author of all things.

John 1:11 It was not as though he arrived on a foreign planet; he came to his own, yet his own did not [1]recognize him. *(Ps 24:1, "The earth is the Lord's and the fullness thereof, the world and those who dwell in it [RSV]." The word, [1]paralambano, comes from para, a preposition indicating close proximity, a thing proceeding from a sphere of influence, with a suggestion of union of place of residence, to have sprung from its author and giver, originating from, denoting the point from which an action originates, intimate connection; and lambano, to comprehend, grasp, to identify with.)*

John 1:12 Everyone who [1]realizes their association in him, [6]convinced that he is their [2]original life and that [7]his name defines them, [5]in them he [3]endorses the fact that they are indeed his [4]offspring, [2]begotten of him; he [3]sanctions the legitimacy of their sonship. *(The word often translated, to receive, [1]lambano, means to comprehend, grasp, to identify with. This word suggests that even though he came to his own, there are those who do not [1]grasp their true [2]origin revealed in him, and like the many Pharisees they behave like children of a foreign father, the father of lies [Jn 8: 44].*

Neither God's legitimate fatherhood of man nor his ownership is in question; man's indifference to his true [2]origin is the problem. This is what the Gospel addresses with utmost clarity in the person of Jesus Christ. Jesus has come to introduce man to himself again; humanity has forgotten what manner of man he is by design! [Jas 1:24, Deut 32:18, Ps 22:27].

The word, [2]genesthai [aorist tense] is like a snapshot taken of an event, from ginomai, to become [See 1:3]. The Logos is the source; everything commences in him. He remains the exclusive Parent reference to their genesis. There is nothing original, except the Word! Man began in God [see also Acts 17:28]. "He has come to give us understanding to know him who is true and to realize that we are in him who is true." [1 Jn 5:20].)

The word, [3]exousia, often translated "power;" as in, he gave "power" to [2]become children of God, is a compound word; and ek, always denoting origin or source and eimi, I am; thus, out of I am! This gives [3]legitimacy and authority to our sonship; [4]teknon, translated as offspring, child.

"He has given," [5]didomi, in this case to give something to someone that already belongs to them; thus, to return. The fact that they already are his own, born from above, they have their [2]beginning and their being in him is now confirmed in their realizing it! Convinced, [6]pisteo; [7]his name onoma, defines man [see Eph 3:15]. "He made to be their true selves, their child-of-God selves." — The Message)

John 1:13 These are they who discover their genesis in God beyond their natural conception! Man began in God. We are not the invention of our parents!

John 1:14 Suddenly the invisible eternal Word takes on [1]visible form! The Incarnation! In him, and now confirmed in us! The most accurate tangible display of God's eternal thought finds expression in human life! The Word became a human being; we are his address; he resides in us! He [2]captivates our gaze! The glory we see there is not a religious replica; he is the [3]authentic begotten son. *([3]monogenes begotten only by the Father and not by the flesh; in him we recognize our true beginning).* The [4]Glory *(that Adam lost)* returns in fullness! Only [5]grace can communicate truth in such complete context! *(In him we discover that we are not here by chance or ac-*

17

cident or by the desire of an earthly parent, neither are we the product of a mere physical conception; we exist by the expression of God's desire to reveal himself in the flesh. His eternal invisible Word, his Spirit-thought, [1]became flesh, [1]ginomai, as in be born and [2]theaomai, meaning to gaze upon, to perceive. We saw his glory, [4]doxa, the display of his opinion, the glory as of the original, authentic begotten of the Father, full of grace and truth. He is both the "only begotten," [3]monogenes; as in the authentic original mold, as well as the first born from the dead [Col 1:18, 1 Pet 1:3]. He is the revelation of our completeness.*

And of his fullness have we all received, grace against grace, [5]garin anti garitos, grace undeserved. For the law was given through Moses, grace and truth came through Jesus Christ. He who is in the bosom of the Father, the only original, authentic begotten of the Father; he is our guide who accurately declares and interprets the invisible God within us. Interesting that the revelation of the Incarnation in verse 14 doesn't follow verse 2 or 3, but verse 12 and 13! Genesis 1:26 is redeemed!)

John 1:15 John the Baptist raised his voice to announce emphatically that Jesus was what his ministry and prophetic message were all about. He declared that Jesus, though younger than him, ranks above him and was "born" before him, since he always was!

John 1:16 He is the source of our completeness. [1]Grace against grace! (*[1]garin anti garitos, grace undeserved. Grace prevailed against the tide of darkness due to Adam's fall. His fullness is the source of all that grace communicates as our portion, against all odds!)*

John 1:17 Against the stark backdrop of the law, with Moses representing the condemned state of mankind, Jesus Christ unveils grace and truth! (*He is the life of our design redeemed in human form).*

John 1:18 Until this moment God remained invisible to man; now the [1]authentic begotten son, (*[1]monogenes, begotten only of God)* the blueprint of man's design who represents the innermost being of God, the son who is in the bosom of the father, brings him into full view! He is the [2]official authority qualified to announce God! (*[2]eksesato, from ek, preposition denoting source, and hegeomai, official authority.)* He is our guide who accurately declares and interprets the invisible God within us.

Heb 4:6 There is only one God. He remains the ultimate Father of the universe. We are because he is. He is present in all; he is above all, through all, and in all. (*He is not far from each one of us; in him we live and move and have our being. We are indeed his offspring. [Acts 17:24-28])*

God is not the product of man's best guess; he is bigger than religion's biggest blunder or eloquence in their attempts to define him. He is beyond extinction or threat and can never be reduced to either our clever or clumsy expression of philosophy or art. Jesus reveals God as Father and Redeemer of the human race.

The New Testament is the revelation of God's initiative and grace gift to mankind. While the law-system addresses mankind in Adam, Grace reveals and addresses the same mankind in Christ.

18

The Romance of the Ages

The central theme and revelation of the Bible celebrates a relationship between God and man of the highest order, a union of absolute integrity, with no hint of distance, inferiority, guilt, condemnation or suspicion. The sacred moment, when for the first time in the history of the universe, the invisible Creator reflected his image and likeness in a fragile vessel of flesh became the reference of a presence and purpose in the earth that would dominate human history and destiny.

The origin of man is forever imprinted in the mind of God. "Before I formed you in the womb, I knew you." Jer.1:5

An inseparable association exists from before the foundation of the earth that identifies mankind in Christ. In Christ we see the original mould and intended shape of our lives, not as in a display window but as in a mirror.

Rom.8:29   He pre-designed and engineered us from the start to be jointly fashioned in the same mold and image of his son according to the exact blueprint of his thought. We see the original and intended pattern of our lives preserved in his Son. He is the firstborn from the same womb that reveals our genesis. He confirms that we are the invention of God. *(We were born anew when he was raised from the dead! [1 Peter 1:3] His resurrection co-reveals our common genesis as well as our redeemed innocence. [Rom 4:25 and Acts 17:31] No wonder then that he is not ashamed to call us his brethren! We share the same origin [Heb 2:11], and, "In him we live and move and have our being, we are indeed his offspring!" [Acts 17:28].)*

You are the expression of the greatest idea that ever was!

Gen 1:26   Then God said, "Let us make man in our image, after our likeness;

Gen 1:27   So God created man in his own image, in the image of God he created him; male and female he created them.

Gen 1:31   And God saw everything that he had made, and behold, it was very good. RSV

Eph 2:10   We are engineered by his design; he molded and manufactured us in Christ. We are his workmanship, his [1]poetry. *(God finds inspired expression of Christ in us. The Greek word for workmanship is [1]poeima.)* We are [2]fully fit to do good, equipped to give attractive evidence of his likeness in us in everything we do. *(God has done everything possible to find spontaneous and effortless expression of his character in us in our everyday lifestyle. The word, [2]proetoimatso, translates a notion that God has prepared a highway for us to lead us out like kings, just like the Oriental custom, where people would go before a king to level the roads to make it possible for the king to journey with ease and comfort. [Isa 40:3-5])*

Col 1:15   In him the image and likeness of God is made visible in human life in order that every one may recognize their true origin in him. He is the firstborn of every creature. *(What darkness veiled from us he unveiled. In him we clearly see the mir-*

ror reflection of our original life. The son of his love gives accurate evidence of his image in human form. God can never again be invisible!)

Col 1:19 The full measure of everything God has in mind for man indwells him. Mirror Bible

("So spacious is he, so roomy, that everything of God finds its proper place in him without crowding." The Message)

Col 2:9 It is in Christ that God finds an accurate and complete expression of himself, in a human body! *(While the expanse cannot measure or define God, his exact likeness is displayed in human form. Jesus proves that human life is tailor-made for God!)*

Col 2:10 Jesus mirrors our completeness and [1]endorses our [2]true identity. He is "I am" in us. *(Isn't it amazing that God packaged completeness in "I am," mirrored in you! Delay is outdated! The word, [1]***arche***, means chief in rank. The word, [2]***exousia***, is often translated as meaning authority; its components are, **ek + eimi**, originating out of "I am." The days are over where our lives were dictated to under the rule of the law of performance and an inferior identity. [See Col 1:19] The full measure of everything God has in mind for man indwells him.* Mirror Bible

("Your own completeness is only realized in him." Phillips Translation.)

The revelation of the Gospel shows how God preserved the blueprint of our design in Christ in spite of humanity's fall into sin. Our eternal association in Christ from before the foundation of the earth was redeemed.

Eph 1:3 Let's celebrate God! He has lavished every blessing heaven has upon us in Christ!

Eph 1:4 He associated us in Christ before [1]the fall of the world! Jesus is God's mind made up about us! He always knew in his love that he would present us again [2]face-to-face before him in blameless innocence. *(The implications of the fall are completely cancelled out, using the word, [1]***katabalo**, meaning "to fall away, to put in a lower place," instead of **themelios**, meaning "foundation" [see 2:20]; thus, translated "the fall of the world," instead of "the foundation of the world," as in most other translations. God found us in Christ before he lost us in Adam! We are presented in blameless innocence before him! The word, [2]***katenopion**, suggests the closest possible proximity, face-to-face!)*

Eph 1:5 He is the architect of our design; his heart dream realized our [1]coming of age in Christ. *(Adoption here is not what it means in our Western society, it is a coming of age, like the typical Jewish Barmitsva. See Galatians 4:1-6, " ... and to seal our sonship the spirit of his son echoes Abba Father in our hearts." This is [1]***huiothesia**.)*

Eph 1:6 His grace-plan is to be celebrated: he greatly endeared us and highly favored us in Christ. His love for his Son is his love for us.

God found us in Christ before he lost us in Adam! Much has been made of Adam's fall, while something of far greater implication deserves our undivided attention.

The message of reconciliation emphasizes the initiative that God undertook and reveals how God succeeded to restore fallen man to himself in absolute innocence.

20

1 Cor 1:30 [1]Of God's doing are we in Christ. He is both the genesis and genius of our wisdom; a wisdom that reveals how righteous, sanctified and redeemed we are in him. *(The preposition, [1]ek, always denotes origin, source. Mankind's association in Christ is God's doing. In God's economy, Christ represents us; what man could never achieve through personal discipline and willpower as taught in every religion, God's faith accomplished in Christ. Of his design we are in Christ; we are associated in oneness with him. Our wisdom is sourced in this union! Also, our righteousness and holiness originate from him. Holiness equals wholeness and seamless harmony of man's spirit, soul, and body. Our redemption is sanctioned in him. He redeemed our identity, our sanity, our health, our joy, our peace, our innocence, and our complete well-being! [See Eph 1:4].) Mirror Bible*

The Knox Translation reads, "It is from him that we take our origin."

2 Cor 5:14 The love of Christ [1]resonates within us and leaves us with only one conclusion: Jesus died humanity's death; therefore, in God's logic every individual simultaneously died. *(The word, [1]sunecho, from sun, meaning together with and echo, meaning to echo, to embrace, to hold, and thus translated, to resonate. Jesus didn't die 99% or for 99%. He died humanity's death 100%! If Paul had to compromise the last part of verse 14 to read: "one died for all therefore only those who follow the prescriptions to qualify, have also died," then he would have had to change the first half of the verse as well! Only the love of Christ can make a calculation of such enormous proportion! Theology would question the extremity of God's love and perhaps prefer to add a condition or two to a statement like that!)*

2 Cor 5:15 Now if all were included in his death they were equally included in his resurrection. This unveiling of his love redefines human life! Whatever reference we could have of ourselves outside of our association with Christ is no longer relevant.

2 Cor 5:16 This is radical! No label that could possibly previously define someone carries any further significance! Even our pet doctrines of Christ are redefined. Whatever we knew about him historically or sentimentally is challenged by this conclusion. *(By discovering Christ from God's point of view we discover ourselves and every other human life from God's point of view!)*

2 Cor 5:17 In the light of your co-inclusion in his death and resurrection, whoever you thought you were before, in Christ you are a brand new person! The old ways of seeing yourself and everyone else are over. Acquaint yourself with the new! *(Just imagine this! Whoever a person was as a Jew, Greek, slave or freeman, Boer, Zulu, Xhosa, British, Indian, Muslim or American, Chinese, Japanese or Congolese; is now dead and gone! They all died when Jesus died! Remember we are not talking law language here! The 'If' in, "If any man is in Christ" is not a condition, it is the conclusion of the revelation of the gospel! Man is in Christ by God's doing [1 Cor 1:30 and Eph 1:4]. The verses of 2 Corinthians 5:14-16 give context to verse 17! For so long we studied verse 17 on its own and interpreted the 'if' as a condition! Paul did not say, "If any man is in Christ," he said "THEREFORE if any man is in Christ ..." The "therefore" immediately includes verses 14 to 16! If God's faith sees every man in Christ in his death, then they were certainly also in Christ in his resurrection. Jesus did not reveal a "potential" you, he revealed the truth about you so that you may know the truth about yourself and be free indeed!)*

2 Cor 5:18 To now see everything as new is to simply see what God has always known in Christ; we are not debating man's experience, opinion, or his contribution; this is 100% God's belief and his doing. In Jesus Christ, God [1]exchanged equivalent value to redeem us to himself. This act of reconciliation is the mandate of our ministry. *(The word, [1]katalasso, translates as reconciliation; a mutual exchange of equal value.)*

2 Cor 5:19 Our ministry declares that Jesus did not act independent of God. Christ is proof that God reconciled the total kosmos to himself. Deity and humanity embraced in Christ; the fallen state of mankind was deleted; their trespasses would no longer count against them! God has placed this message within us. He now announces his friendship with every individual from within us!

2 Cor 5:20 The voice God has in Christ he now has in us; we are God's ambassadors. Our lives exhibit the urgency of God to [1]persuade everyone to realize the reconciliation of their redeemed identity. *(The word, [1]parakaleo, comes from para, a preposition indicating close proximity, a thing proceeding from a sphere of influence, with a suggestion of union of place of residence, to have sprung from its author and giver, originating from, denoting the point from which an action originates, intimate connection, and kaleo, to identify by name, to surname. In Luke 15:28, 31, His father pleaded with him, "My child, you are always with me, and all that I have is yours." "Be reconciled" could not be translated, "Become reconciled!" "Do in order to become" is the language of the Old Testament; the language of the New Testament is, "Be, because of what was done!")*

Rom 1:16 I have no shame about sharing the good news of Christ with anyone; the powerful rescuing act of God persuades both Jew and Greek alike.

Rom 1:17 Herein lies the secret of the power of the Gospel; there is no good news in it until the [1]righteousness of God is revealed! *(The good news is the fact that the Cross of Christ was a success. God rescued [1]the life of our design; he redeemed our [1]innocence. Man would never again be judged righteous or unrighteous by his own ability to obey moral laws! It is not about what man must or must not do but about what Jesus has done!)* God now persuades everyone to believe what he knows to be true about them. *(It is from faith to faith)* The prophets wrote in advance about the fact that God believes that righteousness unveils the life that he always had in mind for us. "Righteousness by his *(God's)* faith defines life." *(And not man's good or bad behavior or circumstances interpreted as a blessing or a curse [Hab 2:4]. Instead of reading the curse when disaster strikes, Habakkuk realizes that the Promise out-dates performance as the basis to man's acquittal. Deuteronomy 28 is out-dated and would no longer be the motivation or the measure of right or wrong behavior! "Though the fig trees do not blossom, nor fruit be on the vines, the produce of the olive fail and the fields yield no food, the flock be cut off from the fold and there be no herd in the stalls, yet I will rejoice in the Lord, I will joy in the God of my salvation. God, the Lord, is my strength; he makes my feet like hinds' feet, he makes me tread upon my high places [Hab 3:17-19 RSV].)*

(In the Gospel the righteousness of God is revealed, from faith to faith. "Look away [from the law of works] to Jesus; he is the Author and finisher of faith." [Heb 12:1]. The gospel is the revelation of the righteousness of God; it declares how God succeeded to put mankind right with him. It is about what God did right, not what Adam did wrong. The word

righteousness comes from the Anglo Saxon word, "rightwiseness;" wise in that which is right. In Greek the root word for righteousness is [1]dike, which means two parties finding likeness in each other. The Hebrew word for righteousness is [1]tzadok, which refers to the beam in a scale of balances. In Colossians 2:9-10, It is in Christ that God finds an accurate and complete expression of himself, in a human body! He mirrors our completeness and is the ultimate authority of our true identity.)

Man exists to be in union with his Maker; in his very make-up he is the God-kind, created for Divine companionship and encounter. Humanity is God's love dream.

Eph 1:3 Let's celebrate God! He has lavished every blessing heaven has upon us in Christ! Mirror Bible

I say ye are gods, all of you are sons of the Most High, why would you die like mere men? Ps 82:6, 7 RSV

You were unmindful of the Rock that begot you, and you forgot the God who gave you birth. Deut 32:18 RSV

In Psalm 22, David prophesies the death of the Messiah-Christ and sees the triumphant outcome in verse 27: All the ends of the earth shall remember and return to the Lord; and all the families of the nations shall worship before Him!

In Christ God dealt with every possible excuse man could have to feel separated and distanced from God. He is the highway in the desert that Isaiah saw: every high place was brought down, every valley filled up, every crooked place made straight, even the rough places were made smooth!

The voice of him that cries in the wilderness, "Prepare the way of the LORD, make straight in the desert a highway for our God. Every valley shall be lifted up, and every mountain and hill shall be made low: and the crooked shall be made straight, and the rough places smooth: And the glory of the LORD shall be revealed, and all flesh shall see it together: for the mouth of the LORD has spoken it." Is 40:3-5.

In his death on the cross he prepares a place for us so that we may forever be where he is, embraced in the bosom of the Father.

And all mankind will see salvation from God's point of view! Lk. 3:4-6

And when I go and prepare a place for you, I will come again and will take you to myself, that where I am you may be also. Jn 14:3

Jn 14:20 In that day you will know that I am in my Father, and you in me, and I in you. RSV

Col 1:21 Your indifferent mind-set alienated you from God into a lifestyle of annoyances, hardships, and labors. Yet he has now fully [2]reconciled and restored you

23

to your original design. *(The word, [1]poneros, comes from annoyances, hardships, and labors, often translated as evil. [See Septuagint: tree of knowledge of good and hard labor!] To reconcile: [2]apokatallasso, fully restored to the original value. [In Thayer Definition: to change, exchange, as coins for others of equivalent value.] Mirror*

"You yourselves are a case study of what he does." — The Message.

Col 1:22 He accomplished this in dying our death in a human body; he fully represented us in order to fully present us again in blameless innocence, face-to-face with God; with no sense of guilt, suspicion, regret, or accusation; all charges against us are officially cancelled. Mirror

Col 3:3 Your union with his death broke the association with that world; see yourselves located in a fortress where your life is hidden with Christ in God! *("In that day you will know that I am in my father, and you in me and I in you." [Jn 14:20] Occupy your mind with this new order of life; you died when Jesus died, whatever defined you before defines you no more. Christ, in whom the fullness of deity dwells, defines you now! The secret of your life is your union with Christ in God! [See Col 2:9, 10]) Mirror Bible*

"Risen, then, with Christ you must lift your thoughts above where Christ now sits at the right hand of God, you must be heavenly minded; not earthly minded, you have undergone death, and your life is hidden away now with Christ in God. Christ is your life, when he is made manifest you are made manifest in his glory." — Knox Translation

2 Co 5:18 All this is from God, who through Christ reconciled us to himself and gave us the ministry of reconciliation;

2 Co 5:19 that is, in Christ God was reconciling the world to himself, not counting their trespasses against them, and entrusting to us the message of reconciliation. RSV

Paul expresses his boundless gratitude towards God for the believers at Corinth whenever he considers the full implication of their faith-union in Christ. He sees them established in favor and grace, and able to communicate spontaneously in order to equally impact others.

1 Cor 1:4 I am always so happy for you when I consider how greatly advantaged you are because of God's grace unveiled in Jesus Christ.

1 Cor 1:5 Your knowledge of Christ is based on so much more than hearsay; every aspect of your life gives eloquent expression to the rich reservoir of your union in him.

1 Cor 1:6 You certainly have the testimony of Christ evidenced in you. Mirror Bible

(You possess full knowledge and give full expression because in you the evidence for the truth of Christ has found confirmation. — NEB Even as the testimony of Christ was confirmed in you. KJV)

Paul encourages us to embrace with confident expectation the full revelation of Christ in us. We may now know beyond doubt that everything we would ever need is already part and parcel of this grace-gift. The testimony of Christ confirmed in you will not leave you stranded half way, but is able to sustain you guiltless in his presence to the end of days. Jesus is the guarantee of your acquittal; his life and testimony is the receipt and documented proof against all accusation and suspicion.

"He is the guarantee of your vindication; he is your warrant against all accusation or indictment." Amplified Bible.

In this light Paul pleads with every believer to be mutually persuaded in the same opinion; he exhorts each and every one of us to speak the same language, because we share the exact same reference.

God's point of view is the only light that dispels the illusion of distance and division.

Psa 36:9 For with thee is the fountain of life; in thy light do we see light. RSV

1 Cor 1:7 In your [1]receiving the [2]revelation of Jesus Christ as the principal influence in your life *(his Lordship)*, you prove that you lack nothing and that his grace gifts fully compliment you. *(This is in such contrast to those days when under-achievement was the rule; when you felt that you were never good enough and always lagging behind. Note: [1]**apekdechomai** is not "eagerly waiting for," but "eagerly accepting" or to welcome with hospitality; [2]**apokalupsis** is the unveiling, disclosure. I don't know why most translations always want to postpone what God has already unveiled!)*

1 Cor 1:8 He establishes you from start to finish; to stand [1]vindicated in your identity in the light of day as evidenced in the Lord Jesus Christ. *(The word, [1]**anegkletos**, means blameless, beyond scrutiny, proved innocent in your original identity.)*

1 Cor 1:9 We are [1]surnamed by God, he is our true lineage; our Leader Jesus Christ has welcomed us to fully participate in the same friendship that he and the Father enjoys. *([1]**kaleo**, to call or identify by name, to surname.)*

1 Cor 1:10 My dear Brothers, because we are surnamed and identified in the name of our master Jesus Christ, I [1]urge you to speak with one voice, *(to say the same thing)* we share the same source as our reference; no division or any sense of distance is tolerated, which makes us a perfect match, accurately joined in the same thought pattern and communicating the same resolve. *(The word, [1]**parakaleo**, is from **para**, a preposition indicating close proximity, a thing proceeding from a sphere of influence, with a suggestion of union of place of residence, to have sprung from its author and giver, originating from, denoting the point from which an action originates, intimate connection and **kaleo**, to surname.)*

1 Cor 1:11 Some of the believers in Chleo's fellowship told me about the controversy in your ranks; this is most disturbing!

1 Cor 1:12 What I was told is that you are divided into groups, where some side with Paul, others with Apollos, still others with Cephas, and even some who say, "we are the Messianic group!"

1 Cor 1:13 This is really ridiculous: can Christ be cut up into little relics? Was Paul crucified for you? Were you baptized into Paul's name?

1 Cor 1:14 Baptism is not my business or emphasis; I am glad that I only baptized

25

Crispus and Gaius amongst you! (*Crispus was his neighbor and leader of the synagogue [see Acts 18:8]. Gaius resided at Corinth. Paul stayed with him when he wrote the Epistle to the Romans [Rom 16:23]; he was also a travel companion of Paul's [Acts 19:29].*)

1 Cor 1:15 Somehow baptism has become a snare to some who wish to win members to their denomination! I distance myself from such folly! Mirror Bible

If possible, so far as it depends upon you, live peaceably with all. Rom 12:18. RSV

Rom 12:18 You have within you what it takes to be everyone's friend, regardless of how they treat you. (*See Rom 1:16, 17. Also Mt 5:44, 45.) Mirror Bible*

Eph 4:21 It is not possible to study Christ in any other context; he is the incarnation, hear him resonate within you! The truth about you has its ultimate reference in Jesus. (*"The truth as it is in Christ." He did not come to introduce a new compromised set of rules; he is not an example for us but of us!*)

Eph 4:22 Now you are free to strip off that old identity like a filthy worn-out garment. Lust corrupted you and cheated you into wearing it. (*Just like an actor who wore a cloak for a specific role he had to interpret; the fake identity is no longer appropriate!*

Eph 4:23 Be renewed in your innermost mind! (*Pondering the truth about you as it is displayed in Christ) will cause you to be completely reprogrammed in the way you think about yourself! (Notice that Paul does not say, "Renew your minds!" This transformation happens in the spirit of your mind, awakened by truth on a much deeper level than a mere intellectual and academic consent. Mirror Bible*

The love dream of God provides the platform for unhindered friendship.

The eye of the fountain preserves and secures the original undiluted thought of God; he is the Word that proceeds from the mouth of God. He is our origin; all our springs of joy are in him!

The Gospel holds the ingredient of the most powerful influence that the consciousness of man could ever encounter. Nothing known to man presents a greater wealth of wisdom than the love of God realized. This great revelation is not only his love for us but also his love in us for others!

We are designed for friendship. Any measure or definition of hostility, distance or loneliness is foreign to our makeup.

"A human being is like a work of art, the more it is admired the more beautiful it grows reflecting the gift of love like light back to the giver"
Elizabeth Goudge.

Let us consider these 5 vital ingredients to meaningful friendship:
1. The love initiative: Unconditional love sets the pace,
2. Integrity inspires trust
3. Innocence: forgiveness, no suspicion, blame or guilt
4. Oneness of mind ~ sharing the same reference
5. Long-term, sustained feedback. (Living happily ever after)

Unconditional Love

The revelation of God's love initiative to reconcile himself with humanity distinguishes true Christianity from every other religion.

Grace takes karma out of the equation!

Religion needs paying and returning customers!

In Africa, no witchdoctor would make any money were the ancestors not always portrayed as unhappy or angry! The angrier the ancestor seems, the more expensive the scapegoat!

The mission of Jesus was not to change God's mind about man but to change man's mind about God! He shocked the Jews with statements like, "No man knows God! The son reveals him! If you have seen me you have seen the Father!"

God is not the product of man's best guess; he is bigger than religion's biggest blunder or eloquence in their attempts to define him. He is beyond extinction or threat and can never be reduced to either our clever or clumsy expression of philosophy or art. Jesus reveals God as Father and Redeemer of the human race.

True Christian faith is not about man attempting to win the favor of deity, or trying to influence the mood of a bad tempered god; it is the revelation of the love of God reconciling a hostile world to himself!

Rom 5:10 Our hostility towards God did not reduce his love for us; he saw equal value in us when he exchanged the life of his son for ours. Now that the act of [1]reconciliation is complete, his life in us saves us from the gutter-most to the uttermost. (Reconciliation, from [1]**katalasso**, meaning a mutual exchange of equal value. Thayer Definition: to exchange, as coins for others of equivalent value. Mirror Bible

"For if while we were enemies we were reconciled to God by the death of his Son, much more, now that we are reconciled, shall we be saved by his life." — RSV)

It is not about a sacrifice that man brings; this is not man with his best lamb; the gospel reveals God's love initiative: Jn 1:29 Behold the Lamb of God who takes away the sin of the world! RSV

Gen 22:7 And Isaac said to his father Abraham, "My father!" And he said, "Here am I, my son." He said, "Behold, the fire and the wood; but where is the lamb for a burnt offering?"

Gen 22:8 Abraham said, "God will provide himself the lamb for a burnt offering, my son."

Gen 22:13 And Abraham lifted up his eyes and looked, and behold, behind him was a ram, caught in a thicket by his horns; and Abraham went and took the ram, and offered it up as a burnt offering instead of his son. RSV

God will himself provide the lamb....and behold, **behind** him was a lamb!!! Jesus the same YESTERDAY! Heb 13:8. I was in the Spirit on the Lord's day, and I heard **behind** me a loud voice like a trumpet. Rev 1:10

Joh 8:56 Your father Abraham rejoiced that he was to see my day; he saw it and was glad."

Joh 8:57 The Jews then said to him, "You are not yet fifty years old, and have you seen Abraham?"

Joh 8:58 Jesus said to them, "Truly, truly, I say to you, before Abraham was, I am." RSV

Isa 53:7 He was oppressed, and he was afflicted, yet he opened not his mouth; like a lamb that is led to the slaughter, and like a sheep that before its shearers is dumb, so he opened not his mouth. RSV

Acts 8:30 So Philip ran to him, and heard him reading Isaiah the prophet, and asked, "Do you understand what you are reading?"

Acst 8:31 And he said, "How can I, unless someone guides me?" And he invited Philip to come up and sit with him.

Acts 8:32 Now the passage of the scripture which he was reading was this: "As a sheep led to the slaughter or a lamb before its shearer is dumb, so he opens not his mouth.

Act 8:33 In his humiliation justice was denied him. Who can describe his generation? For his life is taken up from the earth."

Act 8:34 And the eunuch said to Philip, "About whom, pray, does the prophet say this, about himself or about someone else?"

Acts 8:35 Then Philip opened his mouth, and beginning with this scripture he told him the good news of Jesus. *(See Luk 24:27,44,45, Jn 5:39,40)* RSV

I wrote in the margin of my Bible next to Acts 8:35, when you study or teach scripture, get to the point!

Rom 5:8 Herein is the extremity of God's love gift: mankind was rotten to the core when Christ died their death.

Rom 5:9 If God coulebd love us that much when we were ungodly and guilty, how much more are we free to realize his love now that we know that we are declared innocent by his blood? *(God does not love us more now that we are reconciled to him; we are now free to realize how much he loved us all along! [Col 2:14, Rom 4:25])* Mirror Bible

We love because he first loved us." 1 Jn 4:19 RSV

If sin could separate man from the love of God then redemption would be impossible. Paul declares to the Greek philosophers in Acts 17, that the Creator is not far from each one of us! God is not closer to some than what he is to others; in the incarnation he is equally Emmanuel to every man!

God takes pleasure in mankind. His reference exceeds anything that could possibly disqualify man. In Christ he has broken down every wall of hostility and every excuse we have to feel distant from him.

Eph 4:7 The gift of Christ gives dimension to grace and defines our individual value. *(Grace was given to each one of us according to the measure of the gift of Christ. One measure, one worth! Our worth is defined by his gift not by a reward for our behavior.)* Mirror Bible

1Pe 1:18 You know that you were ransomed from the futile ways inherited from your fathers, not with perishable things such as silver or gold,
1Pe 1:19 but with the precious blood of Christ, like that of a lamb without blemish or spot. We are bought with a price. RSV

Job 7:17 What is man that you should magnify him, and that you should set your heart on him? Literal Translation of the Holy Bible LTHB

What is man that you are mindful of him, and the son of man that you care so much for him?" Ps 8:4.

How precious to me are your thoughts, O God!" How impossible to calculate their sum total; were I to count them my years would have to equal yours!" Ps 139:17, 18. REB *(It will take eternity to calculate the full extent of your thoughts towards us!)*

God's faith sees the fruit of the labor of his love, and feasts upon the thought of our redemption and reconciliation to him. God's faith feasts on the knowledge of mankind's restored union and oneness with him!

Isa 53:3 He was despised and rejected by men; a man of sorrows, and acquainted with grief; and as one from whom men hide their faces he was despised, and we esteemed him not.

Isa 53:4 Surely he has borne our griefs and carried our sorrows; yet we esteemed him stricken, smitten by God, and afflicted.

Isa 53:5 But he was wounded for our transgressions, he was bruised for our iniquities; upon him was the chastisement that made us whole, and with his stripes we are healed.

Isa 53:6 All we like sheep have gone astray; we have turned everyone to his own way; and the LORD has laid on him the iniquity of us all.

Isa 53:11 He shall see the fruit of the travail of his soul and be satisfied; by his knowledge shall the righteous one, my servant, make the multitudes to be accounted righteous; because he shall bear their iniquities.

God rejoices over you with gladness, he renews you in his love; he exults over you with loud singing and spins around in joyful dancing! Zeph 3:17

Love sets faith in motion. Galatians 5:6. MB

Live God's initiative! "I was ready to be found by those who did not seek me; I said, "Here I am, here I am!" I spread out my hands all day long to a rebellious people." Is.65:1,2. RSV

Be God's 'pop-ups' in society. Make known his patient fondness for mankind.

Titus 3:2 Gossip is out! Never have anything bad to say about anyone! You do not have to win every argument; instead, avoid [1]quarrelling, be appropriate, always show perfect courtesy to one and all. *(The word, [1]mache, means controversial, striving. You don't have to wait for people to change before you are nice to them. There is a big difference between "fake politeness" and perfect courtesy!)*

Titus 3:3 Do not be harsh on others. Remember that we, too, were typically foolish; we were stubborn and indifferent to spiritual things, our addiction to the sensual and sexual kept us running around in circles, we were engaged in malice and spiteful jealousies, we were bored and lonely, often utterly disliking ourselves and hating one another!

Titus 3:4 But then, oh happy day! It was the generosity of God and his fondness for mankind that dawned on us like a shaft of light. Our days of darkness were over! Light shone everywhere and we became aware: God rescued the human race! MB

2nd Vital Friendship Ingredient: Integrity

The same God who engineered the sunrise engineered our salvation.

The redemption of man is beyond dispute. God himself guarantees the integrity of this union:
2Ti 2:13 if we are faithless, he remains faithful--for he cannot deny himself. RSV

2 Tim 2:13 Our unbelief does not change what God believes; he cannot [1]contradict himself! *(The word [1]arneomai, means to contradict. See Rom 3:3,4 What we believe about God does not define him; God's faith defines us.)* MB

Rom 3:3 What if some were unfaithful? Does their faithlessness nullify the faithfulness of God?

Rom 3:4 By no means! Let God be true though every man be false, as it is written, "That thou mayest be justified in thy words, and prevail when thou art judged. RSV

Rom 3:3 The question is, how does someone's failure to believe God affect what God believes? Could their unbelief cancel God's faith? *(What we believe about God does not define him; God's faith defines us.)*

Rom 3:4 God's Word is not under threat! In fact if all of humanity fails, truth remains intact. Truth is rooted in God; it is neither challenged nor vindicated by man's experience. *(Truth doesn't become true by popular vote.)* Contradiction does not intimidate or diminish the faith of God. *(What God believes about man does not change through man's unfaithfulness. God remains convinced about us.)* Scripture records that God stands justified in his own word; it confirms that God's promise and purpose are not compromised through man's failure; neither is God's reputation threatened by man's behavior. *(Something doesn't become more true because man believes it. It's already as true as it gets because God believes it; otherwise, there is nothing for man to believe if it wasn't true in the first place. It is from faith to faith, says Paul [Rom 1:17]; there is no gospel in it until the righteousness of God is revealed; "we can do nothing against the truth!" [See 2 Cor 13:5 and 8]. David's sin did not cancel God's promise. "But my mercy I will not take from him" and "his house shall be made sure, and his kingdom for ever before me, and his throne shall be set up forever." [2 Sam 7:15-16].)*

30

God desires to persuade us beyond all dispute about the transparent integrity of his eternal purpose; *(in our human affairs we would swear an oath by the highest authority in order to add conclusive weight to our intentions.)* God employs a similar method in order to drive home his unwavering conviction concerning us; so he swears by himself, there being no higher authority than his own Throne; by implication God's being becomes the immediate guarantee to his word.

Heb 6:13 God could give Abraham no greater guarantee than the integrity of his own being; this makes the promise as sure as God is.

Heb 6:16 It is common practice in human affairs to evoke a higher authority under oath in order to add weight to any agreement between men, thereby silencing any possibility of quibbling. *(Putting an end to all dispute.)*

Heb 6:17 In the same context we are confronted with God's eagerness to go to the last extreme in his dealing with us as heirs of his promise, and to cancel out all possible grounds for doubt or dispute. In order to persuade us of the unalterable character and finality of his resolve, he confined himself to an oath. The promise which already belongs to us by heritage is now also confirmed under oath. *(The Promise is the oath; Jesus is the proof. He desires to show more convincingly to the heirs of the promise the unchangeable character of his purpose. — RSV)*

Heb 6:18 So that we are now dealing with two irreversible facts *(The promise of redemption sustained throughout scripture and the fulfillment of that promise in Jesus)* which make it impossible for anyone to prove God wrong; thus our persuasion as to our redeemed identity is powerfully reinforced. We have already escaped into that destiny; our expectation has come within our immediate grasp!

Heb 6:19 Our hearts and minds are certain; anchored securely within the innermost courts of God's immediate Presence; beyond the *(prophetic)* veil.

Heb 6:20 By going there on our behalf, Jesus pioneered a place for us and removed every type of obstruction that could still distance us from the promise. In him we are represented for all time; he became our High Priest after the order of Melchizedek. We now enjoy the same privileged access he has. *(He said, "I go to prepare a place for you so that you may be where I am. On that day you will no longer doubt that I and the Father are one; you will know that I am in the Father and you in me and I in you!"[Jn 10:30, 14:3, 20])* Mirror

Mankind's redemption is not in the balance neither is it at risk!

The heavens declare his glory, night to night exhibits the giant solar testimony that is mathematically precise, revealing that God knew before time was the exact moment he would enter our history as a man, and the exact moment the Messiah would expire on the cross!

Jesus is God's eternal and final yes to man; in his own person he became the guarantee and fulfillment of every promise God had in mind for humanity! 2Cor 1:18-22. God cannot lie.

Jesus is God's mind made up about you!

Heb 13:8 Take your lead from Jesus. He is your reference to the most complete life. In him yesterday is confirmed today and today mirrors tomorrow. What God spoke to us in Christ is as relevant now as it was in the prophetic past and will always be in the eternal future! *(Jesus is the same yesterday, today, and forever; there is a history to our salvation that carries more authority and relevance than anything that ever happened in our past, or anything present in time or still to happen in the future. See Rom 8:34 What further ground can there possibly be to condemn man? In his death he faced our judgment; in his resurrection he declares our innocence; the implications cannot be undone! He now occupies the highest seat of authority as the executive of our redemption in the throne room of God. See Rom 8: 1, also Rom 4:25. The heavens declare his glory, night to night exhibits the giant solar testimony that is mathematically precise, revealing that God knew before time was the exact moment he would enter our history as a man, and the exact moment the Messiah would expire on the cross and be raised again from the dead!)* Mirror

Tit 1:2, 3 In the hope of eternal life, which God, who cannot lie, promised long ages ago but at the proper time manifested. RSV

Titus 1:2 This is the life of the [1]ages that was anticipated for generations; the life of our original design announced by the infallible resolve of God before [2]time or space existed. *(Man's union with God is the original thought that inspired creation. The word, [1]aionios, means without beginning or end, timeless perpetuity, ages. The word, [2]xronos, means a specific space or portion of time, season. This was before calendar time existed, before the creation of the galaxies and constellations. There exists a greater dimension to eternity than what we are capable of defining within the confines of space and time! God's faith anticipated the exact moment of our redeemed union with him for all eternity!)*

This life was made certain before eternal time. (BBE 1949, Bible in Basic English)

Titus 1:3 My message announces the completeness of time; God's eternal moment realized the logic of our salvation. *(But then the day dawned; the most complete culmination of time! [Gal 4:4] Everything predicted was concluded in Christ!)*

John 1:13 These are they who discover their genesis in God beyond their natural conception! Man began in God. We are not the invention of our parents!

John 1:14 Suddenly the invisible eternal Word takes on [1]visible form! The Incarnation! In him, and now confirmed in us! The most accurate tangible display of God's eternal thought finds expression in human life! The Word became a human being; we are his address; he resides in us! He [2]captivates our gaze! The glory we see there is not a religious replica; he is the [3]authentic begotten son. *([3]monogenes begotten only by the Father and not by the flesh; in him we recognize our true beginning).* The [4]glory *(that Adam lost)* returns in fullness! Only [5]grace can communicate truth in such complete context!

(In him we discover that we are not here by chance or accident or by the desire of an earthly parent, neither are we the product of a mere physical conception; we exist by the expression of God's desire to reveal himself in the flesh. His eternal invisible Word, his Spirit-thought, [1]became flesh, [1]ginomai, as in be born and [2]theaomai, meaning to gaze upon, to perceive. We saw his glory, [4]doxa, the display of his opinion, the glory as of the original, authentic begotten of the Father, full of grace and truth. He is both the "only begotten," [3]monogenes; as in the authentic original mold, as well as the first born from the dead [Col 1:18, 1 Pet 1:3]. He is the revelation of our completeness.

And of his fullness have we all received, grace against grace, ⁵garin anti garitos, grace undeserved. For the law was given through Moses, grace and truth came through Jesus Christ. He who is in the bosom of the Father, the only original, authentic begotten of the Father; he is our guide who accurately declares and interprets the invisible God within us. Interesting that the revelation of the Incarnation in verse 14 doesn't follow verse 2 or 3, but verse 12 and 13! Genesis 1:26 is redeemed!)

Heb 1:1 Throughout ancient times God spoke in many fragments and glimpses of prophetic thought to our fathers.

1:2 Now, the sum total of his conversation with man has finally culminated in a son. He is the official heir of all things. He is, after all, the author of the ages. Jesus is what has been on the tip of the Father's tongue all along! *(The revelation of man's redeemed sonship, as revealed in Jesus, is the crescendo of God's conversation with humanity. Throughout the ages he has whispered his name in disguise to be revealed in the fullness of time as the greatest surprise.*

The exact image of God, his very likeness, the authentic eternal thought, became voice and was made flesh in us. The composer of a concert masterpiece knew that the notes scribbled on a page would finally find its voice in a symphony of instruments.)

Heb 1:3 We have our beginning and our being in him. He is the force of the universe, sustaining everything that exists by his eternal utterance! Jesus is the radiant and flawless expression of the person of God. He makes the glory *(doxa, intent)* of God visible and exemplifies the character and every attribute of God in human form. *(Gen 1:26, 27)* This powerful final utterance of God *(the incarnation revealing our sonship)* is the vehicle that carries the weight of the universe. What he communicates is the central theme of everything that exists. The content of his message celebrates the fact that God took it upon himself to successfully cleanse and acquit humankind. The man Jesus is now his right hand of power, the executive authority seated in the boundless measure of his majesty. He occupies the highest seat of dominion to endorse our innocence! His throne is established upon our innocence. *("Having accomplished purification of sins, he sat down ...")* Mirror Bible

2 Tim 2:13 If we are unfaithful, he remains faithful because he cannot be untrue to himself. GW

2 Tim 2:9 I might be in bonds, but the Word of God is not. *(It might seem to some that my suffering contradicts what I preach, but it cannot! My ministry is measured by the word not by my circumstances. See Col 1:24)*

2 Tim 2:10 This gives me more than enough reason not to quit. I desire for everyone to discover the fact that the life of their ¹design is redeemed in Christ Jesus; this is the timeless intent of God. *(The word ¹eklegomai, ek, source, origin, and legomai from logos, word, thus the life of our design.)*

2 Tim 2:11 The logic of God endorses our faith: we were included in his death and are therefore equally included in his resurrection.

2 Tim 2:12 Whenever we suffer, we already know that we co-reign with him; the Christ-life rules. *(Sufferings do not contradict our joint position with him in the throne room!)* If we ¹contradict ourselves *(behave unlike ourselves)*, he will contradict us and

33

prove us wrong! *(The word ¹arneomai means to contradict.)*

2 Tim 2:13 Our unbelief does not change what God believes; he cannot contradict himself! *(What we believe about God does not define him; God's faith defines us. God cannot be untrue to himself! See Rom 3:3,4.)* Mirror Bible

Heb 10:23 Our conversation echoes his persuasion; his faithfulness backs his promises. *(His integrity inspires our confession.)* Mirror

Abraham showed no hesitation or doubt at God's promise, but drew strength from his faith, confessing God's power *(Greek, **doxa,** opinion)* fully convinced that God was able to perform what he had promised. His faith was thus reckoned virtue. Rom 4:20, 21 Knox.

Rom 4:20 While he had every reason to doubt the promise, he did not hesitate for a moment but instead empowered by faith confidence, he continued to communicate God's opinion. *(His name was his confession: in the Hebrew language, "Abraham"was not a mere familiar sounding name, but a meaningful sentence, a confession of faith authority, against the odds. He did not become embarrassed about his name; he did not change his name to "Abe" for short when there seemed to be no change in his circumstances. Every time he introduced himself or someone called him by his name, it was a bold declaration and repetition of God's promise, calling things that were not as though they were. I would imagine that Sarah spoke his name the most! In fact, every time they addressed one another they spoke the promise, "Mother of nations, kings of peoples shall come from you!" [Gen 17:5, 16]. Abraham, "the father of the multitudes.")*

Rom 4:21 Abraham's confidence was his ¹dress-code; he knew beyond doubt that the power of God to perform was equal to his promise. *(¹plerophoreo, from plero to be completely covered in every part, + phoreo, to wear garments or armor; traditionally translated to be totally persuaded. His faith was his visible identity and armor; he wore his persuasion like he would his daily garments.)* Mirror Bible

1Tim 4:9 The word is certainly true and worthy of our undivided attention. 1Thes 2:13 When you first heard us preach the word, you did not pass it off as just one more human opinion, but you took it to heart as God's true word to you, which it is, God himself at work in you believers! Message.

Heb 12:2 Look away from the shadow dispensation of the law and the prophets and fix your eyes upon Jesus. He is the fountainhead and conclusion of faith. He saw the joy *(of mankind's salvation)* when he braved the cross and despised the shame of it. As the executive authority of God *(the right hand of the Throne of God)* he now occupies the highest seat of dominion to endorse man's innocence! *(Having accomplished purification of sins, he sat down. [Heb 1:3, Isa 53:11])*

2 Cor 1:18 God's certainty is our persuasion; there is no maybe in him!

2 Cor 1:19 The son of God, Jesus Christ, whom I, Paul, Sylvanus, and Timothy boldly announced in you is God's ultimate yes to mankind. Human life is associated in all that he is. In God's mind there exists not even a hint of hesitation about this!

34

2 Cor 1:20 In him the detail of every single promise of God is fulfilled; Jesus is God's yes to your total well being! In our union with him the Amen that echoes in us gives evidence to his glorious intent through us.

2 Cor 1:21 God himself endorses this union that we enjoy in Christ. Mirror Bible

God's faith is the fountainhead of our faith. We do not need to conjure up our own faith when we can have God's; we only need to know what God believes.

Paul says "The joy of the Lord is our strength" We do not need to manufacture our own joy if we can have his. If the joy of the Lord is to our advantage then his joy must be based on something he knows to be true about us! We are God's joy!

What we believe about God does not define him; our doctrines do not even define us, even though they may label us. What God knows to be true about us as demonstrated in Christ alone defines us. Agree with God about you!

Jesus is what God believes about you!

Anything you believe about God that is unlike Jesus is not true about God; Jesus is the image of the invisible God, if you have seen him you have seen the Father.

Any attempt to understand God apart from Jesus Christ isn't theology but my-thology. Jesus is the benchmark from which every truth about the Father must be measured and evaluated. If it doesn't line up with Jesus, "it ain't God." (Steve McVey)

The Bible is all about Jesus; Jesus is all about us!

The Gospel says: THE TRUTH ABOUT YOU! THE TRUTH ABOUT YOU!

Truth persuades naturally!

Something doesn't become more true because man believes it; it's already as true as it gets because God believes it; otherwise there is nothing for man to believe, if it wasn't true in the first place; it is from faith to faith says Paul Rom 1:17, there is no gospel in it until the righteousness of God is revealed!; nothing to do with what Adam or us did wrong, everything to do with what Jesus did right!

Because mankind is the god-kind we are designed to be persuaded; we are faith-compatible;

2Co 4:13 Since we have the same spirit of faith as he had who wrote, "I believed, and so I spoke," we too believe, and so we speak. RSV

The context of this statement is the mirror principle:

2Cor 4:1 Having this ministry by the mercy of God, we do not lose heart. RSV

2Co 4:8 We are afflicted in every way, but not crushed; perplexed, but not driven to despair;

2Co 4:9 persecuted, but not forsaken; struck down, but not destroyed; RSV

The Mirror reads, 2 Cor 4:8 We often feel completely hemmed in on every side but our inner space remains unrestricted; when there seems to be no way out, we escape within! 4:9 At times we are persecuted to the extreme but we are never abandoned. We are knocked down but not knocked out.

Every contradiction becomes an opportunity for the reinforcement and confirmation of the truth, rather than a distraction from it.

Truth realized makes of faith a fortress!

No contradiction has what it takes to persuade otherwise. The content and chief ingredient of our faith is the mirror reflection of mankind in the face of Christ who is the likeness of God.

In the light of God's integrity, the Bible becomes a document of absolute proof to establish the legal platform and guarantee of humanity's redeemed identity and acquittal.

The inscription and image of Caesar distinguishes the piece of metal as legal tender; in the same way, the gospel reveals the inscription and the image of God in the face of Christ as legal tender to redeem mankind. He mirrors every man! The lost coin never lost its original value.

The younger brother of Jesus, James discovers in the resurrection of Christ his own as well as the face of every man's birth. To hear the word of truth is to see the face of your birth as in a mirror, he says.

Then in chapter 3:9 he says, how can we say beautiful things about God the Father but with the same mouth curse a man made in his mirror likeness? The argument is not what the individual did to deserve the insult, but the fact that the image and inscription of our Maker is still intact in every human life! The lost coin never lost its original value!

True worship is to touch someone's life with the same devotion and care you would touch Jesus himself; even if the other person seems a most unlikely candidate.

3rd Vital Friendship Ingredient: Innocence

The sinners were attracted to Jesus not because he introduced a compromised set of rules; something like, "It's all right to sin just don't get caught; or, try and do it less!" Instead he revealed in his person the mirror-reflection of their true origin, their original identity and the integrity of their innocence! They knew that the lie they lived as their identity had no power against the resonance of their own conscience. Jesus didn't say to the prostitute, "Go and sin less," he said to her "Go and sin no more!" Jesus knew something about the life of our design that we had lost sight of! What he revealed, he also redeemed!

Sin –consciousness is what empowers religion. It always amazes me how Simon could not receive the gift of the miraculous abundant catch that Jesus blessed him with; he felt more comfortable with the fact that he caught nothing the previous night because "I am a sinful man!" He accepted his fate as his due because his mind was educated under the law of blessings and curses! (Deuteronomy 28) When he witnessed the word and the miracle of the catch, he slotted back in his familiar 'karma' mode! "Depart from me Jesus! I am a sinful man! I am not worthy!" Luke 5:8.

Thank God! Jesus didn't pick disciples on their performance! It wasn't Simon's skill or reputation as a good fisherman that qualified him to become a fisher of men!

Sin-consciousness empowers the law of performance and contradicts what grace reveals; it inhibits any ground for meaningful friendship. A relationship based upon inferiority, guilt, suspicion or condemnation, has no future. For friendship to be worth anything, innocence is a non negotiable. The innocence Adam walked in before the fall is the same innocence that Christ enjoys in union with his Father, and is now the restored privilege of every human. Every accusation against mankind has been cancelled; humanity stands fully vindicated and acquitted. The prodigal son is not out on probation; he stands justified in his father's love, just as if he had never sinned!

Rom 4:25 Our sins [1]resulted in his death; his resurrection is [1]proof of our righteousness. *(His resurrection is the receipt to our acquittal. This is one of the most important statements in the entire Bible. Why was Jesus handed over to die? Because of [1]dia, our sins. Why was he raised from the dead? Because of, dia, we were justified! His resurrection reveals our righteousness! Here is the equation: his cross = our sins; his resurrection = our innocence! If we were still guilty after Jesus died, his resurrection would neither be possible nor relevant! This explains Acts 10:28 and 2 Cor 5:14 and 16. And in Acts 17:31, "because God had fixed a day on which he would judge the world in righteousness by a man whom he has appointed, and of this he has given assurance to all men by raising him from the dead.")*

Rom 5:1 Righteousness by faith realized means unlimited [1]friendship with God; this is the ultimate conclusion of the Gospel. Jesus Christ is the legal authority *(Lord)* of our testimony. *(In one sentence Paul sums up the previous four chapters. "Therefore, being justified by faith, we have peace with God through our Lord Jesus Christ." — KJV*

[1]Peace is a place of unhindered enjoyment of friendship beyond guilt, suspicion, blame or inferiority. The word, eirene, peace, to join, the "dove-tail" joint in carpentry. The Sabbath rest celebrates God's unhindered enjoyment of man and our unhindered enjoyment of him!)

What did God bear witness to then when he raised Jesus from the dead? (Acts 17:31) "God appointed a day and a person, and on that day in that person he would judge the world in righteousness!" Tenses in the Bible can be most confusing unless we understand the logic of Gods faith! "Before Abraham was I am! The Lamb was slain before the foundation of the world! Our redeemed innocence is the central theme of scripture and the very foundation of God's throne. "Having made purification for sins he sat down!" Jesus is the executive authority of God; seated in the boundless measure of his majesty where he occupies the highest seat of dominion to endorse man's innocence! Heb 1:3.

Repentance is impossible if we do not understand what God believes and thinks, because metanoia is something radical that takes place in your mind, it is a mind shift from darkness, confusion, depression, and guilt to light!

Consider the word *metanoia*, consisting of two components, *meta*, together with, *nous*, mind, suggesting a radical mind shift. This word has been translated regularly as repentance, which is an old English word borrowed from the Latin, which means penance. This gross deception led to the perverted doctrines of indulgences, where naive ignorant people were led to believe that they need to purchase favor from an angry god! Most cathedrals as well as many ministries were and sadly even now are funded with guilt money!

English translations do little to help us understand what repentance truly is. Until Jerome's Latin Vulgate translation, (380 A.D.) the word *metanoia* was commonly used. For instance, Tertullian wrote in 198 A.D., "In Greek, *metanoia* is not a confession of sins but a change of mind." But despite this the Latin fathers begin to translate the word as "do penance" following the Roman Catholic teaching on doing penance in order to win God's favor.

In 1430, Lorenzo Valla, a Catholic theologian, began a critical study of Jerome's Latin Vulgate and Valla pointed out many mistakes that Jerome had made. Sadly, the Vulgate-Only crowd of Valla's day forced him to renounce many of the changes that he noted needed in the Vulgate including the poor translation of metanoia.

Everyone who drinks from the wells of religion will thirst again! The business of religion desperately needs paying and returning customers! They crucified Jesus for this reason; their entire system of keeping people dependent on their hierarchy was challenged and condemned! It was man's sin consciousness and his sense of failure and inferiority that empowered religion for centuries.

Isa 55:8-11 gives meaning to metanoia: your thoughts were distanced from God's thoughts as the heavens are higher than the earth; but just like the rain and the snow would cancel that distance and saturate the soil to awaken its seed, so shall my word be that proceeds from my mouth. (The authentic word from the "eye of the fountain" Genesis 1:26 redeemed! Col 1:15, 2:9,10) In the incarnation the earth was saturated with the ultimate evidence of the image and likeness of God unveiled and redeemed in human form.

The Greek preposition meta means together with; together with implies another influence; this is where the gospel becomes so powerful since it appeals to our conscience to reason together with the Author of our original design, the authentic thought, the mind of God realized again; the distance caused by Adam's fall, (heaven higher than earth), is cancelled in the incarnation. "Come now, let us reason together, says the LORD: though your sins are like scarlet, they shall be as white as snow; though they are red like crimson, they shall become like wool." Isa 1:18 RSV

Paul says categorically that he refuses to tamper with God's word: "With the open statement of the truth, (the unveiled mirror likeness, 2 Cor 3:18) we commend ourselves to every man's conscience!" Greek, suneido, to see together, to co-know, which is the opposite of hades, from ha, negative and ides to see. 2 Cor 4:2.

38

Your belief in God does not define him; his faith in what he knows to be true about you defines you.

In Mark 11:22 Jesus says, "have the faith of God." Unfortunately most translations say, "have faith in God"; there is a vast difference.

God's belief in you gives substance to your faith. Jesus is what God believes about you!

Faith is to the spirit what the senses are to the body; while the one engages with fleeting and fading moments, the other celebrates perfection.

If our point of departure is not God's faith in the finished work of Christ we have no valid gospel to preach! If our faith is not sourced and sustained in him as the mirror image of God revealed and redeemed in us we are deceiving ourselves with yet another religious disguise called Christianity.

He overlooked the times of ignorance and now urges all men everywhere to discover his eternal thoughts about mankind, revealed in Christ, when we were judged in righteousness in one man's death, and raised in his resurrection as the trophy of justice redeemed! Acts 17:30,31 Having made purification for sins he sat down! His throne authority is established upon our redeemed innocence.

God's work in Christ on humanity's behalf has done so much more than the mere forgiveness of sins; He has broken the dominion of sin in our lives!

Isa 1:18 "Come now, let us reason together, says the LORD: though your sins are like scarlet, they shall be as white as snow; though they are red like crimson, they shall become like wool.

Rom 8:1 Now the decisive conclusion is this: in Christ, every bit of condemning evidence against us is cancelled. *("Who walk not after the flesh but after the spirit." This sentence was not in the original text, but later copied from verse 4. The person who added this most probably felt that the fact of Paul's declaration of mankind's innocence had to be made subject again to man's conduct. Religion under the law felt more comfortable with the condition of personal contribution rather than the conclusion of what faith reveals. The "in Christ" revelation is key to God's dealing with man. It is the PIN-code of the Bible. [See 1 Cor 1:30 and Eph 1:4].)*

Rom 8:2 The law of the Spirit is the liberating force of life in Christ. This leaves me with no further obligation to the law of sin and death. Spirit has superseded the sin enslaved senses as the principle law of our lives. *(The law of the spirit is righteousness by faith vs the law of personal effort and self righteousness which produces condemnation and spiritual death which is the fruit of the DIY tree.)*

Rom 8:3 The law failed to be anything more than an instruction manual; it had no power to deliver man from the strong influence of sin holding us hostage in our own bodies. God disguised himself in his son in this very domain where sin ruled man, the human body. The flesh body he lived and conquered in was no different to ours. Thus sin's authority in the human body was condemned. *(Hebrews 4:15, As High Priest he fully identifies with us in the context of our frail human life. Having subjected it to close scrutiny, he proved that the human frame was master over sin. His sympathy*

39

with us is not to be seen as excusing weaknesses that are the result of a faulty design, but rather as a trophy to humanity. He is not an example for us but of us.)

Rom 8:4 The righteousness promoted by the law is now realized in us. Our practical day-to-day life bears witness to spirit inspiration and not flesh domination.

Rom 8:5 Sin's symptoms are sponsored by the senses, a mind dominated by the sensual. Thoughts betray source; spirit life attracts spirit thoughts.

Rom 8:6 Thinking patterns are formed by reference, either the sensual appetites of the flesh and spiritual death, or zoe-life and total tranquillity flowing from a mind addicted to spirit *(faith)* realities.

Rom 8:7 A mind focused on flesh *(the sensual domain where sin held me captive)* is distracted from God with no inclination to his life-laws. Flesh *(self-righteousness)* and spirit *(faith righteousness)* are opposing forces. *(Flesh no longer defines you; faith does!)*

Col 2:11 You were in Christ when he died which means that his death represents your true circumcision. Sin's authority in the human body was stripped off you in him dying your death.

Col 2:12 In the same parallel *(your co-circumcision in his death)* your co-burial and joint-resurrection is now demonstrated in baptism; your co-inclusion in Christ is what God's faith knew when he powerfully raised him from the dead. *(Hos 6:2)*

Col 2:13 You were once spiritually dead, as confirmed in your constant failure; being bound to a lifestyle ruled by the [1]distorted desires of the flesh, but now God has made you alive together with him, having forgiven you all your [2]trespasses. *([1]The uncircumcision of the flesh, i.e., in the Greek, a life controlled by the sexual organs. The word, [2]paraptoma, comes from, para, close proximity, sphere of influence and pipto, to stop flying, from petomai, to fly; thus, to fall from flight or to lose altitude.)*

Col 2:14 His body nailed to the cross hung there as the document of mankind's guilt; in dying our death he [1]deleted the detailed [2]hand-written [3]record of Adam's fall. Every [1]stain that sin left on our conscience was fully blotted out. *(The word, [1]exaleipho, comes from ek, out of, and aleipho, with a, as a particle of union, and liparos, to grease, to leave a stain; guilt was like a grease stain upon the conscience of fallen man. The word, [2]cheirographon, translates as hand-written. The word, [3]dogma, comes from dokeo, a thought pattern; thus thought patterns engraved by human experience of constant failure to do what the law required. In his personal handwriting man endorsed his own death sentence. The hands of fallen man struck the body of Jesus with the blows of their religious hatred and fury when they nailed his bloodied body to the tree; they did not realize that in the mystery of God's economy Jesus was the scapegoat of the entire human race! [Isa 53:4, 5]*

"The slate wiped clean, that old arrest warrant canceled and nailed to Christ's Cross." — The Message)

Col 2:15 His brilliant victory made a public [1]spectacle of every [2]rule and [3]authority empowered by the fall of Adam. The [4]voice of the cross will never be silenced! *(The horror of the Cross is now the eternal trophy of God's triumph over sin! The cross stripped religion of its authority to manipulate man with guilt. Every accusation lost its power to continue to blackmail the human race. The word, ¹apekduomai, is translated from apo, away from, and ekduo, to be stripped of clothing; the religious facade that disguised the law of works as a means of defining man was openly defeated. The dominance of the tree of the knowledge of good and evil (poneros, hard work and labor) was ended. The word, ¹deik-matizo, means to exhibit in public. The word, ⁴parresia, comes from pas, all and rheo, outspokenness, pouring forth speech.*

"He stripped all the spiritual tyrants in the universe of their sham authority at the Cross and marched them naked through the streets." — The Message

See commentary for 1 Corinthians 15:24, The complete conclusion in his work of redemption is celebrated in his yielding the full harvest of his reign to God the Father, having ¹brought to naught the law of works which supported every definition of dominion under the fall, including all ²principalities, all ³authority and every ⁴dynamic influence in society. [He brought to naught the law of works, ¹katargeo, from kata, meaning intensity, and argos, meaning labor; thus free from all self effort to attempt to improve what God has already perfected in Christ. All principalities, ²arche, or chief ranks, i.e., kings, governors; this includes any governing system whereby one is ranked above the other on the basis of their performance or preference. All authority, ³exousia, comes from ek, denoting origin and eimi, I am; in this case, because of what I can do I am defined by what I can do better than you; therefore, I have authority over you. Every dynamic influence in society, ⁴dunamis, means power, in this case, willpower. Every government structure in society will be brought under the dominion of grace where the Christ life rules.]

In 1 Corinthians 2:7-8, We voice words of wisdom that was hidden in silence for timeless ages; a mystery unfolding God's Masterful plan whereby he would redeem his glory in man. Neither the politicians nor the theologians of the day had a clue about this mystery [of mankind's association in Christ]; if they did, they would never have crucified the Lord whose death redeemed our glory!) Mirror Bible

God used Christ's body to condemn sin. CEB   Contemporary English Version

Rom.8:3. He has signed the death warrant of sin. Knox.

1 Cor 1:22 The Jews crave signs *(to confirm their doubts)* while the Greeks revel in philosophical debate! *(Both groups are addicted to the same soul realm.)*

1 Cor 1:23 The crucified Christ is the message we publicly proclaim, to the disgust of the Jews while the Greeks think we are wacky!

1 Cor 1:24 The dynamic of God's wisdom is the fact that both Jew and Greek are equally included and defined in Christ.

1 Cor 1:25 It seems so foolish that God should die man's death on the cross; it seems so weak of God to suffer such insult; yet man's wisest schemes and most powerful display of genius cannot even begin to comprehend or compete with God in his weakest moment on the cross. Mirror Bible

1Cor 2:2 The testimony of God is my only persuasion concerning you: Jesus Christ died your death on the cross! I can see you in no other light! *(For I determined to know nothing in you except Jesus Christ and him crucified.)*

Heb 8:10 Now, instead of documenting my laws on stone, I will chisel them into your mind and engrave them in your inner consciousness; it will no longer be a one-sided affair. I will be your God and you will be my people, not by compulsion but by mutual desire.

Heb 8:11 Knowing me will no longer be a Sunday-school lesson, or something taught by persuasive words of doctrine, neither will they know me on account of family tradition or door to door evangelism *(each one telling his neighbor)*. Everyone, from the most unlikely to the most prominent people in society, will know me inwardly.

Heb 8:12 This knowledge of me will never again be based on a sin-consciousness. My act of mercy, extended in Christ as the new Covenant, has removed every possible definition of sin from my memory!

Heb 9:9 The tabernacle pattern of that time was an analogy of the hitherto imperfect system in which the gifts and sacrifices presented failed completely to cleanse the conscience of the worshipper.

Heb 9:10 All these external rituals pertaining to food and drink and the various ceremonial baptisms and rules for bodily conduct were imposed upon them until the anticipated time of restoration, the foretold moment when ¹all that was crooked would be made straight and restored to its natural and original condition. *(This word, ¹diothosis, is only used in this one place in the New Testament; what was crooked will be made thoroughly straight, restoring to its natural and normal condition something which in some way protrudes or has gotten out of line, as broken or misshapen limbs.)*

Heb 9:11 But now Christ has made his public appearance as High Priest of a perfect tabernacle. The good things that were predicted have arrived. This new tabernacle does not derive from its shadow type, the previous man-made one. It is the reality. *(The restoration of God's original dwelling place in human life is again revealed!)*

Heb 9:12 As High Priest, his permission to enter the Holy Place was not secured by the blood of beasts. By his own blood he obtained access on behalf of the human race. Only one act was needed for him to enter the most sacred place of grace and there to institute a ransom of perpetual consequence. *(The perfection of the redemption he secured needs no further sacrifice. There are no outstanding debts; there is nothing we need do to add weight to what he has accomplished once and for all. The only possible priesthood activity we can now engage in is to continually bring a sacrifice of the fruit of our lips, giving thanks to his Name; no blood, just fruit, even our acts of self-sacrifice, giving of time and money, etc. are all just the fruit of our constant gratitude!)*

Heb 9:13 The blood of beasts and the ashes of the burnt sacrifice of a heifer could only achieve a very temporal and surface cleansing by being sprinkled on the guilty to symbolize their appeal to God for forgiveness. *(This was the best that the law-system had to offer; no inner purging of conscience was possible, only the sense of temporal relief, whilst knowing that the whole process would have to be repeated again and again!)*

Heb 9:14 How much more effective was the blood of Christ when he presented his own flawless life through the eternal Spirit to God in order to purge your conscience from its frustration under the cul-de-sac rituals of the law in your efforts to minister to the living God. *(A dead routine system can never compete with the resurrected Christ now alive in you.)*

1 Pet 4:1,2 Death brings a final end to sin, since Christ suffered for us in the flesh, *(He died our death; you were on his mind throughout)* consider the implication of your co-inclusion in him; thus reinforce your mind to stand fully armed against any onslaught. You may confidently live the rest of your time in the flesh inspired by the determined purpose of God with no further obligation to perverted human lusts.

Col 3:1 You are in fact raised together with Christ! Now ponder with persuasion the consequence of your co-inclusion in him. Relocate yourselves mentally! Engage your thoughts with throne room realities. His resurrection co-raised you to the same position of authority where you are now co-seated in the executive authority of God's right hand.

Col 3:2 Becoming affectionately acquainted with these thoughts will keep you from being distracted again by the earthly *(soul-ruled)* realm. *(A renewed mind conquers the space that was previously occupied by worthless pursuits and habits.)*

Col 3:3 Your union with his death broke the association with that world; see yourselves located in a fortress where your life is hidden with Christ in God! *("In that day you will know that I am in my father, and you in me and I in you." [Jn 14:20] Occupy your mind with this new order of life; you died when Jesus died, whatever defined you before defines you no more. Christ, in whom the fullness of deity dwells, defines you now! The secret of your life is your union with Christ in God! [See Col 2:9, 10])*

"Risen, then, with Christ you must lift your thoughts above where Christ now sits at the right hand of God, you must be heavenly minded; not earthly minded, you have undergone death, and your life is hidden away now with Christ in God. Christ is your life, when he is made manifest you are made manifest in his glory." — Knox Translation)

Col 3:4 The exact life on exhibit in Christ is now repeated in us. We are being [1]co-revealed in the same bliss; we are joined in oneness with him, just as his life reveals you, your life reveals him! *(This verse was often translated to again delay the revelation of Christ to a future event! The word, [1]otan, often translated as "when" is better translated as "every time." Thus, "Every time Christ is revealed we are being co-revealed in his glory." According to Walter Bauer Lexicon, otan is often used of an action that is repeated. Paul declares our joint-glorification in Christ! We are co-revealed in the same bliss. [See 1 Cor 2:7-8, Rom 3:23-24, Rom 8:30, 2 Pet 1:3.] In him we live and move and have our being; in us he lives and moves and has his being! [Acts 17:28])*

Col 3:5 Consider the members of your body as dead and buried towards everything related to the porn industry, sensual uncleanness, longing for forbidden things, lust and greed, which are just another form of idol worship. *(Idol worship is worshipping a distorted image of yourself!)*

Col 3:6 These distorted expressions are in total contradiction to God's design and desire for your life.

Col 3:7 We were all once swept along into a lifestyle of lust and greed.

Col 3:8 But now, because you realize that you co-died and were co-raised together with Christ, you can flush your thoughts with truth! Permanently put these things behind you: things such as violent outbursts of rage, depression, all manner of

43

wickedness, slander *(any attempt to belittle someone else and to cause someone to receive a bad reputation, **blasphemos**)*, and every form of irregular conversation. *(The lifelong association with sin is broken; the dominion of the character of God is revealed again in ordinary life.)*

Col 3:9 That old life was a lie, foreign to our design! Those garments of disguise are now thoroughly stripped off us in our understanding of our union with Christ in his death and resurrection. We are no longer obliged to live under the identity and rule of the robes we wore before, neither are we cheating anyone through false pretensions. *(The garments an actor would wear define his part in the play but cannot define him.)*

Col 3:10 We stand fully identified in the new creation renewed in knowledge according to the pattern of the exact image of our Creator.

Col 3:11 The revelation of Christ in us gives identity to the individual beyond anything anyone could ever be as a Greek or a Jew, American or African, foreigner or famous, male or female, king or pawn. From now on everyone is defined by Christ; everyone is represented in Christ. *(In seeing him not just recorded in history but revealed in us, we discover the face of our birth as in a mirror! [Jas 1:18])*

Heb 10:1 For the law presented to us a faint shadow, outlining the promise of the blessings anticipated in the coming of Christ, even detailing its future significance. The mere sketch however, could never be confused with the actual object that it represented. The annual sacrificial rites as shadow of the eventual object would always leave the worshipper feeling inadequate and be a reminder year after year of the sinfulness of man. *(Barnes Notes on Heb 10:1, "For the law having a shadow: That is, the whole of the Mosaic economy was a shadow; for so the word "Law" is often used. The word "shadow" here refers to a rough outline of anything, a mere sketch, such as a carpenter draws with a piece of chalk, or such as an artist delineates when he is about to make a picture.*

He sketches an outline of the object which he desires to draw, which has "some" resemblance to it, but is not the "very image;" for it is not yet complete. The words rendered "the very image" refer to a painting or statue that is finished, where every part is an exact representation of the original. The "good things to come" here refer to the future blessings which would be conferred on man by the Gospel. The idea is, that under the ancient sacrifices there was an imperfect representation; a dim outline of the blessings which the Gospel would impart to people. They were a typical representation; they were not such that it could be pretended that they would answer the purpose of the things themselves which they were to represent, and would make those who offered them perfect.

Such a rude outline; such a mere sketch, or imperfect delineation, could no more answer the purpose of saving the soul than the rough sketch which an architect makes would answer the purpose of a house, or than the first outline which a painter draws would answer the purpose of a perfect and finished portrait. All that could be done by either would be to convey some distant and obscure idea of what the house or the picture might be, and this was all that was done by the Law of Moses."

The Gospel is no longer a future prediction; it is a now and relevant revelation. We are talking good news, and not just good predictions! News already happened! Every definition of distance or delay is cancelled in Christ)

44

Heb 10:2 If it was possible to present the perfect offering that had the power to successfully remove any trace of a sin-consciousness, then the sacrificial system would surely cease to be relevant. *(The measure of success must be such that God's affirmation of our innocence would be reflected. [See Heb 10:17])*

Heb 10:3 But in the very repetition of these ritual sacrifices the awareness of guilt is reinforced rather than removed.

Heb 10:14 By that one perfect sacrifice he has [1]perfectly [2]sanctified sinful man forever. *(The word, [2]hagiazomenous, means sanctify, the present participle describes an action thought of as simultaneous with the action of the main verb, "perfectly;" [1]teteleioken, in the Perfect Tense denotes an action which is completed in the past, but the effects of which are regarded as continuing into the present. [See Heb 2:11] For he who sanctifies and those who are sanctified have all one origin.)*

Heb 10:15 This is exactly what the Holy Spirit now endorses in us having already foretold it in scripture. *(Jer 31:33, 34)*

Heb 10:16 This is my covenant that I will make with you during those days, says the Lord; I will greatly advantage you by [1]giving my laws in your hearts and engrave them in your inmost thoughts. *(The word, [1]didomi, means to give someone something to their advantage.)*

Heb 10:17 This is final: I have deleted the record of your sins and misdeeds. I no longer recall them. *(Nothing in God's reference of man, reminds him of sin.)*

Heb 10:18 Sins were dealt with in such a thorough manner that no further offerings would ever again be required. Nothing that we can personally sacrifice could add further virtue to our innocence.

Heb 10:19 Brethren, this means that through what the blood of Jesus communicates and represents, we are now welcome to access this ultimate place of sacred encounter with unashamed confidence.

10:20 A brand new way of life has been introduced. Because of his flesh torn on the cross *(our own flesh can no longer be a valid excuse to interrupt the expression of the life of our design).*

Heb 10:21 We have a High Priest in the house!

Heb 10:22 We are free to approach him with absolute confidence, fully persuaded in our hearts that nothing can any longer separate us from him. We are invited to draw near now! We are thoroughly cleansed, inside and out, with no trace of sin's stains on our conscience or conduct. The sprinkled blood purges our inner thought-patterns; our bodies also are bathed in clean water. *(Our behavior bears witness to this.)*

Heb 10:23 Our conversation echoes his persuasion; his faithfulness backs his promises. *(His integrity inspires our confession.)*

Heb 10:24 Let us also think of creative ways by which we can influence one another to find inspired expression in doing things that benefit others. Good actions give voice and volume to the love of God.

Heb 10:25 In the light of our free access to the Father, let us extend that embrace to one another. Our gatherings are no longer a repetition of tradition but an essential fellowship where we remind one another of our true identity. Let us do so with greater urgency now the day has dawned in our understanding. *(The prophetic shadow has been replaced by the light of day.)* Mirror Bible

1Pe 3:18 For Christ also died for sins once for all, the righteous for the unrighteous, that he might bring us to God, being put to death in the flesh but made alive in the spirit; RSV

Rom 6:6 We perceive that our old lifestyle was co-crucified together with him; this concludes that the vehicle that accommodated sin in us, was scrapped and rendered entirely useless. Our slavery to sin has come to an end.

Rom 6:7 If nothing else stops you from doing something wrong, death certainly does.

Rom 6:8 Faith sees us joined in his death and alive with him in his resurrection.

Rom 6:9 It is plain for all to see that death lost its dominion over Christ in his resurrection; he need not ever die again to prove a further point.

Rom 6:10 His appointment with death was [1]once-off. As far as sin is concerned, he is dead. The reason for his death was to take away the sin of the world; his life now exhibits our union with the life of God. *(The Lamb of God took away the sin of the world; [1]efapax, once and for all, a final testimony, used of what is so done to be of perpetual validity and never needs repetition. This is the final testimony of the fact that sin's power over us is destroyed. In Hebrews 9:26, "But Jesus did not have to suffer again and again since the fall (or since the foundation) of the world; the single sacrifice of himself in the fulfillment of history now reveals how he has brought sin to naught." "Christ died once, and faced our judgment! His second appearance (in his resurrection) has nothing to do with sin, but to reveal salvation unto all who eagerly embrace him [Heb 9:28].")*

Rom 6:11 This reasoning is equally relevant to you. [1]Calculate the cross; there can only be one logical conclusion: he died your death; that means you died unto sin, and are now alive unto God. Sin-consciousness can never again feature in your future! You are in Christ Jesus; his Lordship is the authority of this union. *(We are not being presumptuous to reason that we are in Christ! "[1]Reckon yourselves therefore dead unto sin" The word, [1]logitsomai, means logical reasoning [See Eph 1:4 and 1 Cor 1:30].*

"From now on, think of it this way: Sin speaks a dead language that means nothing to you; God speaks your mother tongue, and you hang on every word. You are dead to sin and alive to God. That's what Jesus did." — The Message)

Rom 6:12 You are under no obligation to sin; it has no further rights to dominate your dead declared body. Therefore let it not entice you to obey its lusts. *(Your union with his death broke the association with sin [Col 3:3].)*

Rom 6:13 Do not let the members of your body lie around loose and unguarded in the vicinity of unrighteousness, where sin can seize it and use it as a destructive weapon against you; rather place yourself in [1]readiness unto God, like someone resurrected from the dead, present your whole person as a weapon of righteousness. *(Thus you are reinforcing God's grace claim on mankind in Christ; [1]paristemi, to place in readiness in the vicinity of).*

Rom 6:14 Sin was your master while the law was your measure; now grace rules. *(The law revealed your slavery to sin, now grace reveals your freedom from it.)*

Rom 6:15 Being under grace and not under the law most certainly does not mean that you now have a license to sin.

Rom 6:16 As much as you once gave permission to sin to trap you in its spiral of spiritual death and enslave you to its dictates, the obedience that faith ignites now, introduces a new rule, rightness with God; to this we willingly yield ourselves. *(Righteousness represents everything that God restored us to—in Christ.)*

Rom 6:17 The content of teaching that your heart embraced has set a new ¹standard to become the ¹pattern of your life; the grace of God ended sin's dominance. *(The word, ¹**tupos**, means form, mold. The Doddrich translation translates it as, "the model of doctrine instructs you as in a mold.")*

Rom 6:18 Sin once called the shots; now righteousness rules. Mirror Bible

Rom 5:18 The conclusion is clear: it took just one offense to condemn mankind; one act of righteousness declares the same mankind innocent. Mirror

(Phillips translation: "We see then, that as one act of sin exposed the whole race of men to condemnation, so one act of perfect righteousness presents all men freely acquitted in the sight of God!")

Every accusation against man has been effectively cancelled.
Joh 12:31 Now is the judgment of this world, now shall the ruler of this world be cast out;

Joh 12:32 and I, when I am lifted up from the earth, will draw all judgment to myself.

Joh 12:33 He said this to show by what death he was to die. RSV

Rev 12:9 And the great dragon was thrown down, that ancient serpent, who is called the Devil and Satan, the deceiver of the whole world--he was thrown down to the earth, and his angels were thrown down with him.

Rev 12:10 And I heard a loud voice in heaven, saying, "Now the salvation and the power and the kingdom of our God and the authority of his Christ have come, for the accuser of our brethren has been thrown down, who accuses them day and night before our God.

Rev 12:11 And they have conquered him by the blood of the Lamb and by the word of their testimony, for they loved not their lives even unto death. RSV

Psa 103:1 A Psalm of David. Bless the LORD, O my soul; and all that is within me, bless his holy name!

Psa 103:2 Bless the LORD, O my soul, and forget not all his benefits,

Psa 103:3 who forgives all your iniquity, who heals all your diseases,

Psa 103:4 who redeems your life from the Pit, who crowns you with steadfast love and mercy,

Psa 103:5 who satisfies you with good as long as you live so that your youth is renewed like the eagle's

Psa 103:10 He does not deal with us according to our sins, nor requite us according to our iniquities.

Psa 103:11 For as the heavens are high above the earth, so great is his steadfast love toward those who fear him;

Psa 103:12 as far as the east is from the west, so far does he remove our transgressions from us. RSV

Zec 3:1 Then he showed me Joshua the high priest standing before the angel of the LORD, and Satan standing at his right hand to accuse him.

Zec 3:2 And the LORD said to Satan, "The LORD rebuke you, O Satan! The LORD who has chosen Jerusalem rebuke you! Is not this a brand plucked from the fire?"

Zec 3:3 Now Joshua was standing before the angel, clothed with filthy garments.

Zec 3:4 And the angel said to those who were standing before him, "Remove the filthy garments from him." And to him he said, "Behold, I have taken your iniquity away from you, and I will clothe you with rich apparel."

Zec 3:5 And I said, "Let them put a clean turban on his head." So they put a clean turban on his head and clothed him with garments; and the angel of the LORD was standing by.

Zec 3:8 Hear now, O Joshua the high priest, you and your friends who sit before you, for they are men of good omen: behold, I will bring my servant the Branch.

Zec 3:9 For behold, upon the stone which I have set before Joshua, upon a single stone with seven facets, I will engrave its inscription, says the LORD of hosts, and I will remove the guilt of this land in a single day. RSV

1 Cor 5:8 Our daily life is now the extension of the Passover celebration; feasting on sustained innocence! The old sin conscious-system, the leaven-mind set *(always anticipating and tolerating sin)*, is replaced with an understanding of our unleavened innocence, just like when a diamond is [1]scrutinized in the rays of the sun to confirm its flawless integrity. *(The word, [1]elikrineia, translates as scrutinized in the rays of the sun.)*

4th Vital Friendship Ingredient: Oneness of Mind

There is nothing wrong with the human race because there is nothing wrong with their design nor is there anything wrong with their salvation. In Christ God did enough to rescue his image and likeness, the very blueprint life of our design, in human form.

Mankind cannot become more "saved" than what they already are!

Why is the world and the lives of multitudes of people in such a mess? The problem is not wrong doing as much as it is wrong thinking!

Isa 55:8 For my thoughts are not your thoughts, neither are your ways my ways, says the LORD.

Isa 55:9 For as the heavens are higher than the earth, so are my ways higher than your ways and my thoughts than your thoughts.

We often stop reading there and conclude that God's mind cannot be known!

There is no good news in those verses! Please read on! We are not staring blindly into some vague display window of the ideas and doctrines of men! In Christ every definition of distance is cancelled; every veil is removed!

2 Cor 3:18 The days of window-shopping are over! In him every face is unveiled. In gazing with wonder at the blueprint likeness of God displayed in human form we suddenly realize that we are looking at ourselves! Every feature of his image is mirrored in us! This is the most radical transformation engineered by the Spirit of the Lord; we are led from an inferior mind-set to the revealed endorsement of our authentic identity. Mankind is his glory!

Isa 55:10,11, "For as the rain and the snow come down from heaven, and return not thither but saturate the earth, making it bring forth and sprout, giving seed to the sower and bread to the eater, so shall my word be that goes forth from my mouth; it shall not return to me empty, but it shall accomplish that which I purpose, and prosper in the thing for which I sent it.

Jesus Christ is the word made flesh! In him God lavished every blessing heaven has upon us! Eph 1:3. God owes us nothing! Imagine how this revelation would change someone's prayer life!

In the incarnation God cancelled every definition of distance. He cannot saturate the soil of human life more than what he already did! All the mineral wealth is already deposited in the earth! The word was made flesh in every human life! We have this treasure in earthen vessels! 2 Cor 4:7.

God is not closer to some than what he is to others! He is equally Emmanuel to every individual on planet earth! Paul speaks to a pagan, idol worshipping audience in Acts 17 and make this remarkable statement: The God who created the universe is not far from each one of us! Paul understands that in Christ God already reconciled the world to himself! The world cannot be more reconciled to their Maker than what they already are! In Christ there can never again be an "us" and "them".

Jesus is what God believes about you; Jesus is God's mind made up about every human life!

True Christian faith is not about man attempting to win the favor of deity, or trying to influence the mood of a bad tempered god; it is the revelation of the love of God who accomplished the reconciling of a hostile world to himself through one act of righteousness in one amazing moment! 2012 years ago eternity kissed time!

The appeal of the good news addresses every person's conscience. 2 Cor 4:2. The religious systems of the world blind-folded our minds with unbelief, says Paul in 2 Cor 4:4, to hide from us the revelation of the image of God in us! This is the most priceless treasure that anyone can ever discover! Christ is not hiding in history or in outer space or in the far future; he is not even hiding in the pages of the Bible; he

49

is merely reflected there to be unveiled in you! Col 1:27.

One of the most important words in the Bible is the Greek word, *metanoia*. It is a compound word, *meta* which means, together with, and *nous* meaning mind. Sadly this word was deliberatly translated as repentance, which is a Latin word employed by the religious system to manipulate people with guilt and sell tham the idea that God's favor can be bought!

God's thoughts embraced the human race in Christ; the gospel is the bold unveiling of the love initiative of God! Love awakens faith.

1 Cor 2:13 The impact of our words are not confined to the familiar wisdom of the world taught by human experience and tradition, but communicated by seamless spirit resonance, combining spirit with spirit.

Jesus didn't come to win doctrinal debates, he came to win our hearts!

Within this Divine Romance, oneness of mind is not a luxury option; it is the conclusion of faith.
We do not invent fellowship, we are invited into the fellowship of the `Father and the son.

James 1:23 The difference between a mere spectator and a participator is that both of them hear the same voice and perceive in its message the face of their own genesis reflected as in a mirror;

James 1:24 they realize that they are looking at themselves, but for the one it seems just too good to be true, he departs *(back to his old way of seeing himself)* never giving another thought to the man he saw there in the mirror.

James 1:25 The other one is [1]mesmerized by what he sees; he is [2]captivated by the effect of a law that frees man from the obligation to the old written code that restricted him to his own efforts and willpower. No distraction or contradiction can dim the impact of what he sees in that mirror concerning the law of perfect [3]liberty *(the law of faith)* that now frees him to get on with the act of living the life *(of his original design.)* He finds a new [3]spontaneous lifestyle; the poetry of practical living. *(The law of perfect liberty is the image and likeness of God revealed in Christ, now redeemed in man as in a mirror. Look deep enough into that law of faith that you may see there in its perfection a portrait that so resembles the original that he becomes distinctly visible in the spirit of your mind and in the face of every man you behold. I translated the word, [1]parakupto, with mesmerized from para, a preposition indicating close proximity, originating from, denoting the point from which an action originates, intimate connection, and kupto, to bend, stoop down to view at close scrutiny; [2]parameno, to remain captivated under the influence of; meno, to continue to be present. The word often translated as freedom, [3]eleutheria, means without obligation; spontaneous.)*

James 1:26 Meaningless conversation is often disguised in religious eloquence. Just because it sounds sincere, doesn't make it true. If your tongue is not bridled by what your heart knows to be true about you, you cheat yourself.

Paul sees that oneness in Christ inspires the fine-tuning of our every conversation.

1Co 1:10 I appeal to you, brethren, by the name of our Lord Jesus Christ, that all of you agree and that there be no dissensions among you, but that you be united in the same mind and the same judgment. RSV

1 Cor 1:10 My dear Brothers, because we are surnamed and identified in the name of our master Jesus Christ, I [1]urge you to speak with one voice, *(to say the same thing)* we share the same source as our reference; no division or any sense of distance is tolerated, which makes us a perfect match, accurately joined in the same thought pattern and communicating the same resolve. *(The word, [1]parakaleo, is from para, a preposition indicating close proximity, a thing proceeding from a sphere of influence, with a suggestion of union of place of residence, to have sprung from its author and giver, originating from, denoting the point from which an action originates, intimate connection and kaleo, to surname.)*

2 Co 4:13 Since we have the same spirit of faith as he had who wrote, "I believed, and so I spoke," we too believe, and so we speak, RSV

2 Cor 4:13 We [1]echo the exact same spirit of faith David had when he wrote: "I believe and so I speak!" We too believe and so we speak! Our persuasion is our conversation. *(The word, [1]echo, means to hold or to embrace. Paul quotes David here in Psalm 116; sometimes one's soul wants to gallop away into distraction like a wild horse; David speaks to himself and reminds himself to, "Return, O my soul, to your rest; for the Lord has dealt bountifully with you!" [RSV] "I believe, and so I speak!" God's bountiful dealings with us in Christ is our only valid rest; Sabbath celebrates perfection! And remember God does not employ circumstances to teach us something! The finished work of Christ teaches us; his work on the cross rescued us!)*

Phm 1:6 The fellowship of our faith is ignited by the acknowledging of every good thing that is in us in Christ.

Gal 5:10 In spite of the interference of those "law-church" people, I remain convinced about our like-mindedness in the Lord. It does not matter what high profile position anyone may occupy, do not let their title disturb you! The very law they promote will be their judgment! *(The fermentation process is unavoidable when you host a legalistic mind-set.)* Mirror

Gal 5:10 I have confidence in the Lord that you will take no other view than mine; and he who is troubling you will bear his judgment, whoever he is. RSV

The entire gospel reveals our co-inclusion in Christ. No wonder Paul says that for us to compete with one another or even to measure or compare ourselves with one another is to be without understanding.

2 Co 10:12 Not that we venture to class or compare ourselves with some of those who commend themselves. But when they measure themselves by one another, and compare themselves with one another, they are without understanding. RSV

This concludes that no personal differences, preferences, or prejudices can be tolerated above the wonderful truth of God's work of grace and reconciliation. We are entrusted with world peace! Our ministry is the ministry of reconciliation. God already reconciled a hostile world to himself and now urgently pleads through us and appeals to every man's conscience, in order to make all men see and realize its consequence.

Paul reminds Titus, "To avoid gossip, to speak evil of no one, to quit quarreling, to be gentle, and to show perfect courtesy toward all men. Remember how foolish and hard of hearing we ourselves were; not knowing the truth about ourselves we were led astray, slaves to various passions and pleasures, passing our days in malice and envy, we existed only for our own selfish interests, hated by men and hating one another. But when God overwhelmed us with goodness and his fondness for mankind dawned on us in the gospel, he rescued us, not because of some righteous deeds done by us, but by his own mercy demonstrated in Christ." Tit. 3:2-5. RSV

Titus 3:2 Gossip is out! Never have anything bad to say about anyone! You do not have to win every argument; instead, avoid [1]quarrelling, be appropriate, always show perfect courtesy to one and all. *(The word, [1]mache, means controversial, striving. You don't have to wait for people to change before you are nice to them. There is a big difference between "fake politeness" and perfect courtesy!)*

Titus 3:3 Do not be harsh on others. Remember that we, too, were typically foolish; we were stubborn and indifferent to spiritual things, our addiction to the sensual and sexual kept us running around in circles, we were engaged in malice and spiteful jealousies, we were bored and lonely, often utterly disliking ourselves and hating one another!

Titus 3:4 But then, oh happy day! It was the generosity of God and his fondness for mankind that dawned on us like a shaft of light. Our days of darkness were over! Light shone everywhere and we became aware: God rescued the human race!

Titus 2:11 The grace of God shines as bright as day making the salvation of humankind undeniably visible. Mirror

(For God's undeserved kindness has burst in upon us, bringing a new lease on life for all mankind. — Clarence Jordan)

Rom 12:17 Two wrongs do not make a right. Never retaliate; instead, cultivate the attitude to [1]anticipate only beauty and value in every person you encounter. *([1]pronoew, to know in advance.)*

Rom 12:18 You have within you what it takes to be everyone's friend, regardless of how they treat you. *(See Rom 1:16, 17. Also Mt 5:44, 45.)*

Rom 12:19 Do not bother yourselves to get even, dear ones. Do not let anger or irritation distract you; [1]that which we have in common with one another (righteousness) must set the pace. Scripture confirms that the Lord himself is the [1]revealer of righteousness. *([1]ekdikeo, from ek, a preposition denoting origin, and dikeo, two parties finding likeness in one another. That which originates in righteousness sets the pace in every relationship.)*

Rom 12:20 "If your enemy is hungry, feed him; if he is thirsty, give him something to drink." These acts of kindness will certainly rid your enemy of the dross in his mind and win him as a friend. *(A refiner would melt metal in a crucible and intensify the process by heaping coals of fire on it [Prov 25:21, 22]. This is good strategy; be sensitive to the needs of your enemies. God sees gold in every person. Hostility cannot hide our true*

52

value. He won us while we were hostile towards him [see also Rom 5:8, 10]. His kindness led us to repentance [Rom 2:4].)

Rom 5:8 Herein is the extremity of God's love gift: mankind was rotten to the core when Christ died their death.

Rom 5:9 If God could love us that much when we were ungodly and guilty, how much more are we free to realize his love now that we are declared innocent by his blood? *(God does not love us more now that we are reconciled to him; we are now free to realize how much he loved us all along! [Col 2:14, Rom 4:25])*

Rom 5:10 Our hostility and indifference towards God did not reduce his love for us; he saw equal value in us when he exchanged the life of his son for ours. Now that the act of [1]reconciliation is complete, his life in us saves us from the gutter-most to the uttermost. *(Reconciliation, from [1]**katalasso**, meaning a mutual exchange of equal value. Thayer Definition: to exchange, as coins for others of equivalent value.* Mirror "For if while we were enemies we were reconciled to God by the death of his Son, much more, now that we are reconciled, shall we be saved by his life." RSV)

Rom 2:4 No one can afford to get the wrong idea about God's [2]goodness; he hates sin but loves man! The wealth of his [2]benevolence and his [3]resolute refusal to let go of us in his [4]patient passion is to [5]shepherd everyone into a [1]radical change of mind. *(It is the revelation of the goodness of God that leads us to [1]repentance! Paul often has to remind his readers that his emphasis on the goodness of God is not a cheap excuse for them to continue in sin [see 6:1]. The word, [2]**chrestotetos,** from **chraomai** meaning to receive a loan; life is on loan to us as it were. Life is God's property, and [3]**anoches** comes from **ana**, shows intensity and echo, to hold, or embrace, as in echo. The word, [4]**makrothumias**, means to be patient in bearing the offenses and injuries of others. Literally, passion that goes a long way; from the root word **thuo**, to slay a sacrifice. The word, [5]**ago**, means to lead as a shepherd leads his sheep. The word "repentance" is a fabricated word from the Latin, penance, and to give religion more mileage the English word became re-penance! That is not what the Greek word means at all! The word, [1]**metanoia**, comes from **meta**, meaning together with, and **nous**, mind, together with God's mind. This word suggests a [1]radical mind shift; to return to one's right mind. [See Isa 55:8-10])*
Mirror Bible

2 Cor 5:14 The love of Christ [1]resonates within us and leaves us with only one conclusion: Jesus died humanity's death; therefore, in God's logic every individual simultaneously died. *(The word, [1]**sunecho**, from **sun**, meaning together with and **echo**, meaning to echo, to embrace, to hold, and thus translated, to resonate. Jesus didn't die 99% or for 99%. He died humanity's death 100%! If Paul had to compromise the last part of verse 14 to read: "one died for all therefore only those who follow the prescriptions to qualify, have also died," then he would have had to change the first half of the verse as well! Only the love of Christ can make a calculation of such enormous proportion! Theology would question the extremity of God's love and perhaps prefer to add a condition or two to a statement like that!)*

2 Cor 5:15 Now if all were included in his death they were equally included in his resurrection. This unveiling of his love redefines human life! Whatever reference we could have of ourselves outside of our association with Christ is no longer relevant.

53

2 Cor 5:16 This is radical! No label that could possibly previously define someone carries any further significance! Even our pet doctrines of Christ are redefined. Whatever we knew about him historically or sentimentally is challenged by this conclusion. *(By discovering Christ from God's point of view we discover ourselves and every other human life from God's point of view!)*

2 Cor 5:17 In the light of your co-inclusion in his death and resurrection, whoever you thought you were before, in Christ you are a brand new person! The old ways of seeing yourself and everyone else are over. Acquaint yourself with the new! *(Just imagine this! Whoever a person was as a Jew, Greek, slave or freeman, Boer, Zulu, Xhosa, British, Indian, Muslim or American, Chinese, Japanese or Congolese; is now dead and gone! They all died when Jesus died! Remember we are not talking law language here! The 'If' in, "If any man is in Christ" is not a condition, it is the conclusion of the revelation of the gospel! Man is in Christ by God's doing [1 Cor 1:30 and Eph 1:4]. The verses of 2 Corinthians 5:14-16 give context to verse 17! For so long we studied verse 17 on its own and interpreted the 'if' as a condition! Paul did not say, "If any man is in Christ," he said "THEREFORE if any man is in Christ ..." The "therefore" immediately includes verses 14 to 16! If God's faith sees every man in Christ in his death, then they were certainly also in Christ in his resurrection. Jesus did not reveal a "potential" you, he revealed the truth about you so that you may know the truth about yourself and be free indeed!)*

2 Cor 5:18 To now see everything as new is to simply see what God has always known in Christ; we are not debating man's experience, opinion, or his contribution; this is 100% God's belief and his doing. In Jesus Christ, God [1]exchanged equivalent value to redeem us to himself. This act of reconciliation is the mandate of our ministry. *(The word, [1]**katalasso**, translates as reconciliation; a mutual exchange of equal value.)*

2 Cor 5:19 Our ministry declares that Jesus did not act independent of God. Christ is proof that God reconciled the total kosmos to himself. Deity and humanity embraced in Christ; the fallen state of mankind was deleted; their trespasses would no longer count against them! God has placed this message within us. He now announces his friendship with every individual from within us! Mirror Bible

1Co 2:2 The testimony of God is my only persuasion concerning you: Jesus Christ died your death on the cross! I can see you in no other light! *(For I determined to know nothing in you except Jesus Christ and him crucified.)*

1Co 2:7 We voice words of wisdom that was hidden in silence for timeless ages; a mystery unfolding God's Masterful plan whereby he would redeem his glory in man.

1Co 2:8 Neither the politicians nor the theologians of the day had a clue about this mystery *(of mankind's association in Christ)*; if they did, they would never have crucified the Lord whose death redeemed our glory!

Act 10:15 The voice spoke to him again, "Do not consider anything unclean that God has declared clean." Good News Bible

Acts10: 28. God has shown me that I should not call any man impure or unclean.

1Jn 1:7 but if we walk in the light, as he is in the light, we have fellowship with one another, and the blood of Jesus his Son cleanses us from all sin. RSV

Psa 36:9 For with thee is the fountain of life; in thy light do we see light. RSV

2 Cor 1:18, God's certainty is our persuasion; there is no maybe in him!

2 Cor 1:19 The son of God, Jesus Christ, whom I, Paul, Sylvanus, and Timothy boldly announced in you is God's ultimate yes to mankind. Human life is associated in all that he is. In God's mind there exists not even a hint of hesitation about this!

2 Cor 1:20 In him the detail of every single promise of God is fulfilled; Jesus is God's yes to your total well being! In our union with him the Amen that echoes in us gives evidence to his glorious intent through us. Mirror Bible

Job 22:21 "Agree with God, and be at peace." RSV

Eph 4:2 Meekness and tenderness are the fabric of your make-up; this enables you to show compassion even in seemingly impossible situations, eagerly bearing with one another in an environment where love rules.

Eph 4:3 Being vigilant to guard your oneness of spirit. We are prisoners of peace. We confirm the fact that there is only one body; also that there is only one Spirit.

Eph 4:4 We are identified in one expectation *(hope)*; there is no plan B. We bear the same [1]surname. *(Called, [1]kaleo, to identify by name, to surname.)*

Eph 4:5 We are employed by the same Boss; we share the same faith, and our baptism says the same thing. *(We are equally included in his death and resurrection.)*

Eph 4:6 There is only one God. He remains the ultimate Father of the universe. We are because he is. He is present in all; he is above all, through all, and in all. *(He is not far from each one of us; in him we live and move and have our being. We are indeed his offspring. [Acts 17:24-28])*

Eph 4:7 The gift of Christ gives dimension to grace and defines our individual value. *(Grace was given to each one of us according to the measure of the gift of Christ. One measure, one worth! Our worth is defined by his gift not by a reward for our behavior.)*

Eph 4:8 Scripture confirms that he led us as trophies in his triumphant procession on high; he [1]repossessed his gift *(likeness)* in man. *(See Ephesians 2:6, We are also elevated in his ascension to be equally welcome in the throne room of the heavenly realm where we are now seated together with him in his authority. Quote from the Hebrew text, Ps 68:18, [1]lakachta mattanoth baadam, thou hast taken gifts in man, in Adam. [The gifts which Jesus Christ distributes to man he has received in man, in and by virtue of his incarnation. Commentary by Adam Clarke.] We were born anew in his resurrection. 1 Pet 1:3, Hos 6:2)*

Eph 4:9 The fact that he ascended confirms his victorious descent into the deepest pits of human despair. *(See John 3:13, "No one has ascended into heaven but he who*

[1]descended from heaven, even the son of man." All mankind originate from above; we are [1]anouthen, translated as from above [see Jas 1:17, 18].)

Eph 4:10 He now occupies the ultimate rank of authority from the lowest regions where he stooped down to rescue us to the highest authority in the heavens, having executed his mission to the full. *(Fallen man is fully restored to the authority of the authentic life of his design. [Ps 139:8].)*

Eph 4:11 What God has in us is gift wrapped to the world: some are commissioned to pioneer, others are gifted prophetically, some as announcers of good news, some as shepherds with a real gift to care and nurture, and others have a gift to ignite instruction through revelation knowledge. *(Couriers, communicators, counsellors and coaches. — Rob Lacey)*

Eph 4:12 Each expression of his gift is to fully equip and enable the saints for the work of the ministry so that they may mutually contribute in their specific function to give definition to the visible body of Christ.

Eph 4:13 The purpose of these ministry gifts is to present everyone on par and in oneness of faith; believing exactly what the Son of God believes and knowing accurately what he knows concerning us. Standing face-to-face in equal stature to the measure of the [1]completeness of Christ. *(The word, [1]pleroma, means a life filled to the brim with Christ, like a freight ship carrying its cargo.)* Mirror Bible

James says, "How can say beautiful things about God the Father but with the same mouth curse a man made in his mirror likeness?" Jm 3:9

1Jn 5:9 If we receive the testimony of men, the testimony of God is greater; for this is the testimony of God that he has borne witness to his Son. RSV

1Jn 5:20 And we know that the Son of God has come and has given us understanding, to know him who is true; and we are in him who is true, in his Son Jesus Christ. This is the true God and eternal life. RSV

1Jn 2:7 Beloved, I am writing you no new commandment, but an old commandment which you had from the beginning; the old commandment is the word which you have heard.

1Jn 2:8 Yet I am writing you a new commandment, which is true in him and in you, because the darkness is passing away and the true light is already shining. *(This is the point of the gospel, whatever is true of Jesus is equally true of you! See 1 Jn 4:17," As he is so are we in this world!")*

1Jn 2:9 He who says he is in the light and hates his brother is in the darkness still.

1Jn 2:10 He who loves his brother abides in the light, and in it there is no cause for stumbling. RSV

Heb 2:11 For he who sanctifies and those who are sanctified have all one origin. That is why he is not ashamed to call them brethren. RSV

Rom 13:9 Love makes it impossible for you to commit adultery, or to kill someone, or to steal from someone, speak evil of anyone, or to covet anything that belongs to someone else. Your only option is to esteem a fellow human with equal value to yourself.

Rom 13:10 Everything love does is to the advantage of another; therefore love is the most complete expression of what the law requires. Mirror Bible

True worship is to touch someone's life with the same devotion and care you would touch Jesus himself; even if the other person seems a most unlikely candidate.

I see God in every human being; in his many disturbing disguises! When I wash the leper's wounds, I feel I am nursing the Lord himself. Is it not a beautiful experience? Mother Teresa

If we still see some people as great and some as insignificant we are seeing wrong.

This gospel mobilizes us to be the mirror voice of every person's true redeemed identity and the integrity of their individual value and innocence.

5th Vital Friendship Ingredient: Living happily ever after!

There is no 'sell by date' to this union!

This is not a flash in the pan, hit and run thing! This gospel measures a friendship to be enjoyed with an unhindered, unlimited, uninterrupted future!

Heb 13:8 Take your lead from Jesus. He is your reference to the most complete life. In him yesterday is confirmed today and today mirrors tomorrow. What God spoke to us in Christ is as relevant now as it was in the prophetic past and will always be in the eternal future! *(Jesus is the same yesterday, today, and forever; there is a history to our salvation that carries more authority and relevance than anything that ever happened in our past, or anything present in time or still to happen in the future. Imagine the enormity of eternity in his sameness before time was; and we were there in him all along! See Rom 8:34 What further ground can there possibly be to condemn man? In his death he faced our judgment; in his resurrection he declares our innocence; the implications cannot be undone! He now occupies the highest seat of authority as the executive of our redemption in the throne room of God. See Rom 8: 1, also Rom 4:25. The heavens declare his glory, night to night exhibits the giant solar testimony that is mathematically precise, revealing that God knew before time was the exact moment he would enter our history as a man, and the exact moment the Messiah would expire on the cross and be raised again from the dead!)*

Sixty years after he last saw Jesus in the flesh, John, now in his nineties, reflects on the mystery that was revealed which transformed his life from an illiterate fisherman to a saint. He speaks of an uninterrupted fellowship that he desires for everyone to fully participate in.

He spent most of the latter part of his life (about 30 years) living in Asia Minor and more specifically at Ephesus; much of Paul's emphasis in teaching therefore reflects in John's writing. This he did either from Ephesus or from the Isle of Pathmos where he spent a few years in exile. (Compare Col.1:15-17, John 1:1-

3,16-17, 1Jn 5:20, "He has given us understanding to know him who is true and we are in him who is true!") None of the other disciples better captured the conclusion of the mission of Jesus than what John did in John 14:20, "In that day you will know that I am in the Father and you in me and I in you!"

He has no desire to outwit the others in giving an even more accurate historic account of Christ! The life that was manifest within his sacred gaze and now tangible embrace is a fellowship of the highest order! He must write, he must extend this reality to the next generations!

I am writing this to complete your joy and include you in my delight! 1 Jhn.1:4.

Unlike Mathew and Luke who wrote 30 years prior to John, he did not bother to locate Jesus in the setting of his natural lineage.

Instead he declares, "In the beginning was the Word!" Before history was ever recorded the Word was!

Man pre-existed in the Logic of God! He understands that the Word was both the eternal source and destiny of all things and that nothing could ever reduce or confine the Word to an isolated island experience, neither could the Word be trapped in human doctrine or tradition. No inferior translation or interpretation could compromise God's original intent.

The authentic integrity of God's thought would forever be preserved and celebrated in the incarnation; human life would be the uninterrupted future of the Word. "We are not preaching a new doctrine, but the word that was from the beginning; yet it is new in that what is true in him is equally true in us!" 1 John 2:7+8. In him we discover that we are not here by chance or accident, or by the desire of an earthly parent, neither are we the product of a mere physical conception; we exist by the expression of God's desire to reveal himself in the flesh.

1 John 1:1 The Logos is the source; everything commences in him. The initial reports concerning him that have reached our ears, that which we indeed bore witness to with our own eyes to the point that we became irresistibly attracted, now captivates our gaze. In him we witnessed tangible life in its most articulate form. (To touch, psallo, to touch the string of a musical instrument, thus resonance.)

1 John 1:2 The same life that was with the Father from the beginning, now dawned on us! The infinite life of the Father became visible before our eyes in a human person! (In the beginning "was" the word; eimi, timeless existence)

1 John 1:3 We include you in this conversation; you are the immediate audience of the logic of God! This is the word that always was; we saw him incarnate and witnessed his language as defining our life. In the incarnation Jesus includes mankind in the eternal friendship of the Father and the son! This life now finds expression in an unreserved union.

1 John 1:4 What we enjoy equally belongs to you! I am writing this for your reference, so that joy may be yours in its most complete measure. Mirror

To Job this thought of uninterrupted favor was just too good to be true. Fear and sin-consciousness dominated his relationship with God. When he reflects on his life, he speaks about the "the autumn days of God's friendship." Job 29:2-4 RSV.

This suggests that he lived under the constant fear that the winter would soon interrupt the bliss of this friendship! God has so much more than a seasonal blessing in mind.

Job 1:4 His sons used to go and hold a feast in the house of each on his day; and they would send and invite their three sisters to eat and drink with them.

Job 1:5 And when the days of the feast had run their course, Job would send and sanctify them, and he would rise early in the morning and offer burnt offerings according to the number of them all; for Job said, "It may be that my sons have sinned, and cursed God in their hearts." Thus Job did continually.

Job 3:25 For the thing that I fear comes upon me, and what I dread befalls me.

Job 29:2 "Oh, that I were as in the months of old, as in the days when God watched over me;

Job 29:3 when his lamp shone upon my head, and by his light I walked through darkness;

Job 29:4 as I was in my autumn days, when the friendship of God was upon my tent; RSV

1 Cor 1:8 He establishes you from start to finish; to stand ¹vindicated in your identity in the light of day as evidenced in the Lord Jesus Christ. *(The word, ¹anegkletos, from ana, upwards, en, in and kaleo, to identify by name. Jesus gives evidence to our original identity. Compare anoche from ana + echo in Rom 3:26)* Mirror

Eph 1:3 Let's celebrate God! He lavished every blessing heaven has upon us in Christ!

Eph 1:4 He associated us in Christ before ¹the fall of the world! Jesus is God's mind made up about us! He always knew in his love that he would present us again ²face-to-face before him in blameless innocence. *(The implications of the fall are completely cancelled out. Paul uses the word, ¹katabalo, meaning "to fall away, to put in a lower place," instead of themelios, meaning "foundation" [see 2:20]; thus, translated "the fall of the world," instead of "the foundation of the world," as in most other translations. God found us in Christ before he lost us in Adam! We are presented in blameless innocence before him! The word, ²katenopion, suggests the closest possible proximity, face-to-face!)*

Eph 1:5 He is the architect of our design; his heart dream realized our ¹coming of age in Christ. *(Adoption here is not what it means in our Western society, it is a coming of age, like the typical Jewish Barmitsva. See Galatians 4:1-6, " ... and to seal our sonship the spirit of his son echoes Abba Father in our hearts." This is ¹huiothesia.)*

Eph 1:6 His grace-plan is to be celebrated: he greatly endeared us and highly favored us in Christ. His love for his Son is his love for us. Mirror

Jer 1:5 Before I formed you in the womb I knew you

Ps 139:13 Thou didst knit me together in my mother's womb. RSV

59

Joh 14:20 In that day you will know that I am in my Father, and you in me, and I in you.

1 Cor 13:12 Then we will know even as we have always been known!

1 Cor 13:12 There was a time of [1]suspense, when everything we saw was merely mirrored in the prophetic word, like in an enigma; but then *(when I became a man in the revelation of Christ)* I gaze face-to-face; behold, I am in him! Now I may know even as I have always been known! *(The word, [1]**arti**, comes from **airo**, meaning to keep in suspense. "I knew you before I formed you in your mother's womb!"[Jer 1:5])*

Jesus came to introduce us to ourselves again, "Simon son of Jonah, I say you are Rock! Look to the Rock from which you were hewn and the quarry from which you were dug!" Mt 16:17,18, Is 51:1, Deut 32:18.

He desires for you to know yourself even as you have always been known.

In Christ the Sabbath is no longer a shadow, a token holy day in the week, but the celebration of a perfect redemption in which the exact image and likeness of God is revealed and redeemed in human form. Mankind's original identity and innocence is redeemed. "Having made purification for sins, he sat down..." His throne is established upon the fact of our innocence! God's unhindered enjoyment of man, and man's unhindered enjoyment of God is realized again.

He overlooked the times of ignorance and now urges all men everywhere to discover his eternal thoughts about mankind, revealed in Christ, when we were judged in righteousness in one man's death, and raised in his resurrection as the trophy of justice redeemed! Acts 17:30,31

God's rest is not at risk! He invites us to "enter into his rest", that is to see what his faith sees and knows to be true about the finished work of the cross.

Heb 4:10 God's rest celebrates his finished work; whoever enters into God's rest immediately abandons his own efforts to compliment what God has already perfected. *(The language of the law is "do;" the language of grace is "done.")*

Psa 36:9 For with thee is the fountain of life; in thy light do we see light. RSV

1 Jn 1:5 This is the message we have heard from him and proclaim to you, that God is light and in him is no darkness at all.

1Jn 1:7 but if we walk in the light, as he is in the light, we have fellowship with one another.

1Jn 5:9 If we receive the testimony of men, the testimony of God is greater; for this is the testimony of God that he has borne witness to his Son.

1Jn 5:10 He who believes in the Son of God has the testimony in himself.

To walk in the light as God is in the light means seeing everything exclusively from God's point of view. Now confessing sin takes on a brand new meaning. The Greek word translated, 'to confess', is made up of two words, **homo + logeo**, which means to speak the same thing, so instead of telling God about the detail of your sin, you tell yourself about the detail of your redemption. God does not need the information, you do! You cannot afford to cheat yourself by living a double standard life, acting out "the fellowship thing" while still hosting sin in your life! Address sin in the authority of the light of God's provision in Christ; his shed blood is our constant reference to a clean conscience. You do not need to first get rid of darkness and then bring the light! Light deals most effectively and effortlessly with darkness. The light of the gospel does not reveal sin, it reveals our freedom from it!

John writes to believers at different levels of their maturity, little children, young men and fathers. To the little children he says, "I am writing this so that you may not sin; but if any one does sin, *(sin is the exception, even if you are a young believer)* we have an advocate with the Father, Jesus Christ the Righteous; and he in his own person is the atonement made for our sins, as well as for the sins of the whole world." 1John2:1,12-14.

No one is better qualified to represent you!

Heb 4:14 In the message of the incarnation we have Jesus the Son of God representing humanity in the highest place of spiritual authority. That which God has spoken to us in him is his final word. It is echoed now in the declaration of our confession.

Heb 4:15 As High Priest he fully identifies with us in the context of our frail human lives. Having subjected it to close scrutiny, he proved that the human frame was master over sin. His sympathy with us is not to be seen as excusing weaknesses that are the result of a faulty design, but rather as a trophy to humanity. *(He is not an example for us but of us.)*

Heb 4:16 For this reason we can approach the authoritative throne of grace with bold utterance. We are welcome there in his embrace, and are [1]reinforced with immediate effect in times of trouble. *(The word, [1]boetheia, means to be reinforced, specifically a rope or chain for frapping a vessel in a storm.)*

Heb 9:12 As High Priest, his permission to enter the Holy Place was not secured by the blood of beasts. By his own blood he obtained access on behalf of the human race. Only one act was needed for him to enter the most sacred place of grace and there to institute a ransom of perpetual consequence. *(The perfection of the redemption he secured needs no further sacrifice. There are no outstanding debts; there is nothing we need do to add weight to what he has accomplished once and for all. The only possible priesthood activity we can now engage in is to continually bring a sacrifice of the fruit of our lips, giving thanks to his Name; no blood, just fruit, even our acts of self-sacrifice, giving of time and money, etc. are all just the fruit of our constant gratitude!)*

Heb 9:13 The blood of beasts and the ashes of the burnt sacrifice of a heifer could only achieve a very temporal and surface cleansing by being sprinkled on the guilty to symbolize their appeal to God for forgiveness. *(This was the best that the law-system had to offer; no inner purging of conscience was possible, only the sense of temporal relief, whilst knowing that the whole process would have to be repeated again and again!)*

Heb 9:14 How much more effective was the blood of Christ when he presented his own flawless life through the eternal Spirit to God in order to purge your conscience from its frustration under the cul-de-sac rituals of the law in your efforts to minister to the living God. *(A dead routine system can never compete with the resurrected Christ now alive in you.)*

Rom 6:1 It is not possible to interpret grace as a cheap excuse to continue in sin. It sounds to some that we are saying, "Let's carry on sinning then so that grace may abound." *(In the previous chapter Paul expounds the heart of the gospel by giving us a glimpse of the far-reaching faith of God; even at the risk of being misunderstood by the legalistic mind he does not compromise the message.)*

Rom 6:2 How ridiculous is that! How can we be dead and alive to sin at the same time?

Rom 6:10 His appointment with death was [1]once-off. As far as sin is concerned, he is dead. The reason for his death was to take away the sin of the world; his life now exhibits our union with the life of God. *(The Lamb of God took away the sin of the world; [1]efapax, once and for all, a final testimony, used of what is so done to be of perpetual validity and never needs repetition. This is the final testimony of the fact that sin's power over us is destroyed. In Hebrews 9:26, "But Jesus did not have to suffer again and again since the fall (or since the foundation) of the world; the single sacrifice of himself in the ful-fillment of history now reveals how he has brought sin to naught." "Christ died once, and faced our judgment! His second appearance (in his resurrection) has nothing to do with sin, but to reveal salvation unto all who eagerly embrace him [Heb 9:28].")*

Rom 6:11 This reasoning is equally relevant to you. [1]Calculate the cross; there can only be one logical conclusion: he died your death; that means you died unto sin, and are now alive unto God. Sin-consciousness can never again feature in your future! You are in Christ Jesus; his Lordship is the authority of this union. *(We are not being presumptuous to reason that we are in Christ! "[1]Reckon yourselves therefore dead unto sin" The word, [1]**logitsomai**, means logical reasoning [See Eph 1:4 and 1 Cor 1:30].* The Message Translation says, "From now on, think of it this way: Sin speaks a dead language that means nothing to you; God speaks your mother tongue, and you hang on every word. You are dead to sin and alive to God. That's what Jesus did."*

Rom 8:1 Now the decisive conclusion is this: in Christ, every bit of condemning evidence against us is cancelled. *("Who walk not after the flesh but after the spirit." This sentence was not in the original text, but later copied from verse 4. The person who added this most probably felt that the fact of Paul's declaration of mankind's innocence had to be made subject again to man's conduct. Religion under the law felt more comfortable with the condition of personal contribution rather than the conclusion of what faith reveals. The "in Christ" revelation is key to God's dealing with man. It is the PIN-code of the Bible. [See 1 Cor 1:30 and Eph 1:4].)*

Rom 8:2 The law of the Spirit is the liberating force of life in Christ. This leaves me with no further obligation to the law of sin and death. Spirit has superseded the sin enslaved senses as the principle law of our lives. *(The law of the spirit is righteousness by faith vs the law of personal effort and self righteousness which produces condemnation and spiritual death which is the fruit of the DIY tree.)*

Rom 8:3 The law failed to be anything more than an instruction manual; it had no power to deliver man from the strong influence of sin holding us hostage in our own bodies. God disguised himself in his son in this very domain where sin ruled man, the human body. The flesh body he lived and conquered in was no different to ours. Thus sin's authority in the human body was condemned. *(Hebrews 4:15, As High Priest he fully identifies with us in the context of our frail human life. Having subjected it to close scrutiny, he proved that the human frame was master over sin. His sympathy with us is not to be seen as excusing weaknesses that are the result of a faulty design, but rather as a trophy to humanity. He is not an example for us but of us.)*

Rom 8:4 The righteousness promoted by the law is now realized in us. Our practical day-to-day life bears witness to spirit inspiration and not flesh domination.

Rom 8:5 Sin's symptoms are sponsored by the senses, a mind dominated by the sensual. Thoughts betray source; spirit life attracts spirit thoughts.

Rom 8:6 Thinking patterns are formed by reference, either the sensual appetites of the flesh and spiritual death, or zoe-life and total tranquillity flowing from a mind addicted to spirit *(faith)* realities.

Rom 8:7 A mind focused on flesh *(the sensual domain where sin held me captive)* is distracted from God with no inclination to his life-laws. Flesh *(self-righteousness)* and spirit *(faith righteousness)* are opposing forces. *(Flesh no longer defines you; faith does!)* Mirror Bible

2 Cor 4:18 We are not keeping any score of what seems so obvious to the senses in the natural realm, it is fleeting and irrelevant; it is the unseen eternal realm within us that has our full attention and captivates our gaze!

Titus 1:2 This is the life of the [1]ages that was anticipated for generations; the life of our original design announced by the infallible resolve of God before [2]time or space existed. *(Man's union with God is the original thought that inspired creation. The word, [1]aionios, means without beginning or end, timeless perpetuity, ages. The word, [2]xronos, means a specific space or portion of time, season. This was before calendar time existed, before the creation of the galaxies and constellations. There exists a greater dimension to eternity than what we are capable of defining within the confines of space and time! God's faith anticipated the exact moment of our redeemed union with him for all eternity!)* Mirror This life was made certain before eternal time. *(BBE 1949, Bible in Basic English)*

2 Tim 1:9...Jesus unveils grace to be the [4]eternal intent of God! Grace celebrates our pre-creation innocence and now declares our redeemed union with God in Christ Jesus.

I AM is our past present and future. Enjoy and express him daily in total abandonment!

Paul's Gospel ~ The Success of the Cross

"My mandate and message is to announce the goodness of God to mankind. This message is what the Scriptures are all about. It remains the central prophetic theme and content of inspired writing." Rom 1:1,2

Scripture could never again be interpreted in any other way! The gospel of the success of the cross alone gives content and context to the Bible.

Rom 1:16 I have no shame about sharing the good news of Christ with anyone; the powerful rescuing act of God persuades both Jew and Greek alike.

Rom 1:17 Herein lies the secret of the power of the Gospel; there is no good news in it until the [1]righteousness of God is revealed! The dynamic of the gospel is the revelation of God's faith as the only valid basis for our belief. The prophets wrote in advance about the fact that God believes that righteousness unveils the life that he always had in mind for us. "Righteousness by his (God's) faith defines life." *(The good news is the fact that the Cross of Christ was a success. God rescued [1]the life of our design; he redeemed our [1]innocence. Man would never again be judged righteous or unrighteous by his own ability to obey moral laws! It is not about what man must or must not do but about what Jesus has done! It is from faith to faith, and not man's good or bad behavior or circumstances interpreted as a blessing or a curse [Hab 2:4]. Instead of reading the curse when disaster strikes, Habakkuk realizes that the Promise out-dates performance as the basis to man's acquittal. Deuteronomy 28 would no longer be the motivation or the measure of right or wrong behavior! "Though the fig trees do not blossom, nor fruit be on the vines, the produce of the olive fail and the fields yield no food, the flock be cut off from the fold and there be no herd in the stalls, yet I will rejoice in the Lord, I will joy in the God of my salvation. God, the Lord, is my strength; he makes my feet like hinds' feet, he makes me tread upon my high places [Hab 3:17-19 RSV]. "Look away [from the law of works] to Jesus; he is the Author and finisher of faith." [Heb 12:1]. The gospel is the revelation of the righteousness of God; it declares how God succeeded to put mankind right with him. It is about what God did right, not what Adam did wrong. The word righteousness comes from the Anglo Saxon word, "rightwiseness;" wise in that which is right. In Greek the root word for righteousness is [1]dike, which means two parties finding likeness in each other. The Hebrew word for righteousness is [1]tzadok, which refers to the beam in a scale of balances. In Colossians 2:9-10, It is in Christ that God finds an accurate and complete expression of himself, in a human body! He mirrors our completeness and is the ultimate authority of our true identity.)* Mirror Bible

Paul quotes Habakkuk who prophetically introduced a new era when he realized that righteousness will be founded in what God believes and not in man's clumsy ability to obey the law. From now on righteousness by faith defines life! Hab 2:4.

Hab 3:17 Though the fig tree do not blossom, nor fruit be on the vines, the produce of the olive fail and the fields yield no food, the flock be cut off from the fold and there be no herd in the stalls,

Hab 3:18 yet I will rejoice in the LORD, I will joy in the God of my salvation.

Hab 3:19 GOD, the Lord, is my strength; he makes my feet like hinds feet, he makes me tread upon my high places. To the choirmaster: with stringed instruments. RSV

From Romans chapters 1:18 to 3:20 Paul proceeds to give a graphic display of distorted human behavior. Being a Jew, and therefore to know the law, offers no real advantage since it offers no disguise or defense from sin. It is the same ugliness and deserves the same judgment.

His triumphant statement in v 16,17 of chapter 1 and again reinforced in chapter 3:21-24, is set against this backdrop. The good news declares how the same condemned mankind in Adam is now freely acquitted by God's grace through the redemption that is unveiled in Christ Jesus.

He brings the argument of the ineffectiveness of the law to get man to change his behavior, to a final crescendo in Chapter 7. He states in 7 verse 1 that he is writing to those who are familiar with the law. They have firsthand experience therefore of the weakness of the rule to consistently govern the conduct of man.

The best that the law could offer was to educate and confirm good intentions; but a more powerful law, the law of sin introduced to mankind through one man's transgression, has to be challenged by a greater force than human willpower.

Because sin robbed man of his true identity and awakened in him all kinds of worse-than-animal-like conduct, a set of rules couldn't do it. The revelation of God's righteousness has to be far more effective and powerful than man's slavery to sin.

It is evident that because of man's corrupt behavior, mankind deserves nothing less than condemnation. Yet within this context the grace and mercy of God is revealed; not as mere tolerance from God's side to turn a blind eye and to put up with sin, but as God's triumphant act in Christ to cancel man's guilt and to break sin's spell and dominion over man.

For salvation to be relevant it has to offer mankind a basis and reference for his faith to be launched from. It has to offer a conclusion of greater implication than the stalemate condition he finds himself in under the dispensation of the law.

Rom 7:15 This is how the sell-out to sin affects my life: I find myself doing things my conscience does not allow. My dilemma is that even though I sincerely desire to do that which is good, I don't, and the things I despise, I do.

Rom 7:16 It is obvious that my conscience sides with the law;

Rom 7:17 which confirms then that it is not really I who do these things but sin manifesting its symptoms in me. *(Sin is similar to a dormant virus that suddenly broke out in very visible symptoms.)* It has taken my body hostage.

Rom 7:18 The total extent and ugliness of sin that inhabits me, reduced my life to good intentions that cannot be followed through.

Rom 7:19 Willpower has failed me; this is how embarrassing it is, the most diligent decision that I make to do good, disappoints; the very evil I try to avoid, is what I do.

(If mere quality decisions could rescue man, the law would have been enough. Good intentions cannot save man. The revelation of what happened to us in Christ's death is what brings faith into motion to liberate from within. Faith is not a decision we make to give God a chance, faith is realizing our inclusion in what happened on the Cross and in the resurrection of Christ!)

Rom 7:20 If I do the things I do not want to do, then it is clear that I am not evil, but that I host sin in my body against my will.

Rom 7:21 It has become a predictable principle; I desire to do well, but my mere desire cannot escape the evil presence that dictates my actions.

Rom 7:22 The real person that I am on the inside delights in the law of God. *(The law proves to be consistent with my inner make-up.)*

Rom 7:23 There is another law though, *(foreign to my design)* the law of sin, activating and enrolling the members of my body as weapons of war against the law of my mind. I am held captive like a prisoner of war in my own body.

Rom 7:24 The situation is absolutely desperate for humankind; is there anyone who can deliver me from this death trap?

Rom 7:25 Thank God, this is exactly what he has done through Jesus Christ our Leader; he has come to our rescue! I am finally freed from this conflict between the law of my mind and the law of sin in my body. *(If I was left to myself, the best I could do was to try and serve the law of God with my mind, but at the same time continue to be enslaved to the law of sin in my body. Compromise could never suffice.)*

Rom 8:1 Now the decisive conclusion is this: in Christ, every bit of condemning evidence against us is cancelled. *("Who walk not after the flesh but after the spirit." This sentence was not in the original text, but later copied from verse 4. The person who added this most probably felt that the fact of Paul's declaration of mankind's innocence had to be made subject again to man's conduct. Religion under the law felt more comfortable with the condition of personal contribution rather than the conclusion of what faith reveals. The "in Christ" revelation is key to God's dealing with man. It is the PIN-code of the Bible. [See 1 Cor 1:30 and Eph 1:4].)*

Rom 8:2 The law of the Spirit is the liberating force of life in Christ. This leaves me with no further obligation to the law of sin and death. Spirit has superseded the sin enslaved senses as the principle law of our lives. *(The law of the spirit is righteousness by faith vs the law of personal effort and self righteousness which produces condemnation and spiritual death which is the fruit of the DIY tree.)* Mirror

Paul is convinced that whatever happened to the human race because of Adam's fall is far superseded in every possible proportion by the revelation of mankind's inclusion in the life, death and resurrection of Jesus Christ. He places the fall of Adam and every act of unrighteousness that followed against the one act of righteousness that God performed in Christ as proof of man's acquittal.

The revelation of righteousness by faith unveils how God in Christ represented and redeemed mankind. The etymological essence of the word, 'righteousness' in its root form, *diké*, implies the idea of two parties finding likeness in each other; with no interference of any sense of blame, guilt or inferiority. The Hebrew

66

word for righteousness is the word *tzadok* which refers to the wooden beam in a scale of balances. When Adam lost the glory of God (Hebrew, *kabod*, weight; the consciousness of God's likeness and image) the law proved that no amount of good works could balance the scale again. Grace reveals how God redeemed his image and likeness again in human form; now the scale is perfectly balanced! No wonder Jesus cried out on the cross, "It is finished!"

The law reveals what happened to man in Adam; Grace reveals what happened to the same man in Christ.

Rom 3:27 The law of faith cancels the law of works; which means there is suddenly nothing left for man to boast in. No one is superior to another. *(Bragging only makes sense if there is someone to compete with or impress. "While we compete with one another and compare ourselves with one another we are without understanding. [2 Cor 10:12]. "Through the righteousness of God we have received a faith of equal standing." [See 2 Pet 1:1 RSV]*

Rom 3:28 This leaves us with only one logical conclusion, mankind is justified by faith and not by their ability to keep the law.

Rom 3:29 Which means that God is not the private property of the Jews but belongs equally to all the nations. *(While the law excludes the non-Jewish nations, faith includes us all on level terms.)*

Rom 3:30 There is only one God, he deals with everyone, circumcised or uncircumcised exclusively on the basis of faith.

Rom 3:31 No, faith does not re-write the rules; instead it confirms that the original life-quality meant for mankind as documented in the law, is again realized.

The law presented man with choices, grace awakens belief!

Willpower exhausts, love ignites.

Willpower is the drive of the law of works; love sets faith in motion. Gal 5:6

This is the message that Paul says he owes to the whole world!

Rom 1:5 The grace and commission we received from him, is to bring about a [1]faith-inspired lifestyle in all the nations. [2]His name is his claim on the human race. *(Paul immediately sets out to give new definition to the term, "obedience," no longer by law, but of faith. [1]Obedience, from upo + akoo, means to be under the influence of what is heard, accurate hearing; hearing from above. [2]Every family in heaven and on earth is identified in him (Eph 3:15).*

Rom 16:25 I am not talking "hear-say-theory"; I own the gospel I proclaim! This is my message! I salute God who empowers you dynamically and establishes you to be strong and immovable in the face of contradiction. Jesus Christ is the disclosure of the very mystery that was concealed in silence before [1]time or human [2]history were recorded. *(Titus 1:2 This is the life of the [1]ages that was anticipated for generations; the life of our original design announced by the infallible resolve of God before [2]time or space existed. (Man's union with God is the original thought that inspired creation. The word, [1]aionios, means without beginning or end, timeless perpetuity, ages. The word, [2]xronos, means a specific space or portion of time, season. This was before calendar time existed, before the creation of the galaxies and constellations. There exists a greater dimension to eternity than what we are capable of defining within the confines of space and time! God's faith anticipated the exact moment of our redeemed union with him for all eternity!)*

This life was made certain before eternal time. (BBE 1949, Bible in Basic English)

Paul's gospel does not merely proclaim Christ in history; he announces Christ unveiled in human life; Christ in you! Col 1:27)

Rom 16:26 The mystery mirrored in [1]prophetic scripture is now unveiled. The God of the ages determined to make this mystery known in such a way that all the nations of the earth will hear and realize the [2]lifestyle that faith ignites. *(This gospel breaks the silence of the ages and reveals how God succeeded to redeem his image and likeness in man. [1]Isa 53:4, 5. See note on verse 19. Faith inspires an [2]obedience of spontaneity beyond duty driven obligation.)*

Rom 16:27 Jesus Christ [1]uniquely [2]articulates the [3]wisdom of God; he is the [4]conclusion of the ages. *(Uniquely, [1]monos, alone, Jesus has no competition, this one man represents the entire human race; this is the mystery of the ages. 1 Cor 2:7 We voice words of wisdom that was hidden in silence for timeless ages; a mystery unfolding God's Masterful plan whereby God would redeem his glory in man. 2:8 Neither the politicians nor the theologians of the day had a clue about this mystery (of mankind's association in Christ); if they did, they would never have crucified the Lord whose death redeemed our glory!*

The word, [3]sophos, means clarity, wisdom. He forever broke the silence of the ages! The words, [4]eis aion, means the conclusion of the ages. He is the [2]doxa, opinion; the logos that was before time was; the Word that became flesh and dwells within us [Jn 1:1, 14]. The incarnation (Latin, in carne, in the body) is the final trophy of the eternal logos and doxa of God. (Col 1:15 In him the image and likeness of God is made visible in human life in order that every one may recognize their true origin in him. He is the firstborn of every creature. (What darkness veiled from us he unveiled. In him we clearly see the mirror reflection of our original life. The son of his love gives accurate evidence of his image in human form. God can never again be invisible!) Col 2:3 In Christ the complete treasure of all wisdom and knowledge is sourced. Col 2:9 It is in Christ that God finds an accurate and complete expression of himself, in a human body! (While the expanse cannot measure or define God, his exact likeness is displayed in human form. Jesus proves that human life is tailor-made for God!)

Col 2:10 Jesus mirrors our completeness and [1]endorses our [2]true identity. He is "I am" in us. (Isn't it amazing that God packaged completeness in "I am," mirrored in you! Delay is outdated! The word, [1]arche, means chief in rank. The word, [2]exousia, is often translated as meaning authority; its components are, ek + eimi, originating out of "I am." The days are over where our lives were dictated to under the rule of the law of performance and an inferior identity. [See Col 1:19] The full measure of everything God has in mind for man indwells him.)

The principle of faith is to see what God sees. God called man's salvation when there seemed to be no evidence of it. Sarah's barren womb did not intimidate God's faith. Romans 4:17 "While we look not at the things that the senses observe, but we look at the revelation of the unseen as it is unveiled in our understanding through the mirror revelation of the Gospel of Christ. 2 Cor. 3:18; 2 Cor.4:18

68

Romans 4:17 finds its context in Rom 1:17 and 10:17, "It is clear then that faith's source is found in the content of the message heard; the message is Christ. (We are God's audience; Jesus is God's language!)"

Paul wrote Rom 5:12-21 before any of us preached it; and at the risk of being misunderstood by the legalistic mind as he states in the next verse 6:1, "Shall we continue in sin so that grace may abound?"

What happened to man in Adam is by far surpassed by what happened to man in Christ!

Rom 5:12 One man opened the door to sin. Sin introduced (spiritual) death. Both sin and *(spiritual)* death had a global impact. No one escaped its tyranny.

Rom 5:13 The law did not introduce sin; sin was just not pointed out yet.

Rom 5:14 In the mean time *(spiritual)* death dominated from Adam to Moses, *(2500 years before the law was given)* no one was excluded; even those whose transgression was different from Adam's. The fact is that Adam's offense set sin into motion, and its mark was globally transmitted and stained the whole human race.

Rom 5:15 The only similarity in the comparison between the offense and the gift, is that both Adam and Christ represent the masses; their single action therefore bears global consequence. Spiritual death introduced by one man's transgression is by far superseded by the grace gift lavished upon mankind in the one man Jesus Christ. *(But God's free gift immeasurably outweighs the transgression. For if through the transgression of the one individual the mass of mankind have died, infinitely greater is the generosity with which God's grace, and the gift given in his grace which found expression in the one man Jesus Christ, have been bestowed on the mass of mankind. — Weymouth, 1912)*

Rom 5:16 The difference between the two men is further emphasized in that judgment and condemnation followed a single offense, whereas the free gift of acquittal and righteousness follows innumerable sins.

Rom 5:17 If *(spiritual)* death saw the gap in one sin, and grabbed the opportunity to dominate mankind because of one man, how much more may we now seize the advantage to reign in righteousness in this life through that one act of Christ, who declared us innocent by his grace. Grace is out of all proportion in superiority to the transgression.

Rom 5:18 The conclusion is clear: it took just one offense to condemn mankind; one act of righteousness declares the same mankind innocent. *(Phillips translation: "We see then, that as one act of sin exposed the whole race of men to condemnation, so one act of perfect righteousness presents all men freely acquitted in the sight of God!")*

Rom 5:19 The disobedience of the one man [1]exhibits humanity as sinners; the obedience of another man exhibits humanity as righteous. *([1]kathistemi, to cause to be, to set up, to exhibit. We were not made sinners by our own disobedience; neither were we made righteous by our own obedience.)*

Rom 5:20 The presence of the law made no difference, instead it merely highlighted the offense; but where sin increased, grace superseded it.

Rom 5:21 *(Spiritual)* death provided sin its platform and power to reign from, now grace has taken over sovereignty through righteousness to introduce unthreatened life under the Lordship of Jesus Christ over us. Mirror

We were not made sinners by our own disobedience; neither were we made righteous by our own obedience. The same humanity that fell under the spell of Adam's sin, are now addressed in the Gospel of Jesus Christ!

What God accomplished in Christ is beyond comparison and out of all proportion in effect to Adam's sin. Rom.5:18. Johnson

J.B. Phillips writes (1955) in the preface of his translation of the book of Acts, the following: "Now in much modern evangelism the main plank of the platform is the emphasis, again and again, upon the utter sinfulness of man."
The modern evangelist will shout that the Bible says, "All have sinned", and that, "There is none righteous, no not one." They will shout that the Bible says, "All our righteousness is as filthy rags." However, Luke in writing the Book of Acts seemingly knows nothing about this emphasis. He instead highlights the experience of Peter with Cornelius, when God persuades him to call no man common or unclean! Indeed the modern technique of arousing guilt by quoting isolated texts of Scripture is not found in the Book of Acts at all.

The effect of the "word of his grace" is evident in the Book of the Acts.

Act 6:7 And the word of God increased; and the number of the disciples multiplied greatly in Jerusalem, and a great many of the priests were obedient to the faith.

Act 14:3 So they remained for a long time, speaking boldly for the Lord, who bore witness to the word of his grace, granting signs and wonders to be done by their hands. RSV

The gospel declares man's innocence; it is the receipt that confirms man's acquittal. In any transaction a receipt represents the documented detail and legal reference to effective payment; it is the written acknowledgement of such payment. The legal grounds for such a verdict are detailed in the preaching and teaching of the gospel of grace.

Many Christians can quote Romans 3:23 but sadly fail to memorize the good news is in the next verse! The glory that Adam lost on our behalf is now redeemed.

Rom 3:24 They (the same all of verse 23) are justified by his grace as a gift, through the redemption which is in Christ Jesus. RSV

There is no good news in telling people how condemned they are! The good news reveals how redeemed they are!

Rom 3:22 Jesus is what God believes about mankind. In him the righteousness of God is on display in such a way [1]that all may be equally persuaded about what God believes about them, regardless of who they are; there is no distinction. *(The preposition, [1]eis, indicates a point reached in conclusion.)*

70

Rom 3:23 Everyone is in the same boat; their [1]distorted behavior is proof of a [2]lost [3]blueprint. *(The word sin, is the word [1]hamartia, from ha, negative and meros, form, thus to be without form or identity; [2]hustereo, to fall short, to be inferior, [3]doxa, glory, blueprint, from dokeo, opinion, intent.)*

Rom 3:24 Jesus Christ is proof of God's grace gift; he redeemed the glory of God in human life; mankind condemned is now mankind justified because of the ransom paid by Christ Jesus! *(He proved that God did not make a mistake when he made man in his image amd likeness! Sadly the evangelical world proclaimed verse 23 completely out of context! There is no good news in verse 23, the gospel is in verse 24! All fell short because of Adam; the same 'all' are equally declared innocent because of Christ! The law reveals what happened to man in Adam; grace reveals what happened to the same man in Christ.)*

Rom 3:25 Jesus exhibits God's mercy. His blood propitiation persuades human-kind that God has dealt with the historic record of their sin. What he did vindicates God's righteousness.

Rom 3:26 All along God [1]refused to let go of man. At this very moment God's act of [2]righteousness is [3]pointing mankind to the evidence of their innocence, with Jesus as the [4]source of their faith. *(God's tolerance, [1]anoche, to echo upwards; God continued to hear the echo of his likeness in us. In both these verses [25+26] Paul uses the word, [3]endeixis, where we get the word indicate from. It is also part of the root for the word translated as righteousness, [2]dikaiosune. To point out, to show, to convince with proof. Then follows, [3]ek pisteos iesou, ek, source or origin and iesou which is in the Genetive case, the owner of faith is Jesus! He is both the source and substance of faith! Heb 11:1, 12:2)*

Rom 3:27 The law of faith cancels the law of works; which means there is suddenly nothing left for man to boast in. No one is superior to another. *(Bragging only makes sense if there is someone to compete with or impress. "While we compete with one another and compare ourselves with one another we are without understanding. [2 Cor 10:12]. "Through the righteousness of God we have received a faith of equal standing." [See 2 Pet 1:1 RSV] The OS (operating system) of the law of works is willpower; the OS of the law of faith is love. Gal 5:6 Love sets faith in motion.)* Mirror

How God interprets the death and resurrection of Jesus gives ultimate definition and impact to the gospel. He now desires to capture our gaze to see what he saw in the fruit of the travail of his soul, so that we may know even as we have always been known!

Isa 53:11 He shall see the fruit of the travail of his soul and be satisfied; by his knowledge shall the righteous one, my servant, make many to be accounted righteous; and he shall bear their iniquities. RSV

The highlight of John 10:10 is not the fact that the thief came to steal, kill and destroy, but that Jesus came so that we might have life more abundantly!

Acts 10:28 God has shown me that I should not call any man common or un-clean. RSV

2 Cor 5:14 The love of Christ [1]resonates within us and leaves us with only one conclusion: Jesus died humanity's death; therefore, in God's logic every individual simultaneously died. *(The word, [1]sunecho, from sun, meaning together with and echo, meaning to echo, to embrace, to hold, and thus translated, to resonate. Jesus didn't die*

71

99% or for 99%. He died humanity's death 100%! If Paul had to compromise the last part of verse 14 to read: "one died for all therefore only those who follow the prescriptions to qualify, have also died," then he would have had to change the first half of the verse as well! Only the love of Christ can make a calculation of such enormous proportion! Theology would question the extremity of God's love and perhaps prefer to add a condition or two to a statement like that!) Mirror

No personal ambition, qualification, noble-birth, or achievement gives more distinction or definition to the individual, than the fact of man's identification and co-inclusion in Christ! Phil. 3:4-9.

Paul guards with jealous zeal over this gospel:

Gal 1:6 I am amazed that you can so easily be fooled into swapping the Gospel for a gimmick! The Gospel reveals the integrity of your original identity rescued in Christ; the gimmick is a conglomeration of grace and legalism. A mixture boils down to a do-it-yourself plan of salvation. *(Which is a recipe for disaster.)*

Gal 1:7 There is no other gospel in spite of the many so-called Christian products branded "gospel." If any hint of the law remains, it is not good news but merely religious people's ideas, detracting from the gospel of Christ. *(Some seek to unsettle your minds by perverting the Gospel to accommodate their own opinion.)*

Gal 1:8 I myself or any of my team would stand equally accursed, even if we claim to have had an angelic visitation, if what we preach were to stray ever so slightly from the Gospel of the finished work of Christ.

Gal 1:9 Let me be blatant and clear about this: any gospel that does not emphasize the success of the cross is a counterfeit and produces nothing but the curse!

Gal 1:10 *(In sharp contrast to the time when I needed letters of authority from the religious institutions of the day, endorsing my mission)* God is my complete persuasion. I answer to him alone, not man. I'm employed by Christ; I am addicted to his grace. Popular religious opinion will not influence me to compromise my message. *(What is the point of an impressive CV, when your Maker is not even asking for it?)*

Gal 1:11 I want to make it very clear to you my friends that the message I proclaim is not mere speculation or the product of religious debate.

Gal 1:12 This message is not invented by man; my source was not my formal religious education; I received it by the revelation of Jesus Christ. *(Even though we once knew Christ from a human point of view, we know him thus no longer [2 Cor 5:16].)*

Gal 3:6 Abraham had no other claim to righteousness but simply believing what God declared concerning him! Isaac confirmed God's faith, not Abraham's efforts. This is all we have in common with Abraham. *(Righteousness reveals God's faith as responsible for man's salvation in direct contrast to man doing it himself by keeping moral laws!)*

Gal 3:7 The conclusion is clear; faith and not flesh relates us to Abraham! *(Grace rather than law is our true lineage. Ishmael represents so much more than the Muslim religion. Ishmael represents the clumsy effort of the flesh to compete with faith; the preaching of a mixed message of law and grace.)*

Gal 3:8 Scripture records prophetically that the mass of non-Jewish nations would be justified by faith and not by keeping moral laws. The origin of the gospel is found in this announcement by God over Abraham; he saw all the nations represented in the same principle of the faith that Abraham pioneered. "In you all the nations of the earth are equally represented in the blessing of faith." *([Gen 22:17] I will indeed bless you, and I will multiply your seed as the stars of heaven and as the sand which is on the seashore. And your seed shall possess the gate of their enemies, Gen 22:18 and by your seed shall all the nations of the earth bless themselves. Righteousness by faith is the revelation of the gospel; [Rom 1:17 and Hab 2:4] "the just shall live by his (God's) faith" Righteousness by faith defines your life!)*

Gal 3:9 As did Abraham so do we now find our source in the blessing of faith.

Gal 4:21 Since you are so intrigued by the law, please understand its prophetic message:

Gal 4:22 The law records the fact that Abraham had two sons: one by a slave girl, the other by a free woman.

Gal 4:23 The one is produced by the flesh *(the DIY-tree)*, the other by faith *(the promise)*.

Gal 4:24 There is a parallel meaning in the story of the two sons: they represent two systems, works and grace.

Gal 4:25 Sinai is an Arabian rocky mountain named after Hagar, *(outside the land of promise)*. Its association with the law of Moses mirrors Jerusalem as the capital of Jewish legalism. Hagar is the mother of the law of works.

Gal 4:26 But the mother from above, the true mother of mankind is grace, the free Jerusalem; she is the mother of the promise.

Gal 4:27 For it is written, "Rejoice oh childless one! Erupt in jubilee! For though you have never known travail before, your children will greatly outnumber her who was married *(to the law).*

Gal 4:28 We resemble Isaac: we are begotten of faith, the promise is our parent.

Gal 4:29 Just as when the flesh child persecuted the faith child, so now these Jerusalem Jews in their Christian disguise seek to harass you;

Gal 4:30 however, scripture is clear: "Expel the slave mother and her son; the slave son cannot inherit with the free son." *(In exactly the same way, rid your minds radically from the slave mother and child mentality. Light dispels darkness effortlessly.)*

Gal 4:31 Realize whose children we are my brothers: we are not sons of the slave-mother, the law, but sons of the free mother; we are sons of grace!

1 Cor 1:18 To their own loss the message of the cross seems foolish to some; but to us who discover our salvation there, it is the dynamic of God.

1 Cor 1:19 Isaiah wrote: I will confuse the wisdom of the "so-called" wise and prove their experts wrong! *(Isa 29:14)*

1 Cor 1:20 God's wisdom *(revealed in the success of the cross)* puts the rest out of

business! *(when it comes to real answers to the dilemma of mankind)* they have all closed shop; the philosophers, the academics, the smooth-talkers, the lot!

1 Cor 1:21 By suspicious scrutiny the sense-ruled world surveys the works of God in creation and still do not recognize or acknowledge him; in sharp contrast to this, the foolishness of the message we proclaim brings God's work of redeeming his image in us into faith's focus. *(What we preach cancels every basis for boasting in personal contribution, which seems folly to the DIY systems of this world.)*

1 Cor 1:22 The Jews crave signs *(to confirm their doubts)* while the Greeks revel in philosophical debate! *(Both groups are addicted to the same soul realm.)*

1 Cor 1:23 The crucified Christ is the message we publicly proclaim, to the disgust of the Jews while the Greeks think we are wacky!

1 Cor 1:24 The dynamic of God's wisdom is the fact that both Jew and Greek are equally included and defined in Christ.

1 Cor 1:25 It seems so foolish that God should die man's death on the cross; it seems so weak of God to suffer such insult; yet man's wisest schemes and most powerful display of genius cannot even begin to comprehend or compete with God in his weakest moment on the cross.

1 Cor 1:26 You might as well admit it, my Brothers; it was not your academic qualifications or your good looks or social connections that influenced God to represent you in Christ.

1 Cor 1:27 It is almost as if God deliberately handpicked the wacky of this world to embarrass the wise, the rejects to put to shame the noble.

1:28 The ones with no pedigree of any prominence, the "nobodies" in society, attracted God's initiative to unveil his blueprint opinion in order to redefine man. Thus he rendered any other social standard entirely irrelevant and inappropriate. *(Blueprint opinion, **eklegomai**, from **ek**, meaning origin, source, and **legomai** from **logos**, the logic of God; traditionally translated as "elect.")*

1 Cor 1:29 Every reason for man's boasting in himself dwindles into insignificance before God.

1 Cor 1:30 [1]Of God's doing are we in Christ. He is both the genesis and genius of our wisdom; a wisdom that reveals how righteous, sanctified and redeemed we are in him. *(The preposition, [1]ek, always denotes origin, source. Mankind's association in Christ is God's doing. In God's economy, Christ represents us; what man could never achieve through personal discipline and willpower as taught in every religion, God's faith accomplished in Christ. Of his design we are in Christ; we are associated in oneness with him. Our wisdom is sourced in this union! Also, our righteousness and holiness originate from him. Holiness equals wholeness and harmony of man's spirit, soul, and body. Our redemption is sanctioned in him. He redeemed our identity, our sanity, our health, our joy, our peace, our innocence, and our complete well-being! [See Eph 1:4]. The Knox Translation reads, "It is from him that we take our [1]origin.")*

1 Cor 1:31 He is our claim to fame. *(This is what Jeremiah meant when he wrote: "Let not the wise man glory in his wisdom, let not the mighty man glory in his might, let not the*

rich man glory in his riches; but let him who glories glory in this, that he understands and knows me, that I am the Lord who practice steadfast love, justice, and righteousness in the earth; for in these things do I delight, says the Lord." [Jer 9:23, 24 — RSV])

1 Cor 2:2 The testimony of God is my only persuasion concerning you: Jesus Christ died your death on the cross! I can see you in no other light! *(For I determined to know nothing in you except Jesus Christ and him crucified.)*

1 Cor 2:6 The words we speak resonate revelation wisdom in those who understand how perfectly redeemed they are in Christ, this wisdom supersedes every secular kind; suddenly what once seemed wise and good advice has become useless information. *(All popular programs towards improved moral behavior are now outdated. "Of God's doing are we in Christ. He is both the genesis and genius of our wisdom; a wisdom that reveals how righteous, sanctified, and redeemed we already are in him." In God's economy, Christ represents us; what man could never achieve through personal discipline and willpower as taught in every religion, God's faith accomplished in Christ [1 Cor 1:30].)*

1 Cor 2:7 We voice words of wisdom that was hidden in silence for timeless ages; a mystery unfolding God's Masterful plan whereby he would redeem his glory in man.

1 Cor 2:8 Neither the politicians nor the theologians of the day had a clue about this mystery *(of mankind's association in Christ);* if they did, they would never have crucified the Lord whose death redeemed our glory!

Mankind's inclusion in Christ is the conclusion of grace.

The Prophets saw it:
Who has heard of such a thing? Who has seen such things? Shall the earth be born in one day? Shall all people be brought forth in one moment? Is. 66:8

The only scripture in the entire Old Testament that prophesies the 3rd day resurrection includes us! Hos 6:2 After two days he will revive us; on the third day he will raise us up, that we may live before him. RSV

Our co-inclusion in Jesus' death and resurrection was prophesied 800 years B.C. through Hosea and 700 B.C. by Isaiah.

Isa 52:10 The LORD has bared his holy arm before the eyes of all the nations; and all the ends of the earth shall see the salvation of our God.

Isa 52:14 As many were astonished at him, his appearance was so marred, beyond human semblance, and his form beyond that of the sons of men,

Isa 52:15 so shall he startle many nations; kings shall shut their mouths because of him; for that which has not been told them they shall see, and that which they have not heard they shall understand.

Isa 53:1 Who has believed what we have heard? And to whom has the arm of the LORD been revealed?

Isa 53:2 For he grew up before him like a young plant, and like a root out of dry ground; he had no form or comeliness that we should look at him, and no beauty that we should desire him.

Isa 53:3 He was despised and rejected by men; a man of sorrows, and acquainted with grief; and as one from whom men hide their faces he was despised, and we esteemed him not.

Isa 53:4 Surely he has borne our griefs and carried our sorrows; yet we esteemed him stricken, smitten by God, and afflicted.

Isa 53:5 But he was wounded for our transgressions, he was bruised for our iniquities; upon him was the chastisement that made us whole, and with his stripes we are healed.

Isa 53:6 All we like sheep have gone astray; we have turned everyone to his own way; and the LORD has laid on him the iniquity of us all.

Isa 53:7 He was oppressed, and he was afflicted, yet he opened not his mouth; like a lamb that is led to the slaughter, and like a sheep that before its shearers is dumb, so he opened not his mouth. RSV

Psalm 22 graphically portrays the crucifixion then concludes in verse 27 with, "All the ends of the earth shall remember and turn to the LORD; and all the families of the nations shall worship before him."

Peter saw it:

Acts 10:28 God has shown me that I should not call any man common or unclean. RSV

1Pe 1:3 Blessed be the God and Father of our Lord Jesus Christ! By his great mercy we have been born anew to a living hope through the resurrection of Jesus Christ from the dead. RSV

Peter realized that something happened to mankind in the death and resurrection of Jesus. Flesh and blood did not reveal this to him; he saw that we were hewn out of that same rock tomb!

Luke saw it:

Act 13:32 And we bring you the good news that what God promised to the fathers,

Act 13:33 this he has fulfilled to us their children by raising Jesus; as also it is written in the second psalm, Thou art my Son, today I have begotten thee.

The resurrection of Jesus declares humanity's new birth.

Paul saw it:

Col 2:13 And you, who were dead in trespasses and the uncircumcision of your flesh, God made alive together with him, having forgiven us all our trespasses. RSV

Eph 2:5 This is how grace rescued us: sin left us dead towards God, like spiritual corpses. Long before we knew or believed it, while we were still dead in our sins and indifference, God co-quickened us together with Christ. Sin proved how dead we were *(the law confirmed it!)*; grace reveals how alive we now are *(the gospel announces it!)* Before anyone but God believed it, he made us alive together with him and raised us up together with him. *(We had no contribution to our salvation! God's master-plan unfolded in the mystery of the gospel declaring our joint inclusion in Christ's death and resurrection; God found us in Christ before he lost us in Adam! [Eph 1:4] In the economy of God, when Jesus died we died. God saw us in Christ, in his death and resurrection before we saw ourselves there! He declared our co-resurrection with Christ 800 BC [Hos 6:2]!)*

Eph 2:6 *(As much as we were co-included in his death,)* we are co-included in his resurrection. We are co-raised; we are also elevated in his ascension to be equally welcome in the throne room of the heavenly realm where we are co-seated together with him in his executive authority. We are fully represented in Christ Jesus. *(Our joint position in Christ defines us; this can never again be a distant goal to reach! It is our immediate point of departure. We are not praying towards the Throne room, we pray from the Throne Room. See Col 3:1-4)*

Eph 2:7 *(In a single triumphant act of righteousness God saved us from the "guttermost" to the uttermost. Here we are now, revealed in Christ in the highest possible position of bliss! If man's sad history could not distract from the extravagant love of God,)* imagine how God is now able for timeless perpetuity (the eternal future) to exhibit the trophy of the wealth of his grace demonstrated in his kindness towards us in Christ Jesus. Grace exhibits excessive evidence of the success of the cross.

Eph 2:8 Your salvation is not a reward for good behavior! It was a grace thing from start to finish; you had no hand in it. Even the gift to believe simply reflects his faith! *(You did not invent faith; it was God's faith to begin with! It is from faith to faith, [Rom 1:17] He is both the source and conclusion of faith. [Heb 12:2])*

Eph 2:9 If this could be accomplished through any action of yours then there would be ground for boasting.

Gal 2:19 My co-crucifixion with Christ is valid! I am not making this up. In his death I died to the old system of trying to please God with my own good behavior! God made me alive together with Christ. How can any human effort improve on this! *(Hos 6:2 and Eph 2:5)*

Gal 2:20 The terms, co-crucified and co-alive defines me now. Christ in me and I in him! *(Jn 14:20)* His sacrificial love is evidence of his persuasion of my righteousness! *(The life that I now live in the flesh I live by the faith of the son of God. He believes in my innocence!)*

Rom 6:5 If we were included in his death we are equally included in his resurrection.

Col 2:10 Jesus mirrors our completeness and [1]endorses our [2]true identity. He is "I am" in us. *(Isn't it amazing that God packaged completeness in "I am," mirrored in you! Delay is outdated! The word, [1]arche, means chief in rank. The word, [2]exousia, is often translated as meaning authority; its components are, ek + eimi, originating out of "I am."*

The days are over where our lives were dictated to under the rule of the law of performance and an inferior identity. [See Col 1:19] The full measure of everything God has in mind for man indwells him.

"Your own completeness is only realized in him." — Phillips Translation.)

Col 2:11 You were in Christ when he died which means that his death represents your true circumcision. Sin's authority in the human body was stripped off you in him dying your death.

Col 2:12 In the same parallel *(your co-circumcision in his death)* your co-burial and joint-resurrection is now demonstrated in baptism; your co-inclusion in Christ is what God's faith knew when he powerfully raised him from the dead. *(Hos 6:2)*

Col 2:13 You were once spiritually dead, as confirmed in your constant failure; being bound to a lifestyle ruled by the [1]distorted desires of the flesh, but now God has made you alive together with him, having forgiven you all your [2]trespasses. *([1]The uncircumcision of the flesh, i.e., in the Greek, a life controlled by the sexual organs. The word, [2]paraptoma, comes from, para, close proximity, sphere of influence and pipto, to stop flying, from petomai, to fly; thus, to fall from flight or to lose altitude.)*

Adam's transgression no longer holds the human race hostage. Rom 5:7,8,12-21

Col 3:1 You are in fact raised together with Christ! Now ponder with persuasion the consequence of your co-inclusion in him. Relocate yourselves mentally! Engage your thoughts with throne room realities. His resurrection co-raised you to the same position of authority where you are now co-seated in the executive authority of God's right hand.

Col 3:2 Becoming affectionately acquainted with these thoughts will keep you from being distracted again by the earthly *(soul-ruled)* realm. *(A renewed mind conquers the space that was previously occupied by worthless pursuits and habits.)*

Col 3:3 Your union with his death broke the association with that world; see yourselves located in a fortress where your life is hidden with Christ in God! *("In that day you will know that I am in my father, and you in me and I in you." [Jn 14:20] Occupy your mind with this new order of life; you died when Jesus died, whatever defined you before defines you no more. Christ, in whom the fullness of deity dwells, defines you now! The secret of your life is your union with Christ in God! [See Col 2:9, 10])*

"Risen, then, with Christ you must lift your thoughts above where Christ now sits at the right hand of God, you must be heavenly minded; not earthly minded, you have undergone death, and your life is hidden away now with Christ in God. Christ is your life, when he is made manifest you are made manifest in his glory." — Knox Translation)

Col 3:4 The exact life on exhibit in Christ is now repeated in us. We are being [1]co-revealed in the same bliss; we are joined in oneness with him, just as his life reveals you, your life reveals him! *(This verse was often translated to again delay the revelation of Christ to a future event! The word, [1]otan, often translated as "when" is better translated as "every time." Thus, "Every time Christ is revealed we are being co-revealed in his glory." According to Walter Bauer Lexicon, otan is often used of an action that is repeated. Paul declares our joint-glorification in Christ! We are co-revealed in the same bliss. [See 1 Cor 2:7-8, Rom 3:23-24, Rom 8:30, 2 Pet 1:3.] In him we live and move and have our being; in us he lives and moves and has his being! [Acts 17:28])*

78

"Risen, then, with Christ you must lift your thoughts above where Christ now sits at the right hand of God, you must be heavenly minded; not earthly minded, you have undergone death, and your life is hidden away now with Christ in God. Christ is your life, when he is made manifest you are made manifest in his glory." - Knox Translation

John saw it:

1Jn 5:20 And we know that the Son of God has come and has given us understanding, to know him who is true; and we are in him who is true, in his Son Jesus Christ. This is the true God and eternal life. RSV

1Jn. 2:7, 8 That which is true in him is equally true in us.

1Jn 4:17 As he is so are we in this world. RSV

James the brother of Jesus saw it:

While none of Jesus' brothers believed in him during the three years of his ministry, (John 7:5) his brother James discovers his own true identity when Jesus appears to him after the resurrection (1 Corinthians 15:4-7) and declares, "It was his delightful resolve to give birth to us; we were conceived by the unveiled logic of God." James 1:18.

James sees the mirror mystery of our birth from above. We existed in God before we were formed in our mother's womb. He brought us forth by the word of truth! James 1:17,18. If any man hears this word, *(of our joint resurrection in Christ)* he sees the face of his birth as in a mirror. See 1 Pet 1:3, Eph 2:5.

Now we see it:

Paul spoke in such a manner that many believed.

Act 14:1 And so spoke that a great company believed, both of Jews and of Greeks RSV

Eph 3:9 The mandate of my message is to make all men see. The unveiling of this eternal secret is to bring into public view an association that has always been hidden in God; Jesus Christ is the blueprint of creation.

Eph 3:4 In reading these words you will perceive my insight into the mystery of Christ. *(Insight, understanding, **sunesis**, a joining together like two streams)* Mirror

Eph 1:9 For he has made known to us in all wisdom and insight the mystery of his will, according to his purpose which he set forth in Christ

Eph 1:10 as a plan for the fullness of time, to unite all things in him, things in heaven and things on earth. RSV

Eph 1:10 In the [1]economy of the fullness of time, everything culminates in Christ; all that is in heaven and all that is on earth is reconciled in him. *(The word,[1]**oikonomia**, translates as administration.)* Mirror

Phillips, "All human history shall be consummated in Christ, everything that exists in heaven or earth shall find its perfection and fulfillment in him."

Knox, "All that is in heaven, all that is on earth, summed up in him!"

Eph 1:17 I desire that you will draw directly from the source; that the God of our Lord Jesus Christ, the Father of glory ignites the spirit of wisdom and of revelation in you in the unveiling of his Master Plan *(his intent, **doxa** glory.)* I desire that you know by revelation what he has known about you all along!

Eph 1:18 I pray that your thoughts will be flooded with light and inspired insight; that you will clearly picture his intent in identifying you in him so that you may know how precious you are to him. The saints are his treasure and the glorious trophy of his portion! *(We are God's assets and the measure of his wealth!)*

Eph 1:19 I pray that you will understand beyond all comparison the magnitude of his mighty power towards us who believe. Faith reveals how enormously advantaged we are in Christ.

Eph 1:20 It is the same dynamic energy that he unleashed in Christ when he raised him from the dead and forever established him in the power of his own right hand in the realm of the heavens.

Eph 1:21 Infinitely above all the combined forces of rule, authority, dominion, or governments; he is ranked superior to any name that could ever be given to anyone of this age or any age still to come in the eternal future.

Eph 1:22 I want you to see this: he subjected all these powers under his feet. He towers head and shoulders above everything. He is the head;

Eph 1:23 the [1]church is his body. The completeness of his being that fills all in all resides in us! God cannot make himself more visible or exhibit himself more accurately. *(The word, [1]ekklesia, comes from **ek**, a preposition always denoting origin, and **klesia** from **kaleo**, to identify by name, to surname; his redeemed image and likeness in man.)*

Rom.6:11 Think of yourself as dead to sin. Knox Translation.

Rom 6:11 This reasoning is equally relevant to you. [1]Calculate the cross; there can only be one logical conclusion: he died your death; that means you died unto sin, and are now alive unto God. Sin-consciousness can never again feature in your future! You are in Christ Jesus; his Lordship is the authority of this union. *(We are not being presumptuous to reason that we are in Christ! "[1]Reckon yourselves therefore dead unto sin" The word, [1]logitsomai, means to make a calculation to which there can only be one logical conclusion. [See Eph 1:4 and 1 Cor 1:30].*

"From now on, think of it this way: Sin speaks a dead language that means nothing to you; God speaks your mother tongue, and you hang on every word. You are dead to sin and alive to God. That's what Jesus did." — The Message)

The ends of the earth will see it!

Isa 52:10 The LORD has bared his holy arm before the eyes of all the nations; and all the ends of the earth shall see the salvation of our God.

Habakkuk, (whose name means to embrace) is the prophet who saw righteousness by faith, 2:4; in chapter 2:2 he says,

"Write the vision, and make it plain upon tablets that he may run who reads it."

The Contemporary English Version says,

"I will give you my message in the form of a vision. Write it clearly enough to be read at a glance."

And, then in verse 14 Habakkuk makes this remarkable statement,

For the earth will be filled with the knowledge of the glory of the Lord as the waters cover the sea.

Psalm 98:1-3 records the following song:

Sing unto the Lord a new song, for he has done marvelous things! His right hand and his holy arm have gotten him the victory. The Lord has made known his salvation, his righteousness has he openly shown in the sight of the nations. All the ends of the earth shall see the salvation of our God."

Rom 8:19 Our lives now represent the one event every creature anticipates with held breath, standing on tip-toe as it were to witness the unveiling of the sons of God. Can you hear the drum-roll?

Rom 8:20 Every creature suffered abuse through Adam's fall; they were discarded like a squeezed-out orange. Creation did not volunteer to fall prey to the effect of the fall. Yet within this stark setting, hope prevails.

Rom 8:21 All creation knows that the glorious liberty of the sons of God sets the stage for their own release from decay.

Rom 8:22 We sense the universal agony and pain recorded in history until this very moment. Mirror

All principalities and powers see it:

Eph 2:7 *(In a single triumphant act of righteousness God saved us from the guttermost to the uttermost. Here we are now, revealed in Christ in the highest possible position of bliss! If man's sad history could not distract from the extravagant love of God,)* imagine how God is now able for timeless perpetuity *(the eternal future)* to exhibit the trophy of the wealth of his grace demonstrated in his kindness towards us in Christ Jesus. Grace exhibits excessive evidence of the success of the cross.

Eph 3:10 Every invisible authority and government in the arena of the heavenlies is now confronted with the display of the wisdom of God. The church acts like a prism that disperses the varied magnitude of God in human form. Mirror

Jesus saw his own life mirrored in scripture:

Heb 10:7 "Then I said, I read in your book what you wrote about me; so here I am, I have come to fulfill my destiny." *(Ps 40:7, Lk 4:17, Lk 24:27, 44, Jn 5:39,40, 7:39.)*

"You have your heads in your Bibles constantly because you think you'll find eternal life there. But you miss the forest for the trees. These Scriptures are all about me!" John 5:39 The Message

Heb 5:7 When he faced the horror of his imminent death, he presented his urgent plea to God in an outburst of agonizing emotion and with tears. He prayed with urgent intent to be delivered from death, knowing that God was able to save him. He was heard because of his [1]firm grip on the prophetic word *(not because he feared, as some translations have put it, but because he [1]fully grasped that he was the fulfillment of scripture; he knew that he would be raised on the third day; [Hos 6:2] eu + lambano).*

Heb 5:8 As son, he was in the habit of [1]hearing from above; what he heard [2]distanced him from the effect of what he had suffered. *(The word often translated as obedience is the word, [1]upoakuo, under the influence of hearing, or hearing from above. "By" the things he suffered, [2]apo, away from, distanced. "Then I said, I read in your book what you wrote about me; so here I am, I have come to fulfill your will." [Heb 10:7])*

Heb 5:9 By his perfect hearing he forever freed mankind to hear what he had heard. *(He now makes it possible for us to hear in such a way that we may participate again in the full release of our original identity; the logos finding voice in the incarnation in us.)*

The law of faith reveals how the obedience of Christ cancelled out the effect of the disobedience of Adam.

Joh 12:23 And Jesus answered them, "The hour has come for the Son of man to be glorified. Joh 12:24 Truly, truly, I say to you, unless a grain of wheat falls into the earth and dies, it remains alone; but if it dies, it bears much fruit". RSV

In John 7:37-39, John records how Jesus witnessed the eighth day, the great and final day of the Feast of Tabernacles, when, according to custom, the High Priest would draw water from the Pool of Siloam with a golden jar, mix the water with wine, and then pour it over the altar while the people would sing with great joy from Psalm 118:25-26, and also Isaiah 12:3; "Therefore with joy shall we draw water from the wells of salvation!" Then, Jesus, knowing that he is the completeness of every prophetic picture and promise, cried out with a loud voice: "If anyone is thirsty, let him come to me and drink! If you believe that I am what the scriptures are all about, you will discover that you are what I am all about, and rivers of living waters will gush from your innermost being!" See Rom 5:5)

The logic of God's economy of inclusion:

In the mind of God, Jesus represents the human race.

The pin-code of the Bible are the two words Paul often uses, "in Christ".

Eph 1:3 Let's celebrate God! He lavished every blessing heaven has upon us in Christ!

Eph 1:4 He associated us in Christ before [1]the fall of the world! Jesus is God's mind made up about us! He always knew in his love that he would present us again [2]face-to-face before him in blameless innocence. *(The implications of the fall are completely cancelled out. Paul uses the word, [1]katabalo, meaning "to fall away, to put in a lower place," instead of themelios, meaning "foundation" [see 2:20]; thus, translated "the fall of the world," instead of "the foundation of the world," as in most other translations. God found us in Christ before he lost us in Adam! We are presented in blameless innocence before him! The word, [2]katenopion, suggests the closest possible proximity, face-to-face!)*

Eph 1:5 He is the architect of our design; his heart dream realized our [1]coming of age in Christ. *(Adoption here is not what it means in our Western society, it is a coming of age, like the typical Jewish Barmitsva. See Galatians 4:1-6, " ... and to seal our sonship the spirit of his son echoes Abba Father in our hearts." This is [1]huiothesia.)*

Eph 1:6 His grace-plan is to be celebrated: he greatly endeared us and highly favored us in Christ. His love for his Son is his love for us.

Eph 1:7 Since we are *(fully represented)* in him, his blood is the ransom that secures our redemption. His forgiving us our sins measures the wealth of his grace.

Eph 1:10 In the [1]economy of the fullness of time, everything culminates in Christ; all that is in heaven and all that is on earth is reconciled in him. *(The word,[1]oikonomia, translates as administration.)*

"All human history shall be consummated in Christ, everything that exists in heaven or earth shall find its perfection and fulfillment in him." — Phillips. "All that is in heaven, all that is on earth, summed up in him!" — Knox

Eph 1:11 This is how we fit into God's picture: Christ is the measure of our portion, we are in him, invented and defined in him. God's blueprint intention is on exhibition in us. Everything he accomplishes is inspired by the energy and intent of his affection. *(See Romans 8:29, "He engineered us from the start to fit the mold of sonship and likeness according to the exact blueprint of his design. We see the original and intended shape of our lives preserved in his Son; he is the firstborn from the same womb that reveals our genesis. He confirms that we are the invention of God.")*

Rom 5:18 The conclusion is clear: it took just one offense to condemn mankind; one act of righteousness declares the same mankind innocent.

(Phillips translation: "We see then, that as one act of sin exposed the whole race of men to condemnation, so one act of perfect righteousness presents all men freely acquitted in the sight of God!")

Rom 5:19 The disobedience of the one man [1]exhibits humanity as sinners; the obedience of another man exhibits humanity as righteous. *([1]kathistemi, to cause to be, to set up, to exhibit. We were not made sinners by our own disobedience; neither were we made righteous by our own obedience.)*

The same humanity that fell under the spell of Adam's sin, are now addressed in the Gospel of Jesus Christ!

The immediate implication of the revelation of Christ's obedience releases an authority in us whereby we are empowered to destroy every stronghold *(mindset)* and arrest every thought that would snare us to an inferior opinion or identity.

2Co 10:4 For the weapons of our warfare are not of the flesh, but mighty in God to the casting down of strongholds, 10:5 casting down imaginations, and every high thing that is exalted against the knowledge of God, and bringing every thought into captivity to the obedience of Christ; ASV

Note the correct translation is, "the obedience of Christ," instead of the obedience to Christ like many translations wrongfully suggest.

This makes an enormous difference: to obey Christ keeps one restricted to the same limitations and frustrations experienced under the law of performance; one's own inconsistency and inability bring about the inevitable sense of guilt and failure; whereas the obedience of Christ already achieved every blessing that God has always had in mind for us. The life of our design is redeemed! This is the sharpness of the spear whereby we arrest every thought! The understanding of the obedience of Christ is the best anti-virus protection to harness your mind with. The Greek word, *aichmalotizo* means to arrest at spear point! No contradiction to the implication of his obedience is tolerated. The moment of faith is like the effect of light dispelling darkness, effortlessly! Darkness does not erase the truth, it only hides from view that which already is true. The true light that enlightens every man has come!

John 1:9 A new day for humanity has come. The authentic light of life that illuminates everyone was about to dawn in the world! *(This day would begin our calendar and record the fact that human history would forever be divided into before and after Christ. The incarnation would make the image of God visible in human form. In him who is the blueprint of our lives there is more than enough light to displace the darkness in every human life. He is the true light that enlightens every man! [Col 1:15; 2:9, 10; 2 Cor 4:6])*

2 Cor 4:3 If our message seems vague to anyone, it is not because we are withholding something from certain people! It is just because some are so stubborn in their efforts to uphold an outdated system that they don't see it! They are all equally found in Christ but they prefer to remain lost in the cul-de-sac language of the law!

2 Cor 4:4 The survival and self-improvement programs of the [1]religious systems of this world veil the minds of the unbelievers; exploiting their ignorance about their true origin and their redeemed innocence. The veil of unbelief obstructs a person's view and keeps one from seeing what the light of the gospel so clearly reveals: the [2]glory of God is the image and likeness of our Maker redeemed in human form; this is what the gospel of Christ is all about. *(The god of this [1]aion, age, refers to the religious systems and governing structures of this world. The unbelief that neutralized Israel in the wilderness was the lie that they believed about themselves; "We are grasshoppers, and the 'enemy' is a giant beyond any proportion!" [Num 13:33, Josh 2:11, Heb 4:6] "They failed to possess the promise due to unbelief." The blueprint [2]doxa, glory of God, is what Adam lost on humanity's behalf. [See Eph 4:18])*

2 Cor 4:6 The light source is founded in the same God who said, "Light, be!" And light shone out of darkness! He lit the lamp in our understanding so that we may clearly recognize the features of his likeness in the face of Jesus Christ reflected within us. *(The same God who bade light shine out of darkness has kindled a light in our hearts, whose shining is to make known his glory as he has revealed it in the features of Jesus Christ. — Knox Translation)*

2 Cor 4:7 We have discovered this treasure where it was hidden all along, in these frail skin-suits made of clay. We take no credit for finding it there! It took the enormous power of God in the achievement of Christ to rescue our minds from the lies it believed. *("The kingdom of heaven is like treasure hidden in an agricultural field, which a man found and covered up; then in his joy he goes and sells all that he has and buys that field." [Mt 13:44] God invested all that he has in the redeeming of our original value! He rescued the life of our design. Our inner life hosts the treasure of the life of our design. Jesus*

84

said in John 7:37,38, "If you believe that I am what the scriptures are all about, you will know that you are what I am all about and rivers of living water will gush out of your innermost being!")

Col 1:13 He rescued us from the [1]dominion of darkness *(the sense-ruled world, dominated by the law of performance)* and relocated us into the kingdom where the love of his son rules. *(Darkness is not a force, it is the absence of light. [See Eph 4:18] A darkened understanding veiled the truth of our redeemed design from us; translating [1]exousia, from ek, origin or source, and eimi, I am. Thus, confused about who I am until the day that we heard and understood the grace of God in truth.)*

Col 2:14 His body nailed to the cross hung there as the document of mankind's guilt; in dying our death he [1]deleted the detailed [2]hand-written [3]record of Adam's fall. Every [1]stain that sin left on our conscience was fully blotted out. *(The word, [1]exaleipho, comes from ek, out of, and aleipho, with a, as a particle of union, and liparos, to grease, to leave a stain; guilt was like a grease stain upon the conscience of fallen man. The word, [2]cheirographon, translates as hand-written. The word, [3]dogma, comes from dokeo, a thought pattern; thus thought patterns engraved by human experience of constant failure to do what the law required. In his personal handwriting man endorsed his own death sentence. The hands of fallen man struck the body of Jesus with the blows of their religious hatred and fury when they nailed his bloodied body to the tree; they did not realize that in the mystery of God's economy Jesus was the scapegoat of the entire human race! [Isa 53:4, 5] Mirror*

"The slate wiped clean, that old arrest warrant canceled and nailed to Christ's Cross." — The Message)

Col 2:15 His brilliant victory made a public [1]spectacle of every [2]rule and [3]authority empowered by the fall of Adam. The [4]voice of the cross will never be silenced! *(The horror of the Cross is now the eternal trophy of God's triumph over sin! The cross stripped religion of its authority to manipulate man with guilt. Every accusation lost its power to continue to blackmail the human race. The word, [1]apekduomai, is translated from apo, away from, and ekduo, to be stripped of clothing; the religious facade that disguised the law of works as a means of defining man was openly defeated. The dominance of the tree of the knowledge of good and evil (poneros, hard work and labor) was ended. The word, [1]deikmatizo, means to exhibit in public. The word, [4]parresia, comes from pas, all and rheo, outspokenness, pouring forth speech.*

"He stripped all the spiritual tyrants in the universe of their sham authority at the Cross and marched them naked through the streets." — The Message

The success of the cross is the most dynamic and tangible reference to ordinary people living in victory over sin and temptation; not thru their strong willpower, but by discovering what God believes about them.

There is only one faith that matters, not what we believe about God, but what God believes about us!

The Christ life realized in us is a well of living water, freeing us from within to live the life of our design, uncluttered by the effect of Adams fall.

Identity redeemed

The most tragic consequence of the fall of man was the loss of man's conviction of his true identity. A new dominance was introduced, and man became subject to the judgment of the sense realm. An environment ruled by chance, change and temporal values became his reference.

The greatest distraction and contradiction to our true identity and destiny is to live a life subject to an inferior opinion. We have inherited and adopted a set of values and prejudices that crippled relationships on every level of society.

We have forgotten what manner of people we are. In Adam mankind fell into the maze of a confused identity; he fell from I am into, I'm not!

When Adam 'died' his awareness and consciousness of the divine likeness in him became reduced to him merely knowing himself, his wife and God from a guilt based and performance driven human point of view; he lost the doxa of God and began to live the life of the flesh, with its fading glories like seasonal flowers.

When Jesus tells the stories of the lost sheep, the lost coin and the lost son he emphasis in all 3 parables that neither original ownership, nor original value was lost! The turning point in the prodigal son's life was when he came to himself! Luk 15:17 But when he came to himself he said, 'How many of my father's hired servants have bread enough and to spare, but I perish here with hunger!

We all like sheep have gone astray. Jesus is the good Shepherd, he came to seek and to rescue the lost!

In Psalm 22 David paints a most dramatic prophetic picture of the crucifixion of the Messiah and in verse 27 boldly proclaims the outcome, "All the ends of the earth shall remember and turn to the Lord!" Then in the next Psalm he sings about the Shepherd that leads us to the waters of reflection, where my soul remembers who I am!

Eph 2:10 We are engineered by his design; he molded and manufactured us in Christ. We are his workmanship, his poetry.

We have forgotten the Rock from which we were hewn, the God who gace birth to us! Deut 32:18

You who seek God, *(here is your clue!)* Look to the rock from which you were hewn...Isa 51:1

Col 1:15 In him the invisible God is made visible again; in order that every one may recognize their true origin in him; he is the firstborn of every creature. (What darkness veiled from us he unveiled. In him we clearly see the mirror reflection of our original image and likeness redeemed. The son of his love gives evidence of his image in human form.)

Col 1:19 The full measure of everything God has in mind for man indwells him.

Col 2:9 It is in Christ that God finds an accurate and complete expression of himself, in a human body! (*While the expanse cannot measure or define God, his exact likeness is displayed in human form. Jesus proves that human life is tailor-made for God!*)

Col 2:10 Jesus mirrors our completeness and [1]endorses our [2]true identity. He is "I am" in us. (*Isn't it amazing that God packaged completeness in "I am," mirrored in you! Delay is outdated! The word, [1]arche, means chief in rank. The word, [2]exousia, is often translated as meaning authority; its components are, ek + eimi, originating out of "I am." The days are over where our lives were dictated to under the rule of the law of performance and an inferior identity. [See Col 1:19] The full measure of everything God has in mind for man indwells him.*

"*Your own completeness is only realized in him.*" — Phillips Translation.)

Heb 1:1 Throughout ancient times God spoke in many fragments and glimpses of prophetic thought to our fathers.

Heb 1:2 Now, the sum total of his conversation with man has finally culminated in a son. He is the official heir of all things. He is, after all, the author of the ages. Jesus is what has been on the tip of the Father's tongue all along! (*The revelation of man's redeemed sonship, as revealed in Jesus, is the crescendo of God's conversation with humanity. Throughout the ages he has whispered his name in disguise to be revealed in the fullness of time as the greatest surprise.*

The exact image of God, his very likeness, the authentic eternal thought, became voice and was made flesh in us. The composer of a concert masterpiece knew that the notes scribbled on a page would finally find its voice in a symphony of instruments.)

Heb 1:3 We have our beginning and our being in him. He is the force of the universe, sustaining everything that exists by his eternal utterance! Jesus is the radiant and flawless expression of the person of God. He makes the glory (*doxa, intent*) of God visible and exemplifies the character and every attribute of God in human form. (*Gen 1:26, 27*) This powerful final utterance of God (*the incarnation revealing our sonship*) is the vehicle that carries the weight of the universe. What he communicates is the central theme of everything that exists. The content of his message celebrates the fact that God took it upon himself to successfully cleanse and acquit humankind. The man Jesus is now his right hand of power, the executive authority seated in the boundless measure of his majesty. He occupies the highest seat of dominion to endorse our innocence! His throne is established upon our innocence. (*"Having accomplished purification of sins, he sat down ..."*)
In the culmination of God's eternal thought Jesus exhibits his exact likeness, the radiance of his glory in human form, and redeems man's innocence.

The truth about man is revealed in Christ; this is the mystery of grace: God revealed us in Christ!

The perfect law of liberty frees you to discover your true self beyond all contradiction! James 1:25.

Every human life is equally valued and represented in Christ. He gives context and reference to our being as in a mirror; not as an example for us, but of us. The "ugly duckling" saw reflected in the water the truth that freed the swan!

Gal 1:15 God's eternal [1]love dream separated me from my mother's womb; his grace became my [2]identity. *(The word, [1]eudokeo, means his beautiful intention; the well done opinion. [My mother's womb, my natural lineage and identity as son of Benjamin.] The word, [2]kaleo, means to surname, to summon by name.)*

Gal 1:16 This is the heart of the gospel that I proclaim; it began with an unveiling of sonship [1]in me, freeing me to announce the same sonship [2]in the masses of non-Jewish people. I felt no immediate urgency to compare notes with those who were familiar with Christ from a mere historic point of view.

(The Greek text is quite clear: "It pleased the Father to reveal his son in me in order that I may proclaim him in the nations!" The words, en emoi, translate as "in me," and en ethnos translate as in the Gentile nations, or the masses of non Jewish people! Not "among" the Gentiles as most translations have it. Later, when Barnabas is sent to investigate the conversion of the Greeks in Acts 11, instead of reporting his findings to HQ in Jerusalem, he immediately finds Paul, knowing that Paul's gospel is the revelation of the mystery of Christ in the nations [see Col 1:27]. No wonder then that those believers were the first to be called Christians, or Christ-like!)

Jesus Christ confirms that the son of man is the son of God. "Call no man your father on earth, for you have one Father, who is in heaven." [Mt 23:9] Paul reminds the Greek philosophers in Acts 17 that we live and move and have our being in God; humankind is indeed the offspring of God. He is quoting from their own writings, Aratus, who lived 300 BC. The incorruptible seed of sonship is as much in every man as the seed is already in all soil, even in the desert, waiting for the rain to awaken and ignite its life!

"For as the rain and the snow come down from heaven and water the earth, making it bring forth and sprout, so shall my word be that proceeds from my mouth, it shall not disappoint my purpose, it shall saturate the soil and cause it to bring forth and sprout, instead of the thorn the cyprus and instead of the brier the myrtle!" [Isa 55:8-11, 13]

In Matthew 13:44, Jesus says that the kingdom of heaven is like a treasure hidden in an agricultural field! There is more to the field than what meets the eye! In 2 Corinthians 4:4, 7, Paul says that we have this treasure in earthen vessels! But the god of this world seeks to blind our minds through unbelief [believing a lie about ourselves, Num 13:33] to keep us from seeing the light of the gospel revealing the glory of God in the face of Christ who is the image of God, as in a mirror!

When Jesus speaks of the sinner he speaks of him as the lost sheep, coin, or son. [Lk 15] The inscription and image did not disappear from the coin when it was lost, how can we praise God and with the same mouth curse a man made in his image? [Jas 3:9 and Lk 20:20-26] Mankind forgot what manner of man he is by design; man is the image and likeness bearer of his Maker; this is exactly what Jesus came to reveal and redeem.

We may now behold him with unveiled faces as in a mirror and be immediately transformed [in our understanding] into his likeness. From the glory [opinion] of the flesh to the glory [opinion] of God. Legalistic religion kept the veil in place; the proclaiming of the liberating truth of the Good News, removes the veil! The "ugly duckling" didn't need a face-lift or lessons on how to fake the swan life! It only needed to know the truth about itself to be free indeed.)

Gal 1:17 This is radical! I deliberately distanced myself from Jerusalem and the disciples of Jesus. I landed up in Arabia before I returned again to Damascus. *(The weight of this revelation left me no choice; instead of finding out more about Christ in history, I desire to discover him more in me! [See also 2 Cor 5:16])*

Gal 1:18 Then three years later I ventured into Jerusalem, specifically to meet with [1]Kefas. I ended up staying with him for two weeks. *(In [1]Aramaic the word "rock" is kefas, and in Greek it is petros. Here Paul calls Peter Kefas in order to emphasize the meaning of his name rather than the familiar sound of Peter. Jesus said that the revelation of man's true identity and origin is the rock foundation of the ekklesia, lit. original identity from ek, the preposition denoting origin and kaleo, to surname. [Mt 16:13-18; see also Isa 51:1; Deut 32:18; 1 Peter 2:5 and 1 Kings 6:7])*

Gal 1:19 During this time I did not see any of the other apostles except James, the younger brother of Jesus. *(Saul (Paul), Peter (Kefas) and James shared a vital revelation; all three of them discovered their original identity beyond their natural birth: "Simon son of Jonah, flesh and blood did not reveal to you that I, the son of man am the Christ, the son of God; now that you know who I am, allow me to introduce you to you! I say that you are Rock. [Mt 16:17, 18]*

During the three years of Jesus's ministry none of his brothers believed in him. [Jn 7:5] But in 1 Corinthians 15:7, Paul specifically mentions the fact that Jesus also appeared to James after his resurrection. Suddenly it dawns on James that the Father of light birthed mankind by the eternal Word of truth; the word that became flesh and died humanity's death and who co-raised humankind into newness of life in his resurrection. If any man hears this word he sees the face of his birth as in a mirror! As Peter later admitted "We were born anew when Jesus was raised from the dead!" [1 Pet 1:3] The word that was before time was is our genesis. [Jas 1:17, 18, 23, 24]) Mirror

The days of window-shopping are over! The mirror revelation makes the Bible a new book! A mirror can only reflect the object; likewise the purpose of the page was only to reflect the message, which is "Christ in you"; he completes the deepest longing of every human heart. There is no more accurate translation of Scripture than the Incarnation.

Paul reminds the Greek philosophers in Acts 17 that we live and move and have our being in God; humankind is indeed the offspring of God. He is quoting from their own writings, Aratus, who lived 300 BC. The incorruptible seed of sonship is as much in every man as the seed is already in all soil, even in the desert, waiting for the rain to awaken and ignite its life!

Israel dies in the desert not because of an inferior redemption out of slavery, but because they believed a lie about themselves! "We are grasshoppers compared to the giants. Num 13:33

They did not realize that those giants were already defeated and paralysed with fear! Josh 2:11.

The church have preached a defeated devil back into bussiness for many years!

The devil is not the parent of a single person, he is the father of lies!

Mal 2:10 Have we not all one father? Has not one God created us?

Jesus has come to reveal that the son of man is the son of God. "If you have seen me you have seen the Father! Mat 23:9 "Call no man your father on earth, for you have one Father, who is in heaven." He says to Simon, "Flesh-and-blood cannot reveal to you who the son of man is, but my Father who is in heaven; blessed are you, Simon son of Jonah, I give you a new name that reveals your original identity: you are Rock! *(petros, hewn out of the rock, petra (Isa 51:1, Deut 32:3, 4, 18).* This revelation is the rock foundation upon which I will build my identity, *(my image and likeness)* and the strong gates of *hades, (ha + ideis, not to see)* that trapped man into the walled city of the senses will not prevail against the voice that surnames and summons man again. *(Mt 16:13, 17) Church, ekklesia, from ek, denoting source or origin and klesia from kaleo, to surname or identify by name.)*

In him we discover that we are not here by chance or accident, or by the desire of an earthly parent, neither are we the product of a mere physical conception; we exist by the expression of God's desire to reveal himself in the flesh. His eternal, invisible Word, his Spirit-thought, became *(egeneto, from ginomai, be born)* flesh. James says: "Of his own will he brought us forth by the word of truth ... if any man hears this word, he sees the face of his birth as in a mirror." (Jas 1:17, 18, 23 RSV). Now we may know even as we have always been known (1 Cor 13:12).

God never compromised his original thought. "The word became flesh and took up residence *(tabernacled)* in us, and we gazed with wonder and amazement upon the mystery of our inclusion in him *(theaomai, to gaze upon, to perceive).* We saw his glory *(doxa, the display of his opinion);* the glory as of the original, authentic begotten of the Father, full of grace and truth." *(The original mind, or opinion of God, preserved and now revealed in Christ. He is both the "only begotten," monogenes, as in the authentic original mold, as well as the first born from the dead [Col 1:18, 1Pet 1:3].)*

1 John 1:1 The Logos is the source; everything commences in him. The initial reports concerning him that have reached our ears, that which we indeed bore witness to with our own eyes to the point that we became irresistibly attracted, now captivates our gaze. In him we witnessed tangible life in its most articulate form. *(To touch, psallo, to touch the string of a musical instrument, thus resonance.)*

1 John 1:2 The same life that was with the Father from the beginning, now dawned on us! The infinite life of the Father became visible before our eyes in a human person! *(In the beginning "was" the word; eimi, timeless existence)*

1 John 1:3 We include you in this conversation; you are the immediate audience of the logic of God! This is the word that always was; we saw him incarnate and witnessed his language as defining our lives. In the incarnation Jesus includes mankind in the eternal friendship of the Father and the son! This life now finds expression in an unreserved union.

1 John 1:4 What we enjoy equally belongs to you! I am writing this for your reference, so that joy may be yours in its most complete measure. *(In all these years since the ascension of Jesus, John now ninety years old continues to enjoy unhindered friendship with God and desires to extend this same fellowship to everyone through this writing.)*

Man comes from above. "I knew you before I formed you in your mother's womb." (Jer 1:5). In our make-up we are the god-kind with an appetite for more than what bread and the senses could satisfy. Jesus proves that we come from above. It would not be possible for man to access the heavenly sphere if man did not originate from there; the son of man is in heavenly places in the bosom of his Father whilst on this planet in an earthly body (Jn 3:13). His death and resurrection prepared a place for us so that we may be where he is! The fullness of Deity bodily indwells him (Col 2:9)! Jesus said to Nicodemus, "Unless you're born from above, *anouthen (meaning unless you originate from above),* you could not access heavenly realities; you would have no appetite for heavenly things!" (Jn 3:3).

John records how Jesus defended his message when he declared, to the disgust of the religious leaders, "I and the Father are one!" (Jn 10:30 RSV) He quoted Psalm 82:6 (RSV), "I say you are gods, sons of the Most High, all of you!"

Man began in God; we are not the invention of our parents!

Jesus declares the climax of his mission where in his death and resurrection every possible definition of separation will be cancelled: "In that day you will know that I am in my Father, and you in me and I in you!" (Jn 14:20 RSV).

John 1:12 Everyone who [1]realizes their association in him, [6]convinced that he is their [2]original life and that [7]his name defines them, [5]in them he [3]endorses the fact that they are indeed his [4]offspring, [2]begotten of him; he [3]sanctions the legitimacy of their sonship. *(The word often translated, to receive, [1]lambano, means to comprehend, grasp, to identify with. This word suggests that even though he came to his own, there are those who do not [1]grasp their true [2]origin revealed in him, and like the many Pharisees they behave like children of a foreign father, the father of lies [Jn 8: 44].*

Neither God's legitimate fatherhood of man nor his ownership is in question; man's indifference to his true [2]origin is the problem. This is what the Gospel addresses with utmost clarity in the person of Jesus Christ. Jesus has come to introduce man to himself again; humanity has forgotten what manner of man he is by design! [Jas 1:24, Deut 32:18, Ps 22:27].

The word, [2]genesthai [aorist tense] is like a snapshot taken of an event, from ginomai, to become [See 1:3]. The Logos is the source; everything commences in him. He remains the exclusive Parent reference to their genesis. There is nothing original, except the Word! Man began in God [see also Acts 17:28]. "He has come to give us understanding to know him who is true and to realize that we are in him who is true." [1 Jn 5:20].)

The word, [3]exousia, often translated "power;" as in, he gave "power" to [2]become children of God, is a compound word; and ek, always denoting origin or source and eimi, I am; thus, out of I am! This gives [3]legitimacy and authority to our sonship; [4]teknon, translated as offspring, child.

"He has given," [5]didomi, in this case to give something to someone that already belongs to them; thus, to return. The fact that they already are his own, born from above, they have their [2]beginning and their being in him is now confirmed in their realizing it! Convinced, [6]pisteo; [7]his name onoma, defines man's true identity. [see Eph 3:15]. Mirror

"He made to be their true selves, their child-of-God selves." — The Message)

Christ is the most exhaustive and authentic expression of God in human form. Nothing feeds us more and imparts life more dynamically than what the revelation of the incarnation does.

God's Strategy ~ Asia in one man

Paul writes in Rom 16:5 "Salute my dear friend Epaenetus. He represents the whole of Asia to me since he was my first convert there."

God always sees the many in the one. In God's economy "one died for all; therefore all died!" 2 Cor 5:14

God's faith sees every human life equally included and represented in Christ.

The law reveals what happened to man in Adam;

Grace reveals what happened to the same man in Christ.

God found us in Christ before he lost us in Adam!

1 Cor 2:7 We voice words of wisdom that was hidden in silence for timeless ages; a mystery unfolding God's Masterful plan whereby he would redeem his glory in man.

1 Cor 2:8 Neither the politicians nor the theologians of the day had a clue about this mystery *(of mankind's association in Christ)*; if they did, they would never have crucified the Lord whose death redeemed our glory!

John 1:29 "Behold, the Lamb of God, who takes away the sin of the world!" This is not mankind's clumpsy attemt to save himself; this is God's doing!

Heb 1:3 When he had by himself purged our sins, sat down on the right hand of the Majesty on high; KJV The throne of God is established upon our innocence!

History recorded the death and resurrection of one man; eternity recorded the death and resurrection of the human race.

Rom 4:25 Our sins [1]resulted in his death; his resurrection is [1]proof of our righteousness. *(His resurrection is the receipt to our acquittal. This is one of the most important statements in the entire Bible. Why was Jesus handed over to die? Because of [1]dia, our sins. Why was he raised from the dead? Because of **dia**, we were justified! His resurrection reveals our righteousness! Here is the equation: his cross = our sins; his resurrection = our innocence! If we were still guilty after Jesus died, his resurrection would neither be possible nor relevant! This explains Acts 10:28 and 2 Cor 5:14 and 16. And in Acts 17:31, "because God had fixed a day on which he would judge the world in righteousness by a man whom he has appointed, and of this he has given assurance to all men by raising him from the dead.")*

Paul boldly announces to the idol worshipping Greek philosophers in Acts 17 that the Creator "is not far from each one of us! In him we live and move and have our being! We are indeed his offspring!" He understands that in Christ God cancelled every definition of distance! In the incarnation God embraced the human race! He is equally Emmanuel for everyone! In the light of the incarnation there can no longer be an "us" and "them!" This message claims the most radical mind-shift! (the word translated repent is a very unfortunate and deliberate mistake! It comes from the Latin word, pennance and in order to squeeze even more mileage and guilt money out of people a "re" was added to make it repennance! The Greek word *metanoia* suggests a radical mindshift! It is a compound word, *meta* means together with and *nous*, is mind, to realize God's thoughts! The good news confronts mankind with Jesus as the mind of God made up about us!

Paul makes this powerful statement to these philosophers in Acts 17:30,31, "The times of ignorance God overlooked, but now he implores **all men everywhere** to discover God's thoughts towards them, *(not, repent, as the translations suggest, but, metanoia),* because he has fixed a day and appointed a person, and on that day in that person he would judge the world in righteousness, and of this he has given proof to **all men** by raising him from the dead."

The resurrection of Jesus Christ announces mankind's innocence! This is the heart of the gospel!

In dramatic fashion God re-writes Peters doctrine and changes his appetite! Acts 10:28 God has shown me that I should not call any man common or unclean.

1 Pet 1:3 Blessed be the God and Father of our Lord Jesus Christ! By his great mercy we have been born anew to a living hope through the resurrection of Jesus Christ from the dead.

2 Co 5:16 From now on, therefore, we regard no one from a human point of view; even though we once regarded Christ from a human point of view, we regard him thus no longer. RSV

Eph 1:3 Let's celebrate God! He lavished every blessing heaven has upon us in Christ!

Eph 1:4 He associated us in Christ before the fall of the world! Jesus is God's mind made up about mankind! He always knew in his love that he would present us again face-to-face before him in blameless innocence. *The word, katenopion, suggests the closest possible proximity, face-to-face!* Mirror

The concept of association is a very powerful one; it suggests that it is impossible to bring the one party to mind without immediately and on equal terms include the other. The one immediately reminds of the other!

Col 1:25 I am an administrator in God's economy; my mission is to make his word known to you with utmost clarity.

Col 1:26 The element of prophetic mystery was concealed for ages and generations but is now fully realized in our redeemed innocence.

Col 1:27 In us God desires to exhibit the priceless treasure of Christ's indwelling; every nation will recognize him as in a mirror! The unveiling of Christ in human life completes man's every expectation. *(He is not hiding in history, or in outer space nor in the future, neither in the pages of scripture, he is merely mirrored there to be unveiled within you. Mt 13:44, Gal 1:15, 16)*

Col 1:28 This is the essence and focus of our message; we [1]awaken every man's mind, instructing every individual by bringing them into [2]full understanding *(flawless clarity)* in order that we may [3]prove *(present)* everyone [4]perfect in Christ. *(Translating [1]vous + tithemi as to re-align every mind with God's mind. The word, [2]sophos,*

93

*comes from **sophes** meaning clear, clarity. The word, [3]**paristano**, comes from **para**, sphere of influence, closest possible association, and **histemi**, meaning to stand, to exhibit with evidence. The word, [4]**teleios**, means perfect, without shortcoming and fully efficient.)*

Col 1:29 [1]Your completeness in Christ is my point of departure! My labor now exceeds any zeal that I previously knew under the law of willpower and duty. I am laboring beyond the point of exhaustion, striving with intense resolve with all the energy that he mightily inspires within me. *([1]eis, a point reached in conclusion.)* Mirror

Gal 3:8 Scripture records prophetically that the mass of non-Jewish nations would be justified by faith and not by keeping moral laws. The origin of the gospel is found in this announcement by God over Abraham; he saw all the nations represented in the same principle of the faith that Abraham pioneered. "In you all the nations of the earth are equally represented in the blessing of faith." *([Gen 22:17] I will indeed bless you, and I will multiply your seed as the stars of heaven and as the sand which is on the seashore. And your seed shall possess the gate of their enemies, Gen 22:18 and by your seed shall all the nations of the earth bless themselves. Righteousness by faith is the revelation of the gospel; [Rom 1:17 and Hab 2:4] "the just shall live by his (God's) faith" Righteousness by faith defines your life!)*

Heb 12:2 Look away from the shadow dispensation of the law and the prophets and fix your eyes upon Jesus. He is the fountainhead and conclusion of faith. He saw the joy *(of mankind's salvation)* when he braved the cross and despised the shame of it. As the executive authority of God *(the right hand of the Throne of God)* he now occupies the highest seat of dominion to endorse man's innocence! *(Having accomplished purification of sins, he sat down. [Heb 1:3, Isa 53:11])*

Rom 4:16 Therefore since faith sponsors the gift of grace, the promise is equally secured for all the children. The law has no exclusive claim on anyone *(the reward system cannot match the gift principle)*. Faith is our source, and that makes Abraham our father. *(God's persuasion is the source of faith. Heb 12:2)*

Rom 4:17 When God changed Abram's name to Abraham, he made a public statement that he would be the father of all nations. *(Genesis 17:5)* Here we see Abraham faced with God's faith; the kind of faith that resurrects the dead and calls things which are not *(visible yet)* as though they were. *(Note that most of Abram's ancestors were allready fathers by the time that they had turned 30 or 35; yet Terah was 70 years old before he had Abram; his name suggests that Terah acknowledged that he could not claim parenthood of this son, he was 'fathered from above'! [Gen 11:12-26] Now imagine how nervous Abram was when eventually he was 75 and still without child! That was when God met with him and added to his name the 'ha' of Jaweh's (Jehovah) own name! In Arabic the word raham means drizzling and lasting rain. The innumerable drops of water in a drizzling rain are like the stars mentioned in Gen 15:5 ("look toward heaven, and number the stars, if you are able to number them . . . so shall your seed be") now imagine those innumerable stars raining down upon the earth and each one becomes a grain of sand! So shall your seed be! Gen 22:17 ("I will indeed bless you, and I will multiply your descendants as the stars of heaven and as the sand which is on the seashore"). Abraham's identity, his name, was the echo of God's faith and his bold confession in the absence of Isaac. The name change, similar to that of Simon to Rock, reminds man to realize his original identity as son of God, hewn out of the Rock [Deut 32:18, Isa 51:1, 2].)*

Rom 4:18 Faith gave substance to hope when everything seemed hopeless; the words, "so shall your seed be" conceived in him the faith of fatherhood. *(Abraham's case here pictures the hopelessness of fallen man, having lost their identity, and faced with the impossibility to redeem themselves.)*

Gal 3:16 It is on record that the promise *(of the blessing of righteousness by faith)* was made to Abraham and to his seed, singular, *(thus excluding his effort to produce Ishmael.)* Isaac, the child of promise and not of the flesh mirrors the Messiah.

Rom 1:16 I have no shame about sharing the good news of Christ with anyone; the powerful rescuing act of God persuades both Jew and Greek alike.

Rom 1:17 Herein lies the secret of the power of the Gospel; there is no good news in it until the [1]righteousness of God is revealed! The dynamic of the gospel is the revelation of God's faith as the only valid basis for our belief. The prophets wrote in advance about the fact that God believes that righteousness unveils the life that he always had in mind for us. "Righteousness by his (God's) faith defines life." *(The good news is the fact that the Cross of Christ was a success. God rescued [1]the life of our design; he redeemed our [1]innocence. Man would never again be judged righteous or unrighteous by his own ability to obey moral laws! It is not about what man must or must not do but about what Jesus has done! It is from faith to faith, and not man's good or bad behavior or circumstances interpreted as a blessing or a curse [Hab 2:4]. Instead of reading the curse when disaster strikes, Habakkuk realizes that the Promise out-dates performance as the basis to man's acquittal. Deuteronomy 28 would no longer be the motivation or the measure of right or wrong behavior! "Though the fig trees do not blossom, nor fruit be on the vines, the produce of the olive fail and the fields yield no food, the flock be cut off from the fold and there be no herd in the stalls, yet I will rejoice in the Lord, I will joy in the God of my salvation. God, the Lord, is my strength; he makes my feet like hinds' feet, he makes me tread upon my high places [Hab 3:17-19 RSV]. "Look away [from the law of works] unto Jesus; he is the Author and finisher of faith." [Heb 12:1].*

*The gospel is the revelation of the righteousness of God; it declares how God succeeded to put mankind right with him. It is about what God did right, not what Adam did wrong. The word righteousness comes from the Anglo Saxon word, "rightwiseness;" wise in that which is right. In Greek the root word for righteousness is [1]**dike**, which means two parties finding likeness in each other. The Hebrew word for righteousness is [1]**tzadok**, which refers to the beam in a scale of balances. In Colossians 2:9-10, It is in Christ that God finds an accurate and complete expression of himself, in a human body! He mirrors our completeness and is the ultimate authority of our true identity.*

Isa 9:2 The people who walked in darkness have seen a great light; those who dwelt in a land of deep darkness, on them has light shined.

Isa 9:3 Thou hast multiplied the nation, thou hast increased its joy; they rejoice before thee as with joy at the harvest, as men rejoice when they divide the spoil.

Isa 9:4 For the yoke of his burden, and the staff for his shoulder, the rod of his oppressor, thou hast broken as on the day of Midian. *(Gideon's victory Jdg 7:8)*

Isa 9:6 For to us a child is born, to us a son is given; and the government will be upon his shoulder, and his name will be called "Wonderful Counselor, Mighty God, Everlasting Father, Prince of Peace."

Isa 9:7 Of the increase of his government and of peace there will be no end, upon the throne of David, and over his kingdom, to establish it, and to uphold it with justice and with righteousness from this time forth and for evermore. The zeal of the LORD of hosts will do this. RSV

The zeal of the Lord is in total contrast to a religious zeal for God. The zeal of God is fueled by the revelation of righteousness by faith. While the one exhausts the other ignites!

Rom 10:2 I have been there myself. I know their zeal and devotion; their problem is not their passion, but their ignorance.

Rom 10:3 They are tirelessly busy with their own efforts to justify themselves while blatantly ignoring the fact that God already justified them in Christ.

Rom 10:4 Christ is the conclusion of the law, everything the law required of man was fulfilled in him; he thus represents the righteousness of the human race, based upon faith *(and not personal performance)*.

Rom 10:5 Moses is the voice of the law; he says that a man's life is only justified in his doing what the law requires.

Rom 10:6 But faith finds its voice in something much closer to man than his most disciplined effort to obey the law. Faith understands that Christ is no longer a distant promise; neither is he reduced to a mere historic hero. He is mankind's righteousness now! Christ is no longer hidden somewhere in the realm of heaven as a future hope. For the Jews to continue to ask God to send the Messiah is a waste of time! That is not the language of faith.

Rom 10:7 Faith knows that the Messiah is not roaming somewhere in the region of the dead. "Who will descend into the abyss to bring Christ back from the dead," is not the language of faith. *(Those who deny the resurrection of Christ would wish to send someone to go there and confirm their doubts, and bring back final proof that Jesus was not the Messiah. Faith announces a righteousness that reveals that humankind has indeed been co-raised together with Christ; the testimony of the risen Christ is confirmed in the heart and life of every believer.)*

Rom 10:8 Faith-righteousness announces that every definition of distance in time, space, or hostility has been cancelled. Faith says, "The Word is near you. It is as close to you as your voice and the conviction of your heart." We publicly announce this message *(because we are convinced that it belongs to every man)*.

Rom 10:9 Now your salvation is realized! Your own [1]words echo God's voice. The unveiling of the masterful act of Jesus forms the words in your mouth, inspired by the conviction in your heart that God indeed raised him from the dead. *(In his resurrection, God co-raised us [Hos 6:2]. His resurrection declares our innocence [Rom 4:25]. Salvation is not reduced to a recipe or a "sinners prayer" formula; it is the spontaneous inevitable conversation of a persuaded heart! To confess, [1]***homologeo, homo,*** *the same thing +* ***logeo,*** *to say)*

Rom 10:10 Heart-faith confirms our redeemed righteousness and ignites the kind of conversation consistent with salvation. *(He restored us to blameless innocence! It is impossible not to boldly announce news of such global consequence [Isa 40:9].)*

96

1 Cor 15:10 While my own doing completely disqualified me; his doing now defines me. I am what I am by the grace of God. I am because he is! His grace was not wasted on me; instead I am inspired to labor beyond the point of exhaustion, more than anything I ever did under the law of performance; whatever it is that I accomplish now has grace written all over it. I take no credit for it. Mirror

Psa 2:7 You are my son, today I have begotten you.

Psa 2:8 Ask of me, and I will make the nations your heritage, and the ends of the earth your possession. RSV

1Pe 1:3 Blessed be the God and Father of our Lord Jesus Christ! By his great mercy we have been born anew to a living hope through the resurrection of Jesus Christ from the dead. RSV

Hos 6:1 "Come, let us return to the LORD; for he has torn, that he may heal us; he has stricken, and he will bind us up. [See Isa 53:4,5]

Hos 6:2 After two days he will revive us; on the third day he will raise us up, that we may live before him.

Hos 6:3 Let us know, let us press on to know the LORD; his going forth is sure as the dawn; he will come to us as the showers, as the spring rains that water the earth." RSV

Eph 2:5 even when we were dead through our trespasses, God made us alive together with Christ *(by grace you have been saved)*,

Eph 2:6 and raised us up with him, and made us sit with him in the heavenly places in Christ Jesus, RSV

2 Cor 5:15 Now if all were included in his death they were equally included in his resurrection. This unveiling of his love redefines human life! Whatever reference we could have of ourselves outside of our association with Christ is no longer relevant. Mirror

In Psalm 22 David paints a most dramatic prophetic picture of the crucifixion of the Messiah and in verse 27 boldly proclaims the outcome, "All the ends of the earth shall remember and turn to the Lord!" And in verse 31 he declares, his deliverance will be proclaimed to a people yet unborn, they will hear that he has wrought it.

Then in the next Psalm David sings about the Shepherd that leads us to the waters of reflection, "where my soul remembers who I am!"

The remotest parts of the earth will witness the salvation that God has brought about.

Isa 42:6 "I am the LORD, I have called you in righteousness, I have taken you by the hand and kept you; I have given you as a covenant to the people, a light to the nations,

Isa 42:7 to open the eyes that are blind, to bring out the prisoners from the dungeon, from the prison those who sit in darkness.

Picture the body language of the messengers returning from the battlefield with the glad tidings of victory!

Isa 52:7 How beautiful upon the mountains are the feet of him who brings good tidings, who publishes peace, who brings good tidings of good, who publishes salvation, who says to Zion, "Your God reigns."

Isa 52:8 Hark, your watchmen lift up their voice, together they sing for joy; for eye to eye they see the return of the LORD to Zion.

Isa 52:9 Break forth together into singing, you waste places of Jerusalem; for the LORD has comforted his people, he has redeemed Jerusalem.

Isa 52:10 The LORD has bared his holy arm before the eyes of all the nations; and all the ends of the earth shall see the salvation of our God. RSV

Isa 60:1 Arise, shine; for your light has come, and the glory of the LORD has risen upon you.

Isa 60:2 For behold, darkness shall cover the earth, and thick darkness the peoples; but the LORD will arise upon you, and his glory will be seen upon you.

Isa 60:3 And nations shall come to your light, and kings to the brightness of your rising.

Isa 60:21 Your people shall all be righteous; they shall possess the land for ever, the shoot of my planting, the work of my hands, that I might be glorified.

Isa 60:22 The least one shall become a clan, and the smallest one a mighty nation; I am the LORD; in its time I will hasten it.

Isa 61:1 The Spirit of the Lord GOD is upon me, because the LORD has anointed me to bring good tidings to the afflicted; he has sent me to bind up the broken hearted, to proclaim liberty to the captives, and the opening of the prison to those who are bound;

Isa 61:2 to proclaim the year of the LORD's favor, and the day of vengeance of our God; to comfort all who mourn;

Luk 4:18,19 "The Spirit of the Lord is upon me, because he has anointed me to preach good news to the poor. He has sent me to proclaim release to the captives and recovering of sight to the blind, to set at liberty those who are oppressed, to proclaim the acceptable year of the Lord."

Luk 4:20 And he closed the book, and gave it back to the attendant, and sat down; and the eyes of all in the synagogue were fixed on him.

Luk 4:21 And he began to say to them, "Today this scripture has been fulfilled in your hearing."

If the gospel was to be measured geographically then the ends of the earth can be the only conclusion. The breadth, length, height, and depth of the love of Christ, which surpasses knowledge addresses every human as included in God's audience. This gospel is every man's portion.

Luk 2:10 And the angel said unto them, Be not afraid; for behold, I bring you good tidings of great joy which shall be to all the people:

Luk 2:11 for there is born to you this day in the city of David a Saviour, who is Christ the Lord. ASV

Luk 2:14 "Glory to God in the highest, and on earth peace among men with whom he is pleased!" RSV

The destiny of the good news is to win the world.

Php 2:9 Therefore God has highly exalted him and bestowed on him the name which is above every name,

Php 2:10 that at the name of Jesus every knee should bow, in heaven and on earth and under the earth,

Php 2:11 and every tongue confess that Jesus Christ is Lord, to the glory of God the Father. RSV

Act 4:20 We cannot but speak of what we have seen and heard.

Job 32:8 But it is the spirit in a man, the breath of the Almighty, that makes him understand.

Job 32:18 For I am full of words, the spirit within me constrains me.

Job 32:19 Behold, my heart is like wine that has no vent; like new wineskins, it is ready to burst.

Job 32:20 I must speak, that I may find relief; RSV

Psa 39:3 My heart became hot within me. As I mused, the fire burned; then I spoke with my tongue. RSV

Luk 24:32 They said to each other, "Did not our hearts burn within us while he talked to us on the road, while he opened to us the scriptures?" RSV

Our beholding him as in a mirror, gives volume to our voice! The revelation of grace fuels the fire within!

Isa 40:9 Get you up to a high mountain, O Zion, herald of good tidings; lift up your voice with strength, O Jerusalem, herald of good tidings, lift it up, fear not; say to the cities of Judah, "Behold your God!" RSV

Col 3:1 You are in fact raised together with Christ! Now ponder with persuasion the consequence of your co-inclusion in him. Relocate yourselves mentally! Engage your thoughts with throne room realities. His resurrection co-raised you to the same position of authority where you are now co-seated in the executive authority of God's right hand.

Col 3:2 Becoming affectionately acquainted with these thoughts will keep you from being distracted again by the earthly (soul-ruled) realm. (A renewed mind conquers the space that was previously occupied by worthless pursuits and habits.)

Col 3:3 Your union with his death broke the association with that world; see yourselves located in a fortress where your life is hidden with Christ in God!

The secret and success of Paul's ministry was not in his articulate or persuasive speech or the size of his budget or audience, but in the revelation of the redeemed image and likeness of God in man, and the love of Christ constraining him.

2 Cor 10:10 For they say, "His letters are weighty and strong, but his bodily presence is weak, and his speech of no account."

2 Cor 11:6 Even if I am unskilled in speaking, I am not in knowledge; in every way we have made this plain to you in all things. RSV

1 Cor 2:1 My intention in visiting you was not to engage with you in theological debate or to impress you with clever words guessing about the evidence of God.

1 Cor 2:2 The testimony of God is my only persuasion concerning you: Jesus Christ died your death on the cross! I can see you in no other light! *(For I determined to know nothing in you except Jesus Christ and him crucified.)*

1 Cor 2:3 I felt completely inadequate; you know that it was not my eloquent speech that persuaded you; I was so nervous that my whole body was trembling with stage fright

1 Cor 2:4 My message was not with persuasive arguments based on secular wisdom, since my aim was [1]not to point people to me but rather to the powerful working of the Spirit in them. *(Thayer's Greek definition of [1]**apodeiknumi** is to point away from one's self. Previous translations of this word have often given the impression that the great, miracle-working man of God would steal the show and entertain the crowds! This was so unlike Jesus and Paul! Paul never writes about how many people he had healed and brought to faith, etc. His all-consuming concern was that the eyes of our understanding would be illuminated with the revelation of Christ in us.*

Note 2 Corinthians 10:10 [RSV], "For they say, 'His letters are weighty and strong, but his bodily presence is weak, and his speech of no account.'" Also, 2 Corinthians 11:6, "Even if I am unskilled in speaking, I am not in knowledge." — RSV)

1 Cor 2:5 Man's wise schemes of influence could never match the power of God as reference to your faith.

1 Cor 2:6 The words we speak resonate revelation wisdom in those who understand how perfectly redeemed they are in Christ, this wisdom supersedes every secular kind; suddenly what once seemed wise and good advice has become useless information. *(All popular programs towards improved moral behavior are now outdated. "Of God's doing are we in Christ. He is both the genesis and genius of our wisdom; a wisdom that reveals how righteous, sanctified, and redeemed we already are in him." In God's economy, Christ represents us; what man could never achieve through personal discipline and willpower as taught in every religion, God's faith accomplished in Christ [1 Cor 1:30].)*

Paul's ministry was so much more than a mere career choice; he was compelled by love and joy because of what he knew to be true, in spite of severe contradiction.

1Cor 15:10 While my own doing completely disqualified me; his doing now defines me. I am what I am by the grace of God. I am because he is! His grace was not wasted on me; instead I am inspired to labor beyond the point of exhaustion, more than anything I ever did under the law of performance; whatever it is that I accomplish now has grace written all over it. I take no credit for it.

2 Cor 4:1 Since we are employed by the mercy of God, and not by our own quali-fications, quitting is not an option.

2 Cor 4:2 We have renounced hidden agendas *(employing a little bit of the law in an attempt to "balance" out grace)*; we have distanced ourselves from any obscure crafti-ness to manipulate God's word to make it mean what it does not say! With truth on open display in us, we highly recommend our lives to every one's [1]conscience! Truth finds its most authentic and articulate expression in human life. This beats any doctrinal debate! *(It is our passion for all to see what is so completely obvious in the mirror of our redeemed likeness and innocence! [1]Conscience in Latin means to know together; in the Greek, [1]suneido, it translates as joint seeing; which is the opposite of hades, not to see.)*

2 Cor 4:3 If our message seems vague to anyone, it is not because we are withhold-ing something from certain people! It is just because some are so stubborn in their efforts to uphold an outdated system that they don't see it! They are all equally found in Christ but they prefer to remain lost in the cul-de-sac language of the law!

2 Cor 4:4 The survival and self-improvement programs of the [1]religious systems of this world veil the minds of the unbelievers; exploiting their ignorance about their true origin and their redeemed innocence. The veil of unbelief obstructs a person's view and keeps one from seeing what the light of the gospel so clearly reveals: the [2]glory of God is the image and likeness of our Maker redeemed in human form; this is what the gospel of Christ is all about. *(The god of this [1]aion, age, refers to the religious systems and governing structures of this world. The unbelief that neutralized Israel in the wilderness was the lie that they believed about themselves; "We are grasshop-pers, and the 'enemy' is a giant beyond any proportion!" [Num 13:33, Josh 2:11, Heb 4:6] "They failed to possess the promise due to unbelief." The blueprint [2]doxa, glory of God, is what Adam lost on humanity's behalf. [See Eph 4:18])*

2 Cor 4:5 Even though we recommend ourselves with great confidence, it is not with arrogance; we do not preach ourselves! We preach Christ Jesus the Lord; we are salvation junkies; employed by Jesus for your sakes.

2 Cor 4:6 The light source is founded in the same God who said, "Light, be!" And light shone out of darkness! He lit the lamp in our understanding so that we may clearly recognize the features of his likeness in the face of Jesus Christ reflected within us. *(The same God who bade light shine out of darkness has kindled a light in our hearts, whose shining is to make known his glory as he has revealed it in the features of Jesus Christ. — Knox Translation)*

2 Cor 4:7 We have discovered this treasure where it was hidden all along, in these frail skin-suits made of clay. We take no credit for finding it there! It took the enor-mous power of God in the achievement of Christ to rescue our minds from the lies it believed. *("The kingdom of heaven is like treasure hidden in an agricultural field, which a man found and covered up; then in his joy he goes and sells all that he has and buys that field." [Mt 13:44] God invested all that he has in the redeeming of our original value! He rescued the life of our design. Our inner life hosts the treasure of the life of our design. Jesus said in John 7:37,38, "If you believe that I am what the scriptures are all about, you will know that you are what I am all about and rivers of living water will gush out of your in-nermost being!")*

2 Cor 4:8 We often feel completely hemmed in on every side but our inner space remains unrestricted; when there seems to be no way out, we escape within!

2 Cor 4:9 At times we are persecuted to the extreme but we are never abandoned. We are knocked down but not knocked out.

2 Cor 4:10 Wherever we go, whatever we encounter in our bodies, we bear witness within us of the fact that Jesus died our death; in this same body, we now exhibit his life. The fact that we co-died in his death confirms that we now co-live in his resurrection!

2 Cor 4:11 Our day-to-day experience continues to exhibit that even in the face of death, our association with the death Jesus already died remains the inspiration of his life made so clearly visible within us. This is in such contrast to the circumstances that we are often faced with.

2 Cor 4:12 Living aware of our co-crucifiction with Christ *(the thought of our mutual death)* in the face of death threatening circumstances [1]inspires life in you! *(The word, [1]energeo, translates as energy trigger.)*

2 Cor 4:13 We [1]echo the exact same spirit of faith David had when he wrote: "I believe and so I speak!" We too believe and so we speak! Our persuasion is our conversation. *(The word, [1]echo, means to hold or to embrace. Paul quotes David here in Psalm 116; sometimes one's soul wants to gallop away into distraction like a wild horse; David speaks to himself and reminds himself to, "Return, O my soul, to your rest; for the Lord has dealt bountifully with you!" [RSV] "I believe, and so I speak!" God's bountiful dealings with us in Christ is our only valid rest; Sabbath celebrates perfection! And remember God does not employ circumstances to teach us something! The finished work of Christ teaches us; his work on the cross rescued us!)*

2 Cor 4:14 The resurrection life we enjoy in Jesus fully includes you.

2 Cor 4:15 Whatever we go through in the gospel is to advantage you! We live for you! As grace abounds in more and more people so does the volume of gratitude in the accomplished mission of Jesus break through the sound barrier to exhibit the [1]heart dream of God. (*The word, [1]doxa, means glory, from dokeo, meaning intent opinion, the heart dream of God is his image and likeness redeemed in man.)*

2 Cor 4:16 We have much reason to be brave! There might be a lot of wear and tear on the outside; but don't be distracted by that! On the inside we are celebrating daily revival!

2 Cor 4:17 We are fully engaged in an exceedingly superior reality; the extent and weight of this glory makes any degree of suffering vanish into insignificance! The suffering is fleeting and ever so slight by comparison to the weight and enduring effect of this glory we participate in for all eternity. *(In Afrikaans: Ons is totaal oorweldig deur die verbysterende ewige dimensies van heerlikheid wat reeds ons deel is en nooit onderskep kan word deur hierdie kortstondige ligte verdukking nie.)*

2 Cor 4:18 We are not keeping any score of what seems so obvious to the senses in the natural realm, it is fleeting and irrelevant; it is the unseen eternal realm within us that has our full attention and captivates our gaze! *(See John 1:18 Until this mo-*

*ment God remained invisible to man; now the [1]authentic begotten son, [1]**monogenes,** begotten only of God) the blueprint of man's design who represents the innermost being of God, the son who is in the bosom of the father, brings him into full view! He is the [2]official authority qualified to announce God! He is our guide who accurately declares and interprets the invisible God within us. Official guide, [2]**eksegesato,** from **ek,** preposition denoting source, and **hegeomai,** the strengthened form of **ago,** to lead as a shepherd leads his sheep; thus hegeomai means to be officially appointed in a position of authority.)*

2 Cor 3:18 The days of window-shopping are over! In him every face is unveiled. In gazing with wonder at the blueprint likeness of God displayed in human form we suddenly realize that we are looking at ourselves! Every feature of his image is mirrored in us! This is the most radical transformation engineered by the Spirit of the Lord; we are led from an inferior mind-set to the revealed endorsement of our authentic identity.

2 Cor 11:23 Are they servants of Christ? I am a better one--I am talking like a madman--with far greater labors, far more imprisonments, with countless beatings, and often near death.

2 Cor 11:24 Five times I have received at the hands of the Jews the forty lashes less one.

2 Cor 11:25 Three times I have been beaten with rods; once I was stoned. Three times I have been shipwrecked; a night and a day I have been adrift at sea;

2 Co 11:26 on frequent journeys, in danger from rivers, danger from robbers, danger from my own people, danger from Gentiles, danger in the city, danger in the wilderness, danger at sea, danger from false brethren;

2 Co 11:27 in toil and hardship, through many a sleepless night, in hunger and thirst, often without food, in cold and exposure.

2 Co 11:28 And, apart from other things, there is the daily pressure upon me of my anxiety for all the churches.

2 Co 11:29 Who is weak, and I am not weak? Who is made to fall, and I am not indignant?

2 Co 11:30 If I must boast, I will boast of the things that show my weakness. RSV

Php 4:11 Not that I complain of want; for I have learned, in whatever state I am, to be content.

Php 4:12 I know how to be abased, and I know how to abound; in any and all circumstances I have learned the secret of facing plenty and hunger, abundance and want.

Temporal setbacks and lack are no threat to the overwhelming conviction of God's love.

Rom 8:37 On the contrary, in the thick of these things our triumph remains beyond dispute. His love has placed us above the reach of any onslaught.

Rom 8:38 This is my conviction, no threat whether it be in death or life; be it angelic beings, demon powers or political principalities, nothing known to us at this time, or even in the unknown future;

Rom 8:39 no dimension of any calculation in time or space, nor any device yet to be invented, has what it takes to separate us from the love of God demonstrated in Christ. Jesus is our ultimate authority.

Paul felt urged and indebted to persuade both the learned Greeks and the illiterate masses of their inclusion in Christ.

Rom 1:5 The grace and commission we received from him, is to bring about a faith-inspired lifestyle in all the nations. His name is his claim on the human race. *(Paul immediately sets out to give new definition to the term, 'obedience', no longer by law, but of faith. Obedience, upo + akuo lit. under the influence of what is heard, accurate hearing, hearing from above. Every family in heaven and on earth, is identified in him. Eph 3:15.)*

Rom 1:14 I am so convinced of everyone's inclusion; I am indebted both to the Greeks as well as those many foreigners whose languages we do not even understand. I owe this message to everyone, it is not a matter of how literate and educated people are; the illiterate are equally included in the benefit of the good news. *(To be indebted obliges one to return something to someone that belongs to them in the first place.)*

Rom 1:15 Because of this compelling urgency I am so keen to preach to you Romans also.

He continued to labor with his own hands not to put any burden on the people he ministered to; yet he was never known as Paul the tentmaker; even his apostleship was not a formal title but rather a description of his passion; he was driven by the word to make all men see.

1 Cor 4:1 This is how one should regard us *(so called, Apostles)*: we are the [1]under-rowers of Captain Christ; responsible for the engine room as it were! We are entrusted with the administration of the mysteries of God. *(The unveiling of the mystery of the gospel of man's association in Christ is the driving force of the Church. The word, [1]huperetes, means an under-rower, who was one who was in the trireme, quadrireme, or quinquereme galleys and rowed in one of the undermost benches; those who were the lowest ranked slaves and often the most invisible part of the whole operation. We are not hiding behind fancy titles or impressive CV's to try and win your applause or financial support. We are not here to impress you with us; our mandate is to impress you with how complete you are in Christ because of God's doing. [See 1 Cor 1:30, 2:6-9].)*

1 Cor 4:2 *(Our title might be unimpressive, but our job is most significant.)* For this reason our ministry is of unquestionable integrity.

1 Cor 4:3 The authority of my ministry is not based upon your scrutiny of my life or even any cross examination by a human court. Neither is it by my own assumption;

1 Cor 4:4 even though I know of nothing against my conscience, I am not thereby acquitted. The point is not how self righteous I appear in my own eyes; the Lord's judgment is the only valid reference to our innocence.

Rom 16:25 I am not talking "hear-say-theory"; I own the gospel I proclaim! This is my message! I salute God who empowers you dynamically and establishes you to be strong and immovable in the face of contradiction. Jesus Christ is the disclosure of the very mystery that was concealed in silence before [1]time or human [2]history were recorded. *(Titus 1:2 This is the life of the [1]ages that was anticipated for generations; the life of our original design announced by the infallible resolve of God before [2]time or space existed. (Man's union with God is the original thought that inspired creation. The word, [1]aionios, means without beginning or end, timeless perpetuity, ages. The word, [2]xronos, means a specific space or portion of time, season. This was before calendar time existed, before the creation of the galaxies and constellations. There exists a greater dimension to eternity than what we are capable of defining within the confines of space and time! God's faith anticipated the exact moment of our redeemed union with him for all eternity!)*

This life was made certain before eternal time. (BBE 1949, Bible in Basic English)

Paul's gospel does not merely proclaim Christ in history; he announces Christ unveiled in human life: Christ in you! Col 1:27)

Rom 16:26 The mystery mirrored in [1]prophetic scripture is now unveiled. The God of the ages determined to make this mystery known in such a way that all the nations of the earth will hear and realize the [2]lifestyle that faith ignites. *(This gospel breaks the silence of the ages and reveals how God succeeded to redeem his image and likeness in man. [1]Isa 53:4, 5. See note on verse 19. Faith inspires an [2]obedience of spontaneity beyond duty driven obligation.)*

Rom 16:27 Jesus Christ [1]uniquely [2]articulates the [3]wisdom of God; he is the [4]conclusion of the ages. *(Uniquely, [1]monos, alone, Jesus has no competition, this one man represents the entire human race; this is the mystery of the ages. 1 Cor 2:7 We voice words of wisdom that was hidden in silence for timeless ages; a mystery unfolding God's Masterful plan whereby God would redeem his glory in man. 2:8 Neither the politicians nor the theologians of the day had a clue about this mystery (of mankind's association in Christ); if they did, they would never have crucified the Lord whose death redeemed our glory!)*

In Chapter 16 of the book of Romans the names of 37 individual believers are personally honored in this chapter of salutation. Seven home churches are also specifically mentioned, five in Rome and two in Corinth. Since Paul never visited Rome before, these people were all acquaintances, converts, fellow prisoners, or travel companions of his before they moved to Rome.

Since Prisca and Aquila originally came from Rome (Acts 18:2, 26 and 1 Cor 16:19), they possibly purposefully returned there to start or strengthen the ekklesia together with a strong team of believers. Their strategy was to scatter several home-fellowships throughout the city. This is reflected in Paul's letter to the Corinthians where he says, "Our expectation is that as your faith increases, our field amongst you will be greatly enlarged so that we may preach the gospel also in lands beyond you." (2 Cor 10:15, 16)

Act 18:2 And he found a Jew named Aquila, a native of Pontus, lately come from Italy with his wife Priscilla, because Claudius had commanded all the Jews to leave Rome. And he went to see them;

Act 18:3 and because he was of the same trade he stayed with them, and they worked, for by trade they were tentmakers.

Act 18:4 And he argued in the synagogue every Sabbath, and persuaded Jews and Greeks.

Act 18:5 When Silas and Timothy arrived from Macedonia, Paul was occupied with preaching, testifying to the Jews that the Christ was Jesus.

1 Th 2:7 But we were gentle among you, like a nurse taking care of her children.

1 Th 2:8 So, being affectionately desirous of you, we were ready to share with you not only the gospel of God but also our own selves, because you had become very dear to us.

1 Th 2:9 For you remember our labor and toil, brethren; we worked night and day, that we might not burden any of you, while we preached to you the gospel of God.

Act 20:33 I coveted no one's silver or gold or apparel.

1 Th 4:11 to aspire to live quietly, to mind your own affairs, and to work with your hands, as we charged you;

1 Th 4:12 so that you may command the respect of outsiders, and be dependent on nobody. RSV

2 Th 3:6 Now we command you, brethren, in the name of our Lord Jesus Christ, that you keep away from any brother who is living in idleness and not in accord with the tradition that you received from us.

2 Th 3:7 For you yourselves know how you ought to imitate us; we were not idle when we were with you,

2 Th 3:8 we did not eat any one's bread without paying, but with toil and labor we worked night and day, that we might not burden any of you.

2 Th 3:9 It was not because we have not that right, but to give you in our conduct an example to imitate.

2 Th 3:10 For even when we were with you, we gave you this command: If any one will not work, let him not eat.

2 Th 3:11 For we hear that some of you are living in idleness, mere busybodies, not doing any work.

2 Th 3:12 Now such persons we command and exhort in the Lord Jesus Christ to do their work in quietness and to earn their own living.

2 Th 3:13 Brethren, do not be weary in well-doing.

To Paul life in the flesh meant fruitful labor; everything that happened to him only served to advance the gospel.

Php 1:12 I want you to know, brethren, that what has happened to me has really served to advance the gospel,

Php 1:13 so that it has become known throughout the whole praetorian guard and to all the rest that my imprisonment is for Christ;

Php 1:14 and most of the brethren have been made confident in the Lord because of my imprisonment, and are much more bold to speak the word of God without fear.

2 Tim 1:10 Everything that grace pointed to is now realized in Jesus Christ and brought into clear view through the gospel: Jesus is what grace reveals. He took death out of the equation and re-defines life; this is good news indeed!

2 Tim 1:11 Grace is my commission; it is my job and joy to proclaim this message and guide the nations into a full understanding of the love initiative of God.

2 Tim 1:12 What I suffer because of this does not frighten me at all; faith has made him so [1]apparent. I am absolutely persuaded that I am safe in him. We are no longer looking for a future event, or another day, the day has come! Death is not doomsday; nothing can interrupt what he has done! *(Greek, [1]eido, Latin, video, to see, to know)*

2 Tim 2:7 Ponder my words; the Lord will give you insight that will inspire you in every contradiction that you face.

2 Tim 2:8 Make my gospel emphasis the focus of your thoughts: Jesus Christ is the seed of David, he is the promised Messiah; his resurrection from the dead is the proof. *(It is the evidence that he completed the salvation of mankind by defeating death. Hos 6:2, Eph 2:5)*

2 Tim 2:9 I might be in bonds, but the Word of God is not. *(It might seem to some that my suffering contradicts what I preach, but it cannot! My ministry is measured by the word not by my circumstances. See Col 1:24)*

2 Tim 2:10 This gives me more than enough reason not to quit. I desire for everyone to discover the fact that the life of their [1]design is redeemed in Christ Jesus; this is the timeless intent of God. *(The word [1]eklegomai, ek, source, origin, and legomai from logos, word, thus the life of our design.)*

2 Tim 2:11 The logic of God endorses our faith: we were included in his death and are therefore equally included in his resurrection.

2 Tim 2:12 Whenever we face suffering, we already know that we co-reign with him; the Christ-life rules. *(Sufferings do not distract us, neither do they contradict our joint position with him in the throne room!)* If we [1]contradict ourselves *(behave unlike ourselves)*, he will contradict us and prove us wrong! *(The word [1]arneomai means to contradict.)*

2 Tim 2:13 Our unbelief does not change what God believes; he cannot contradict himself! *(See Rom 3:3,4 What we believe about God does not define him; God's faith defines us. God cannot be untrue to himself!)*

Col 1:24 This is why no form of suffering can interfere with my joy. Every suffering on your behalf is just another opportunity to reinforce that which might still be lacking *(in your understanding)* of the affliction of Christ on behalf of his body which is the church. *(The inconvenience that Paul might be suffering on behalf of the believers is not to add to the sufferings of Christ—as though the sufferings of Christ on our behalf were insufficient but it is to further emphasize and confirm the principle of unselfish love that constrains New Testament ministry.)*

1 Corinthians 9:13 It is common knowledge that the people engaged in temple ministry eat what is sacrificed there.

1 Cor 9:14 The same principle goes for those who proclaim the gospel; and this is not just someone's good idea it is endorsed by the Lord.

1 Cor 9:15 The reason for my writing about these issues is not to bring you under any kind of obligation; on the contrary, I want to be very clear about this, the fact that I do things differently by not expecting anyone to pay me for my ministry is to emphasize my urgency to remove any possible excuse from anyone's mind that I might have ulterior motives! I am dead serious about this gospel!

1 Cor 9:16 I live to preach; it consumes my total being; your money is not going to make any difference since this gospel has my arm twisted and locked behind my back! *(anagke)* In fact, my life would be reduced to utter misery if it were not possible for me to preach the good news!

1 Cor 9:17 If this was a mere career choice, then surely you could hire or fire me! But I am not for sale; I am employed by the economy of persuasion!

1 Cor 9:18 So what's in it for me? You may ask! The pleasure of declaring the gospel of Christ at no expense is priceless! No, I am not cheating anyone or myself by foregoing the rights I might have as a preacher.

1 Cor 9:19 So in a sense I am free from anyone's expectation or management; yet I have voluntarily enslaved myself to all people; this beats any other motivation to influence people.

1 Cor 9:20 I am like a Jew to the Jew to win them; I am disguised as a legalist to win those stuck under the law!

1 Cor 9:21 To the Gentiles who have no regard for Jewish sentiment, I became like one without any obligation to Jewish laws; to win them! Don't get me wrong; I am not sinning to identify with the sinners! I am in the law of Christ! *(The agape law!)*

1 Cor 9:22 I am so persuaded about every person's inclusion in Christ that I desire to be everything I need to be in order to win everyone's understanding of their union with Christ; I do not present myself as super strong to the weak but would expose myself to their weakness in order to win them. I do not distance myself from anyone; my mission is to be exactly what is required of me in every possible situation to bring salvation to [1]every kind of person, whoever they are! *(Traditionally translated, "in order to save some", this is not what Paul is saying! Greek, [1]tis, suggests every single kind.)*

1 Cor 9:23 The gospel explains my lifestyle; it is so much more than a pulpit ministry to me; my life is inseparably joined to you in the fellowship of the good news!

1 Cor 9:24 An athlete runs a race to win; his aim is to receive the prize not just to compete! This why I preach, to persuade you and not just to entertain you! *(A soccer player can do magic with his footwork and ball skills, but it is no good if he cannot take the gap and score the goal!)*

1 Cor 9:25 The athlete knows how to draw from focused inner strength in order to win the crown; for them all their effort translates into a mere moment celebrated by a fading wreath of honor; for us to win your faith is of imperishable value!

1 Cor 9:26 I run with certain victory in my every step! I am not shadow boxing when I preach!

1 Cor 9:27 I deliberately compare myself to the sacrifice and dedication of a champion athlete; in similar fashion I would pommel my body and subdue it! I would deny myself many things in my pursuit to win your faith so that you will not have any excuse to reject my message. I want you not your money! *(Paul is not saying this because he is worried about God's approval; it is his audience's approval that he is after, "becoming all things to all types of people in order to win every single one of them!" See 1Co 9:12, we would rather suffer lack than insisting on our rights and in the process cause you to be distracted from the gospel of Christ.)*

1 Cor 15:58 Therefore, my beloved brethren, be steadfast, immovable, always abounding in the work of the Lord, knowing that in the Lord your labor is not in vain. RSV

The Mirror Translation reads, :58 For this reason you can afford to be absolutely settled and rock-solid in faith's persuasion and always ready to go beyond where you would have gone before; your doing now is inspired by your knowing that you are in him; if his resurrection is yours then his victory over sin and death is equally yours.

2 Cor 10:12 Not that we venture to class or compare ourselves with some of those who commend themselves. But when they measure themselves by one another, and compare themselves with one another, they are without understanding.

2 Cor 10:13 But we will not boast beyond limit, but will keep to the limits God has apportioned us, to reach even to you.

2 Cor 10:14 For we are not overextending ourselves, as though we did not reach you; we were the first to come all the way to you with the gospel of Christ.

2 Cor 10:15 We do not boast beyond limit, in other men's labors; but our hope is that as your faith increases, our field among you may be greatly enlarged,

2 Cor 10:16 so that we may preach the gospel in lands beyond you, without boasting of work already done in another's field. RSV

2 Tim 2:2 and what you have heard from me before many witnesses entrust to faithful men who will be able to teach others also. RSV

2 Tim 2:2 What you have learnt from me is not a theory, you have witnessed ample evidence that confirms the integrity of my message. See the future of this gospel in everyone you influence; their persuasion is also their competence to instruct others in the same revelation. *(See Titus 1:9)* Mirror

Titus 1:7 An overseer must be above reproach; if he has a bad reputation in the community you do not want him to be part of your leadership team! A leader administrates God's economy and must therefore be a competent manager of God's business. A person with his own selfish agenda, or one who loses his temper easily, or someone that is known to over indulge in food or wine, or a bully, or greedy for money is certainly not a candidate.

Titus 1:8 He must be [1]fond of strangers and able to make people feel immediately at home. Your leader must be a [2]caring person and one who shows [3]unselfish devotion to the welfare of others. Someone [3]sober-minded, whose thought-life is sorted out; one who walks in the [4]revelation of the finished work of Christ; a man of [5]mercy and who is strong in spirit. *(The word, [1]philoxenos, means fond of strangers. The word, [2]philagathos, translates as benevolent, good, kind, humane, generous, liberal, benign, philanthropic, altruistic. The word, [3]sophrone, means a saved mind. The word, [4]dikaion, translates as righteousness, the revelation of the finished work of Christ, and the word, [5]hosios, is translated as mercy as in Acts 13:44, which is a quote from Isaiah 55:3 from the Hebrew word, ghesed, for mercy)*

Titus 1:9 The overseer [1]mirrors the persuasion of the word he was taught and is competent to instruct with accuracy and to entreat and convince those who oppose the message. *(The word, [1]antechomai, comes from anti meaning against, standing opposite, and echo; thus one who mirrors the word.)*

Titus 1:10 There are many who engage in worthless debates about their Jewish sentiments and playing mind-games in order to snare new believers into legalism.

Titus 1:11 By entreating and persuading them with wisdom, their influence will be silenced. The rot must be stopped since they have already confused entire families with their teachings and robbed them financially in the process.

Titus 3:2 Never have anything bad to say about anyone! You do not have to win every argument; instead, avoid [1]quarrelling, be appropriate, always show perfect courtesy to one and all. *(The word, [1]mache, means controversial, striving. You don't have to wait for people to change before you are nice to them. There is a big difference between "fake politeness" and perfect courtesy!)*

Titus 3:3 Do not be harsh on others. Remember that we, too, were typically foolish; we were stubborn and indifferent to spiritual things, our addiction to the sensual and sexual kept us running around in circles, we were engaged in malice and spiteful jealousies, we were bored and lonely, often utterly disliking ourselves and hating one another!

Titus 3:4 But then, oh happy day! It was the generosity of God and his fondness for mankind that dawned on us like a shaft of light. Our days of darkness were over! Light shone everywhere and we became aware: God rescued the human race!

Titus 2:11 The grace of God shines as bright as day making the salvation of humankind undeniably visible. Mirror

(For God's undeserved kindness has burst in upon us, bringing a new lease on life for all mankind. — Clarence Jordan)

Jesus never underestimated the individual, regardless of their reputation; he reaches the city of Sychar through one woman.

Joh 4:40 So when the Samaritans came to him, they asked him to stay with them; and he stayed there two days.

Joh 4:41 And many more believed because of his word.

Joh 4:42 They said to the woman, "It is no longer because of your words that we believe, for we have heard for ourselves, and we know that this is indeed the Savior of the world."

Mar 5:18 And as he was getting into the boat, the man who had been possessed with demons begged him that he might be with him.

Mar 5:19 But he refused, and said to him, "Go home to your friends, and tell them how much the Lord has done for you, and how he has had mercy on you."

Mar 5:20 And he went away and began to proclaim in the Decapolis how much Jesus had done for him; and all men marveled.

Here Jesus sees ten cities in one man's testimony! (Decapolis = 10 cities.)

God saw so much more in Gideon than what Gideon saw in himself. Before he encountered the word of the Lord, his life was reduced to mere survival.

Jdg 6:11 Now the angel of the LORD came and sat under the oak at Ophrah, which belonged to Joash the Abiezrite, as his son Gideon was beating out wheat in the wine press, to hide it from the Midianites.

Jdg 6:12 And the angel of the LORD appeared to him and said to him, "The LORD is with you, you mighty man of valor."

Jdg 6:14 And the LORD turned to him and said, "Go in this might of yours and deliver Israel from the hand of Midian; do not I send you?"

Jdg 6:15 And he said to him, "Pray, Lord, how can I deliver Israel? Behold, my clan is the weakest in Manasseh, and I am the least in my family."

Jdg 6:16 And the LORD said to him, "But I will be with you, and you shall smite the Midianites as one man." RSV

God watches over His word to perform it! Jer.1:5-12. Jeremiah sees an almond tree; the Hebrew name for an almond tree is the tree that has woken up, since it is the first tree to blossom while all the other trees are still in their winter sleep! Phillip is led by the Spirit on a lonely road to introduce one Ethiopian to Christ; God sees the continent of Africa in one man! Acts 8:26-40.

Paul is not led by open doors, but by the knowledge that God always leads us in triumph and through us spreads the fragrance of the knowledge of him everywhere.

2 Co 2:12 When I came to Troas to preach the gospel of Christ, a door was opened for me in the Lord;

2 Co 2:13 but my mind could not rest because I did not find my brother Titus there. So I took leave of them and went on to Macedonia.

2 Co 2:14 But thanks be to God, who in Christ always leads us in triumph, and through us spreads the fragrance of the knowledge of him everywhere. RSV

2 Cor 2:14 I am overwhelmed with gratitude! Wherever my travels take me I am

so aware that God leads us as trophies in his victory parade. What he knows to be true about us diffuses through us like a perfume of sweet aroma everywhere we go, celebrating the success of the cross. *(In ancient triumphs, abundance of perfumes and wreaths of sweet smelling flowers were used in their victory celebrations.)*

2 Cor 2:15 We are a sweet savor of Christ unto God evident in everyone we meet. The fragrance of Christ is recognized in all unto salvation. The same gospel that announces the fragrant victory of Christ declares the odor of death; the [1]defeat of [2]destruction in everyone! *(This parade of victory is a public announcement of the defeat of the religious systems and structures based on the law of works. Just like it is in any public game where the victory celebration of the winning team is an embarrassment for the losing team. The death of evil is announced in resurrection life! The word, **apollumi**, is derived from [1]**apo**, away from, and [2]**ollumi**, to destroy, to ruin.)*

2 Cor 2:16 The message we communicate is a fragrance with an immediate association; to darkness, it is the smell of doom *(the death of death)*; to life it is the familiar fragrance of life itself.

2 Cor 2:17 We are not competing with those who have added their [1]price tag to the gospel. Our conversation has its source in Christ; we communicate from the transparent innocence of a face to face encounter with God. *(The law of personal performance or [1]**kapeleuo**, meaning retail.)*

How we have wasted time playing for time! "You say there are yet four months then comes the harvest! I say you are looking at the wrong harvest! The bread you labor for cannot satisfy; lift up your eyes and see the harvest that is already ripe!" The seed in the fruit already matches the seed that was sown. We cannot even begin to preach the gospel without a revelation of the finished work of the cross! The only possible address of God is human life! No temple or any structure that man can build or organize can replace the living epistle.

Joh 2:19 Jesus answered them, "Destroy this temple, and in three days I will raise it up."

Hos 6:2 After two days he will revive us; on the third day he will raise us up, that we may live before him.

The human body is again redeemed as the only worthy tabernacle of God.

Joh 4:35 Do you not say, 'There are yet four months, then comes the harvest'? I tell you, lift up your eyes, and see how the fields are already white for harvest.

Joh 4:38 I sent you to reap that for which you did not labor; others have labored, and you have entered into their labor." RSV

2 Cor 5:14 The love of Christ [1]resonates within us and leaves us with only one conclusion: Jesus died humanity's death; therefore, in God's logic every individual simultaneously died. *(The word, [1]**sunecho**, from **sun**, meaning together with and **echo**, meaning to echo, to embrace, to hold, and thus translated, to resonate. Jesus didn't die 99% or for 99%. He died humanity's death 100%! If Paul had to compromise the last part of verse 14 to read: "one died for all therefore only those who follow the prescriptions to qualify, have also died," then he would have had to change the first half of the verse as well! Only the love of Christ can make a calculation of such enormous proportion! Theology*

would question the extremity of God's love and perhaps prefer to add a condition or two to a statement like that!)

2 Cor 5:15 Now if all were included in his death they were equally included in his resurrection. This unveiling of his love redefines human life! Whatever reference we could have of ourselves outside of our association with Christ is no longer relevant.

2 Cor 5:16 This is radical! No label that could possibly previously define someone carries any further significance! Even our pet doctrines of Christ are redefined. Whatever we knew about him historically or sentimentally is challenged by this conclusion. *(By discovering Christ from God's point of view we discover ourselves and every other human life from God's point of view!)*

2 Cor 5:17 In the light of your co-inclusion in his death and resurrection, whoever you thought you were before, in Christ you are a brand new person! The old ways of seeing yourself and everyone else are over. Acquaint yourself with the new! *(Just imagine this! Whoever a person was as a Jew, Greek, slave or freeman, Boer, Zulu, Xhosa, British, Indian, Muslim or American, Chinese, Japanese or Congolese; is now dead and gone! They all died when Jesus died! Remember we are not talking law language here! The 'If' in, "If any man is in Christ" is not a condition, it is the conclusion of the revelation of the gospel! Man is in Christ by God's doing [1 Cor 1:30 and Eph 1:4]. The verses of 2 Corinthians 5:14-16 give context to verse 17! For so long we studied verse 17 on its own and interpreted the 'if' as a condition! Paul did not say, "If any man is in Christ," he said "THEREFORE if any man is in Christ ..." The "therefore" immediately includes verses 14 to 16! If God's faith sees every man in Christ in his death, then they were certainly also in Christ in his resurrection. Jesus did not reveal a "potential" you, he revealed the truth about you so that you may know the truth about yourself and be free indeed!)*

2 Cor 5:18 To now see everything as new is to simply see what God has always known in Christ; we are not debating man's experience, opinion, or his contribution; this is 100% God's belief and his doing. In Jesus Christ, God [1]exchanged equivalent value to redeem us to himself. This act of reconciliation is the mandate of our ministry. *(The word, [1]**katalasso**, translates as reconciliation; a mutual exchange of equal value.)*

2 Cor 5:19 Our ministry declares that Jesus did not act independent of God. Christ is proof that God reconciled the total kosmos to himself. Deity and humanity embraced in Christ; the fallen state of mankind was deleted; their trespasses would no longer count against them! God has placed this message within us. He now announces his friendship with every individual from within us!

2 Cor 5:20 The voice God has in Christ he now has in us; we are God's ambassadors. Our lives exhibit the urgency of God to [1]persuade everyone to realize the reconciliation of their redeemed identity. (The word, [1]parakaleo, comes from para, a preposition indicating close proximity, a thing proceeding from a sphere of influence, with a suggestion of union of place of residence, to have sprung from its author and giver, originating from, denoting the point from which an action originates, intimate connection, and kaleo, to identify by name, to surname. In Luke 15:28, 31, His father pleaded with him, "My child, you are always with me, and all that I have is yours." "Be reconciled" could not be translated, "Become reconciled!"

"Do in order to become" is the language of the Old Testament; the language of the New Testament is, "Be, because of what was done!"

2 Cor 5:21 This is the divine exchange: he who knew no [1]sin embraced our distortion; he appeared to be without form; this was the mystery of God's prophetic [2]poetry. He was disguised in our distorted image, marred with our iniquities; he took our sorrows, our pain, our shame to his grave and birthed his righteousness in us. He took our sins and we became his innocence. *(The word, [1]hamartia, comes from ha, without, and meros, form. The word, [2]poema, from we were born anew in his resurrection from the dead.*

Isaiah 52:10 The Lord has bared his holy arm before the eyes of all the nations, and all the ends of the earth shall see the salvation of our God. :14-15 Just as many were astonished at you—so was he marred in his appearance, more than any human, and his form beyond that of human semblance—so will he startle many nations. Kings will shut their mouths at him; for what had not been told them they will see, and what they had not heard they will understand. 53:4-5 Surely he has borne our griefs, and carried our sorrows; yet we esteemed him stricken, smitten of God, and afflicted. But surely he was wounded for our transgressions; he was bruised for our iniquities; the chastisement of our peace was on him; and with his stripes we ourselves are healed. RSV

Deuteronomy 32:5, 6 They have corrupted themselves; they did not behave as his children, they have become a distorted generation of people, twisted out of their true pattern; they are a crooked and perverse generation. (Paul quotes this very verse in Phil 2:15.)Deuteronomy 32:18 You were unmindful of the Rock that begot you and have forgotten the God who danced with you. (Hebrew: kgheel means to dance)

Romans 8:29 He pre-designed and engineered us from the start to be jointly fashioned in the same mold and image of his son according to the exact blueprint of his thought. We see the original and intended pattern of our lives preserved in his Son. He is the firstborn from the same womb that reveals our genesis. He confirms that we are the invention of God. (We were born anew when he was raised from the dead! [1 Peter 1:3] His resurrection co-reveals our common genesis as well as our redeemed innocence. [Rom 4:25 and Acts 17:31] No wonder then that he is not ashamed to call us his brethren! We indeed share the same origin [Heb 2:11}, and, "In him we live and move and have our being, we are indeed his offspring!" [Acts 17:28].)

Romans 8:30 Jesus reveals that man pre-existed in God; he defines us. He justified us and also glorified us. He redeemed our innocence and restored the glory we lost in Adam. [Romans 3:23, 24: the word, prohoritso, means pre defined, like when an architect draws up a detailed plan; and the word, kaleo, to surname, identify by name.]

Titus 2:11 The grace of God shines as bright as day making the salvation of humankind undeniably visible.) Mirror

Isa 26:12 O LORD, thou hast wrought for us all our works. RSV

Rom 10:12 Nothing distinguishes the Jew from the Greek when it comes to the generosity of God. He responds with equal benevolence to everyone who sees themselves identified in him *(they realize that God defines them and not their cultural identity.)*

Rom 10:13 Salvation is to understand that every person's [1]true identity is revealed in Christ. *(Whosoever shall [1]call upon the Name of the Lord shall be saved; [1]epikaleomai, to entitle; to identify by name, to surname.)*

Rom 10:14 How is it possible to convince people of [1]their identity in him while they do not believe that he represents them? How will they believe if they remain ignorant about who they really are? How will they understand if the Good News of their inclusion is not announced? *(The word, [1]epikaleomai, traditionally translates as "to call upon," from kaleo, which literary means to surname, or to identify by name. This is also the root word in ekklesia, with ek being a preposition that denotes origin, and kaleo. In the context of Matthew 16 where Jesus introduces this word, he reveals that the son of man is indeed the son of God, "I say to you Simon, son of Jonah, you are petros [Rock] and upon this petra I will build my ekklesia!" [See note on Rom 9:33].)*

Rom 10:15 What gives someone the urgency to declare these things? It is recorded in prophetic scripture, "How lovely on the mountains *(where the watchmen were stationed to witness the outcome of a war)* are the feet of them leaping with the exciting news of victory. Because of their eyewitness encounter they are qualified to run with the Gospel of peace and announce the consequent glad tidings of good things that will benefit everyone."

Rom 10:16 It is hard to imagine that there can yet be a people who struggle to hear and understand the good news. Isaiah says, "Lord, who has believed our report?"

Rom 10:17 It is clear then that faith's [1]source is found in the content of the message heard; the message is Christ. *(We are God's audience; Jesus is God's language! The Greek, [1]ek, is a preposition that denotes source or origin; thus, faith comes out of the word that reveals Christ. The word "Christ" appears in the best manuscripts. Herein lies the secret of the power of the gospel; there is no good news in it until the righteousness of God is revealed! [See Rom 1:17] The good news is the fact that the cross of Christ was a success. God rescued the life of our design; he redeemed our innocence. Man would never again be judged righteous or unrighteous by his own ability to obey moral laws! It is not about what man must or must not do but about what Jesus has done! God now persuades everyone to believe what he knows to be true about them. [It is from faith to faith.] The prophets wrote in advance about the fact that God believes that righteousness unveils the life that he always had in mind for us. "Righteousness by his (God's) faith defines life." [Hab 2:4].)*

Rom 10:18 Has God not given man a fair chance to hear? Psalm 19 says, "His voice goes thru the whole world like the rays of the sun; nothing is hid from its heat; yes, truly their resonance sounded in all the earth, and their words unto the ends of the earth."

Our ability to obey and believe is superseded by his. It is what he did and believes that inspires our action and faith!

Uneducated, ordinary men turned their world upside down.

Act 1:5 for John baptized with water, but before many days you shall be baptized with the Holy Spirit."

Act 1:8 But you shall receive power when the Holy Spirit has come upon you; and you shall be my witnesses in Jerusalem and in all Judea and Samaria and to the end of the earth."

Act 4:13 Now when they saw the boldness of Peter and John, and perceived that they were uneducated, common men, they wondered; and they recognized that they had been with Jesus.

Act 17:6 And when they could not find them, they dragged Jason and some of the brethren before the city authorities, crying, "These men who have turned the world upside down have come here also,

1Cor 1:22 The Jews crave signs (to confirm their doubts) while the Greeks revel in philosophical debate! *(Both groups are addicted to the same soul realm.)*

1 Cor 1:23 The crucified Christ is the message we publicly proclaim, to the disgust of the Jews while the Greeks think we are wacky!

1 Cor 1:24 The dynamic of God's wisdom is the fact that both Jew and Greek are equally included and defined in Christ.

1 Cor 1:25 It seems so foolish that God should die man's death on the cross; it seems so weak of God to suffer such insult; yet man's wisest schemes and most powerful display of genius cannot even begin to comprehend or compete with God in his weakest moment on the cross.

1 Cor 1:26 You might as well admit it, my Brothers; it was not your academic qualifications or your good looks or social connections that influenced God to represent you in Christ.

1 Cor 1:27 It is almost as if God deliberately handpicked the wacky of this world to embarrass the wise, the rejects to put to shame the noble.

1 Cor 1:28 The ones with no pedigree of any prominence, the "nobodies" in society, attracted God's initiative to unveil his blueprint opinion in order to redefine man. Thus he rendered any other social standard entirely irrelevant and inappropriate. *(Blueprint opinion, **eklegomai**, from **ek**, meaning origin, source, and **legomai** from **logos**, the logic of God; traditionally translated as "elect.")*

1 Cor 1:29 Every reason for man's boasting in himself dwindles into insignificance before God.

1 Cor 1:30 [1]Of God's doing are we in Christ. He is both the genesis and genius of our wisdom; a wisdom that reveals how righteous, sanctified and redeemed we are in him. *(The preposition, [1]ek, always denotes origin, source. Mankind's association in Christ is God's doing. In God's economy, Christ represents us; what man could never achieve through personal discipline and willpower as taught in every religion, God's faith accomplished in Christ. Of his design we are in Christ; we are associated in oneness with him. Our wisdom is sourced in this union! Also, our righteousness and holiness originate from him. Holiness equals wholeness and harmony of man's spirit, soul, and body. Our redemption is sanctioned in him. He redeemed our identity, our sanity, our health, our joy, our peace, our innocence, and our complete well-being! [See Eph 1:4]. The Knox Translation reads, "It is from him that we take our [1]origin.")*

Heb 12:1 So now the stage is set for us: all these faith-heroes cheer us on as it were like a great multitude of spectators in the amphitheater. This is our moment. As with an athlete who is determined to win, it would be silly to carry any baggage of the old law-system that would weigh one down. Make sure you do not get your feet clogged up with sin-consciousness. Become absolutely streamlined in faith. Run the race of your spiritual life with total persuasion. *(Persuaded in the success of the cross.)*

Heb 12:2 Look away from the shadow dispensation of the law and the prophets and fix your eyes upon Jesus. He is the fountainhead and conclusion of faith. He saw the joy *(of mankind's salvation)* when he braved the cross and despised the shame of it. As the executive authority of God *(the right hand of the Throne of God)* he now occupies the highest seat of dominion to endorse man's innocence! *(Having accomplished purification of sins, he sat down. [Heb 1:3, Isa 53:11])*

Heb 12:3 [1]Ponder how he overcame all the odds stacked against him; this will boost your soul-energy when you feel exhausted. *([1]analogitsomai, upwards calculation.)*

Act 8:5 Philip went down to a city of Samaria, and proclaimed to them the Christ.

Act 8:6 And the multitudes with one accord gave heed to what was said by Philip, when they heard him and saw the signs which he did.

Act 8:7 For unclean spirits came out of many who were possessed, crying with a loud voice; and many who were paralyzed or lame were healed.

All of Asia both Jews and Greeks heard the word within two years as a result of focused ministry coming from one school!

Act 19:8 And he entered the synagogue and for three months spoke boldly, arguing and pleading about the kingdom of God;

Act 19:9 but when some were stubborn and disbelieved, speaking evil of the Way before the congregation, he withdrew from them, taking the disciples with him, and argued daily in the hall of Tyrannus.

Act 19:10 This continued for two years, so that all the residents of Asia heard the word of the Lord, both Jews and Greeks.

Act 19:11 And God did extraordinary miracles by the hands of Paul,

Isa 40:9 Get you up to a high mountain, O Zion, herald of good tidings; lift up your voice with strength, O Jerusalem, herald of good tidings.

Pondering the revelation of Christ in you gives volume to your voice. Engaging your thoughts with throne room realities where you are seated together with Christ is the highest mountain for strategic altitude! Col 3:1-3,16. Christ is the language of God's logic. Let his message sink into you with unlimited vocabulary; taking wisdom to its most complete conclusion. This makes your fellowship an environment of instruction in an atmosphere of music. Every lesson is a reminder, echoing in every song you sing, whether it be a psalm (raving about God in praise and worship accompanied by musical instruments) or a hymn (a testimony song) or a song in the spirit (a new spontaneous prophetic song). Grace fuels your heart with inspired music to the Lord.

Isa 52:7 How beautiful upon the mountains are the feet of him who brings good tidings, who publishes peace, who brings good tidings of good, who publishes salvation.

If you believe that I am what the scriptures are all about, you will know that you are what I am all about and rivers of living water will flow out of your innermost being. Jn 7:37,38 And the earth shall be filled with the knowledge of the glory of the Lord as the waters cover the sea.

One wonders why God showed Ezekiel a valley of bleached bones? Zero sign of life left! and then ask the question, "Can these bones live?" And why God waited till Sarah's womb was dead! and why God only created Adam on the 6th day when all his work was done? Jesus didnt die 99% or for 99% He died humanity's death! If Paul had to compromise the last part of verse 14 of 2 Cor 5, to read: "one died for all therefore only those who follow the prescriptions to qualify, have also died," then he would have had to change the first half of the verse as well!

Only the love of Christ can make a calculation of such enormous proportion!

How can we underestimate such a great salvation!

How can anyone possibly be lost if they are already found in Christ! Let's tell people how found they are! LUKE 15

The revelation of the initiative of God to bring an end to hostility is the dominant theme of the Gospel of redemption. If we can fully grasp the implication of this it would make divorce not only unnecessary but impossible! It would cause wars to cease to the ends of the earth!

We are entrusted with world peace! Our ministry is the ministry of reconciliation. God already reconciled a hostile world to himself and now urgently pleads through us and appeals to every man's conscience, in order to make all men see and realize its consequence.

While every effort is spent in the research of possible solutions to the horror threat of diseases such as AIDS and TB, the greatest quest to meaningful life, friendship with substance, of spontaneity and continuity, is either neglected or ignored. Often the very cancer of promiscuity and immorality that destroys relationship is not only tolerated but accepted or even promoted in a corrupt society.

The Gospel is the unveiling of a friendship of the highest expression of integrity and quality, within every man's reach!

We have underestimated the Gospel of Jesus Christ for centuries, because we have adopted an interpretation that robbed us of the true impact of salvation in its relation to life in the here and now on planet earth. We have felt more comfortable with a faith that refers us to a place in heaven one day rather than to see faith as the now and relevant substance of things we always longed for and the evidence of unseen realities within us and within our immediate grasp.

There is nothing wrong with the human race!

In October 2010 I was ministering in Budapest when I woke up one night at 2 am with this startling thought, "There is nothing wrong with the human race, because there is nothing wrong with their design and there is nothing wrong with their salvation. There is only something horribly wrong with man's thinking!"

Jesus is proof that God has done enough to rescue his image and likeness in man and restore fallen humanity to a place of blameless innocence.
Why is the world in such a mess then if the cross was indeed a success?

We are thinking wrong!

Just like Israel did when, after their amazing deliverance from Pharao and slavery they continued to believe a lie about themselves and died neutralized in a desert. The challenges that we are faced with both individually as well as a global humanity seem to dwarf us into insignificance. Num 13:33

God says it as it is in Isa 55:8 For my thoughts are not your thoughts, neither are your ways my ways, says the LORD.

Isa 55:9 For as the heavens are higher than the earth, so are my ways higher than your ways and my thoughts than your thoughts.

We often stop reading there and conclude that God's thoughts and ways are meant to be incomprehendible. That makes no sense at all! Thank God for the next two verses, the whole of the good news is wrapped up in this statement:

Isa 55:10 "For as the rain and the snow come down from heaven, and return not thither but saturate the earth, making it bring forth and sprout, giving seed to the sower and bread to the eater,

Isa 55:11 so shall my word be that goes forth from my mouth; it shall not return to me empty, but it shall accomplish that which I purpose, and prosper in the thing for which I sent it.

Jesus Christ is the incarnate word; he is God's thoughts most perfectly packaged and unveiled in human form. In him the word became flesh. Every definition of distance is cancelled! The word cannot become more flesh than what it did in the man Jesus Christ. As head of the human race Jesus Christ is proof that the destiny of the word was fulfilled in him on behalf of the human race. He did not come as an example for us but of us!

2 Cor 3:18 The days of window-shopping are over! In him every face is unveiled. In gazing with wonder at the blueprint likeness of God displayed in human form we suddenly realize that we are looking at ourselves! Every feature of his image is mirrored in us! This is the most radical transformation engineered by the Spirit of the Lord; we are led from an inferior mind-set to the revealed endorsement of our authentic identity. Mankind is his glory!

The appeal of the good news message is to straighten out mankind's think-ing! This is what the Greek word, *metanoia* means! It means to discover God's thoughts about you! It does not mean to repent as all the English translations have it! Repent comes from a Latin word which means pennance! Religion delib-erately squeezed this word into the Bible to make money out of people's misery!

Jer 29:11 For I know the thoughts that I think toward you, says the LORD, thoughts of peace and not of evil, to give you a future and a hope.

Jesus is God's mind made up about mankind!

What about the sinful Nature?

"We often read, especially in theological books, about the nature of man. (It's interest-ing that this term is not used in the scriptures.) So I did some research as to what most theologians mean by 'nature of man'. It means the truth or reality of man!

That is such a clear and simple definition - the problem is that many try to find the truth and reality of man in Adam's fall. We should look a bit further back and discover Gen 1:26 - The truth and reality of man came out of God. His nature was the origin of our nature. His reality is the substance we were made from!

The key to understanding the mystery of God-and-man-in-the-one-person-of-Christ, is to realize that he designed man for this very purpose of unity with God. There is no conflict in God's design between the nature of man and the nature of God." Andre Rabe

We theologically created the idea of man being 'sinful by nature' as if humans are flawed by design. In fact it is a distorted mindset that we inherited from Adam that Jesus had to free us from. This mindset was sponsored by the tree of the knowledge of good and evil. We were alienated and hostile in mind, do-ing evil deeds sponsored by the law of sin and death that lodged in our bodies hosting a foreign influence, foreign to our design. Just like a virus would attach itself to a person and display its symptoms. Someone might host a virus but at no point does the patient become the virus!

Rom 3:23 Everyone is in the same boat; their [1]distorted behavior is proof of a [2]lost [3]blueprint. *(The word sin, is the word [1]hamartia, from ha, negative and meros, form, thus to be without form or identity; [2]hustereo, to fall short, to be inferior, [3]doxa, glory, blueprint, from dokeo, opinion, intent.)*

All have sinned and fallen short of the 'glory' of God; the word, glory is the Greek word doxa, which comes from the word dokeo, to form an opinion, intent; it speaks of a mental picture and suggests the exact blueprint that God had in mind when he said, "Let us make man in our image and in our likeness."

We have forgotten our true identity. Deu 32:18 You were unmindful of the Rock that begot you, and you forgot the God who gave you birth.

James 1:23 The difference between a mere spectator and a participator is that both of them hear the same voice and perceive in its message the face of their own gen-esis reflected as in a mirror;

James 1:24 they realize that they are looking at themselves, but for the one it seems just too good to be true, he departs *(back to his old way of seeing himself)* and immediately forgets what manner of person he is; never giving another thought to the one he saw there in the mirror.

James 1:25 The other one is [1]mesmerized by what he sees; he is [2]captivated by the effect of a law that frees man from the obligation to the old written code that restricted him to his own efforts and willpower. No distraction or contradiction can dim the impact of what he sees in that mirror concerning the law of perfect [3]liberty *(the law of faith)* that now frees him to get on with the act of living the life *(of his original design.)* He finds a new [3]spontaneous lifestyle; the poetry of practical living. *(The law of perfect liberty is the image and likeness of God revealed in Christ, now redeemed in man as in a mirror. Look deep enough into that law of faith that you may see there in its perfection a portrait that so resembles the original that he becomes distinctly visible in the spirit of your mind and in the face of every man you behold. I translated the word,* [1]***parakupto,*** *with mesmerized from* **para***, a preposition indicating close proximity, originating from, denoting the point from which an action originates, intimate connection, and* **kupto***, to bend, stoop down to view at close scrutiny;* [2]***parameno***, *to remain captivated under the influence of;* **meno***, to continue to be present. The word often translated as freedom,* [3]***eleutheria***, *means without obligation; spontaneous.)*

God's thoughts are most accurately expressed in the incarnation; not as in a display window but as in a mirror, so that we now may behold his glory with unveiled faces; the eyes of our understanding enlightened with the true light that enlightens every man.

Eph 4:17 My most urgent appeal to you in the Lord is this: you have nothing in common with the folly of the empty-minded [1]masses; the days of conducting your lives and affairs in a meaningless way are over! *(The Gentiles,* [1]***ethnos***, *the masses of people who are walking in the vanity of their minds.)*

Eph 4:18 The life of their design seems foreign to them because their minds are darkened through a hardened heart ruled by ignorance. They are blinded by the illusion of the senses as their only reference, stubbornly wearing a blindfold in broad daylight. *(Hardness of heart is the result of a darkened understanding; a mind veiled through unbelief. [See 2 Cor 4:4])*

Eph 4:19 Having become conditioned to a life distanced from God; they are calloused in spirit, and are lust and greed driven; they have totally abandoned themselves to outrageous shameless living.

Rom 1:19 even though God is not a stranger to anyone, for what can be known of God is already manifest in them. *(The law reveals how guilty and sinful man is, while the gospel reveals how forgiven and restored to his original blueprint man is.)*

Rom 1:20 God is on display in creation; the very fabric of visible cosmos appeals to reason. It clearly bears witness to the ever present sustaining power and intelligence of the invisible God, leaving man without any valid excuse to ignore him. *(Psalms 19:1-4, God's glory is on tour in the skies, God-craft on exhibit across the horizon. Madame Day holds classes every morning, Professor Night lectures each evening. Their words aren't heard, their voices aren't recorded, But their silence fills the earth: unspoken truth is spoken everywhere. — The Message)*

Rom 1:21 Yet man only knew him in a philosophical religious way, from a distance, and failed to give him credit as God. Their taking him for granted and lack of gratitude veiled him from them; they became absorbed in useless debates and discussions, which further darkened their understanding about themselves.

Rom 1:22 Their wise conclusions only proved folly.

Rom 1:23 Their losing sight of God, made them lose sight of who they really were. In their calculation the image and likeness of God became reduced to a corrupted and distorted pattern of themselves. Suddenly man has more in common with the "creepy crawlies" than with his original blueprint.

Rom 1:24 It seemed like God abandoned mankind to be swept along by the lusts of their own hearts to abuse and defile themselves. *(Their most personal possession, their own bodies, became worthless public property.)*

Rom 1:25 Instead of embracing their Maker as their true identity they preferred the deception of a warped identity, religiously giving it their affection and devotion.

Rom 1:26 By being confused about their Maker they became confused about themselves;

Eph 4:17 Now this I affirm and testify in the Lord, that you must no longer live as the Gentiles do, in the futility of their minds;

Eph 4:18 they are darkened in their understanding, alienated from the life of God because of the ignorance that is in them, due to their hardness of heart; RSV

The physical life we've 'inherited' as it were comes with its 'tendencies and traits' which 'traits and tendencies' have been imprinted genetically into us thru generations of behavioral patterns that were inconsistent with the life of our design.

Then we are raised within fixed cultural and social molds that further established our thinking patterns and behavioral inclinations.

Eph 2:1 Picture where God found us. We were in a death trap of an inferior lifestyle, constantly living below the [1]blueprint measure of our lives. *([1]Sin is **hamartia**, which comes from **ha** + **meros**, meaning without form or without our allotted portion.)*

Eph 2:2 We were all part of a common pattern, swept along under a powerful invisible influence, a spirit-energy that adopted us as sons to its dictate through unbelief.

Eph 2:3 Throughout that time everyone of us were warped and corrupted in our conduct snared in a jumble of forbidden lusts, driven by the desires of the senses, totally engaged in an expression of a life ruled by mind games; it was as if a twisted passion parented a universal breed of people.

Eph 2:4 None of this could distract from the extravagant love of God; he continued to love us with the exact same intensity.

Eph 2:5 This is how grace rescued us: sin left us dead towards God, like spiritual corpses; yet in that state of deadness and indifference, God co-quickened us together with Christ. Sin proved how dead we were *(the law confirmed it!)* Grace reveals how alive we now are *(the gospel announces it!)* Before anyone but God believed it, he made us alive together with him and raised us up together with him. *(We had no contribution to our salvation! God's master-plan unfolded in the mystery of the gospel declaring our joint inclusion in Christ's death and resurrection; God found us in Christ before he lost us in Adam! [Eph 1:4] In the economy of God, when Jesus died we died. God saw us in Christ, in his death and resurrection before we saw ourselves there! He declared our co-resurrection with Christ 800 BC [Hos 6:2]!)*

Eph 2:6 *(As much as we were co-included in his death,)* we are co-included in his resurrection. We are also elevated in his ascension to be equally present in the throne room of the heavenly realm where we are co-seated with him in his executive authority. We are fully represented in Christ Jesus. *(Our joint position in Christ defines us; this can never again be a distant goal to reach but our immediate point of departure.)*

Eph 2:7 *(In a single triumphant act of righteousness God saved us from the "guttermost" to the uttermost. Here we are now, revealed in Christ in the highest possible position of bliss! If man's sad history could not distract from the extravagant love of God,)* imagine how God is now able for timeless perpetuity (the eternal future) to exhibit the trophy of the wealth of his grace demonstrated in his kindness towards us in Christ Jesus. Grace exhibits excessive evidence of the success of the cross.

Eph 2:8 Your salvation is not a reward for good behavior! It was a grace thing from start to finish; you had no hand in it. Even the gift to believe simply reflects his faith! *(You did not invent faith; it was God's faith to begin with! It is from faith to faith, [Rom 1:17] He is both the source and conclusion of faith. [Heb 12:2])*

Eph 2:9 If this could be accomplished through any action of yours then there would be ground for boasting.

Eph 2:10 We are engineered by his design; he molded and manufactured us in Christ. We are his workmanship, his [1]poetry. *(God finds inspired expression of Christ in us. The Greek word for workmanship is [1]poema.)* We are [2]fully fit to do good, equipped to give attractive evidence of his likeness in us in everything we do. *(God has done everything possible to find spontaneous and effortless expression of his character in us in our everyday lifestyle. The word, [2]**proetoimatso**, translates a notion that God has prepared a highway for us to lead us out like kings, just like the Oriental custom, where people would go before a king to level the roads to make it possible for the king to journey with ease and comfort. [Isa 40:3-5])*

Adam's mind changed not God's.

No decent doctor will slap his patient and command him to stop coughing! At no point does the patient become the virus!

When Adam 'died' his awareness and consciousness of the divine likeness in him became reduced to him merely knowing himself, his wife and God from a guilt-based and performance-driven human point of view; he lost sight of the doxa (glory) of God and began to live the life of the flesh, with its fading glories like seasonal flowers. 2 Cor 3:7-11, Isa 40:5-7

Question: Why did Jesus have to DIE for that? If it's merely a "mind matter", if God didn't ever see mankind different, then why could Jesus not just come, reveal himself and introduce us to our original design again?

This is the whole point of the gospel: If one could merely make a quality decision to change one's life then the law would be the saviour of man.

Rom 7:15 This is how the sell-out to sin affects my life: I find myself doing things my conscience does not allow. My dilemma is that even though I sincerely desire to do that which is good, I don't, and the things I despise, I do.

Rom 7:16 It is obvious that my conscience sides with the law;

Rom 7:17 which confirms then that it is not really I who do these things but sin manifesting its symptoms in me. *(Sin is similar to a dormant virus that suddenly broke out in very visible symptoms.)* It has taken my body hostage.

Rom 7:18 The total extent and ugliness of sin that inhabits me, reduced my life to good intentions that cannot be followed through.

Rom 7:19 Willpower has failed me; this is how embarrassing it is, the most diligent decision that I make to do good, disappoints; the very evil I try to avoid, is what I do. *(If mere quality decisions could rescue man, the law would have been enough. Good intentions cannot save man. The revelation of what happened to us in Christ's death is what brings faith into motion to liberate from within. Faith is not a decision we make to give God a chance, faith is realizing our inclusion in what happened on the Cross and in the resurrection of Christ!)*

Rom 7:20 If I do the things I do not want to do, then it is clear that I am not evil, but that I host sin in my body against my will.

Rom 7:21 It has become a predictable principle; I desire to do well, but my mere desire cannot escape the evil presence that dictates my actions.

Rom 7:22 The real person that I am on the inside delights in the law of God. *(The law proves to be consistent with my inner make-up.)*

Rom 7:23 There is another law though, *(foreign to my design)* the law of sin, activating and enrolling the members of my body as weapons of war against the law of my mind. I am held captive like a prisoner of war in my own body.

Rom 7:24 The situation is absolutely desperate for humankind; is there anyone who can deliver me from this death trap?

Rom 7:25 Thank God, this is exactly what he has done through Jesus Christ our Leader; he has come to our rescue! I am finally freed from this conflict between the law of my mind and the law of sin in my body. *(If I was left to myself, the best I could do was to try and serve the law of God with my mind, but at the same time continue to be enslaved to the law of sin in my body. Compromise could never suffice.)*

Rom 8:1 Now the decisive conclusion is this: in Christ, every bit of condemning evidence against us is cancelled. *("Who walk not after the flesh but after the spirit." This sentence was not in the original text, but later copied from verse 4. The person who added this most probably felt that the fact of Paul's declaration of mankind's innocence had to be made subject again to man's conduct. Religion under the law felt more comfort-*

able with the condition of personal contribution rather than the conclusion of what faith reveals. The "in Christ" revelation is key to God's dealing with man. It is the PIN-code of the Bible. [See 1 Cor 1:30 and Eph 1:4].)

Rom 8:2 The law of the Spirit is the liberating force of life in Christ. This leaves me with no further obligation to the law of sin and death. Spirit has superseded the sin enslaved senses as the principle law of our lives. *(The law of the spirit is righteousness by faith vs the law of personal effort and self righteousness which produces condemnation and spiritual death which is the fruit of the DIY tree.)*

Rom 8:3 The law failed to be anything more than an instruction manual; it had no power to deliver man from the strong influence of sin holding us hostage in our own bodies. God disguised himself in his son in this very domain where sin ruled man, the human body. The flesh body he lived and conquered in was no different to ours. Thus sin's authority in the human body was condemned. *(Hebrews 4:15, As High Priest he fully identifies with us in the context of our frail human life. Having subjected it to close scrutiny, he proved that the human frame was master over sin. His sympathy with us is not to be seen as excusing weaknesses that are the result of a faulty design, but rather as a trophy to humanity. He is not an example for us but of us.)*

Rom 8:4 The righteousness promoted by the law is now realized in us. Our practical day-to-day life bears witness to spirit inspiration and not flesh domination.

Rom 8:5 Sin's symptoms are sponsored by the senses, a mind dominated by the sensual. Thoughts betray source; spirit life attracts spirit thoughts.

Rom 8:6 Thinking patterns are formed by reference, either the sensual appetites of the flesh and spiritual death, or zoe-life and total tranquillity flowing from a mind addicted to spirit *(faith)* realities.

Rom 8:7 A mind focused on flesh *(the sensual domain where sin held me captive)* is distracted from God with no inclination to his life-laws. Flesh *(self-righteousness)* and spirit *(faith righteousness)* are opposing forces. *(Flesh no longer defines you; faith does!)*

Gal 2:15 Sin is not a respecter of persons! Sin is sin whether you're Jew or Gentile.

Gal 2:16 As Jews we should be the first to know that no one will achieve a blameless standing before God through personal performance according to the requirements of the Law. [1]What Jesus Christ believes concerning our innocence matters most; he is persuaded that he did enough to declare man righteous. Our best intentions to do good cannot add any weight to our righteousness. Righteousness is not a reward for our good behavior. As Jewish believers we know this! We have no advantage over any other person. Jew and Gentile alike were equally guilty, now we are equally justified because of Jesus and for no other reason! *(Paul uses the [1]objective genitive - "faith of." "He is the author and finisher of faith; he is both the origin and conclusion of faith" [Heb. 12:2]; "from faith to faith" [Rom 1:17]. It is God's persuasion in the merit of his Son's achievement that awakens faith in man.")*

Gal 2:17 However, if in our quest to discover righteousness by faith in what Christ did for us, we find that it is still possible to stumble; do not now label yourself a sinner yet again! The fact that you sinned does not cancel the cross of Christ and gives you no reason to abandon justification by faith as if Christ is to be blamed for your distraction! That would be absurd! *(Now all of a sudden you want to keep the law again to further add to your righteousness as if Christ did not achieve enough. Do not let your experience deceive you to invent a new doctrine.)*

Gal 2:18 Only a con artist will try to be a law-man and a grace-man at the same time!

Gal 2:19 My co-crucifixion with Christ is valid! I am not making this up. In his death I died to the old system of trying to please God with my own good behavior! God made me alive together with Christ. How can any human effort improve on this! *(Hos 6:2 and Eph 2:5)*

Gal 2:20 The terms, co-crucified and co-alive defines me now. Christ in me and I in him! *(Jn 14:20)* His sacrificial love is evidence of his persuasion of my righteousness! *(The life that I now live in the flesh I live by the faith of the son of God. He believes in my innocence!)*

Gal 2:21 It is an insult to the grace of God to prefer Moses to Jesus! If the law could justify you then Jesus wasted his time dying your death! *(That would reduce salvation to a ludicrous contest between your obedience and the obedience of Christ! [Rom 5:19])*

Gal 3:7 The conclusion is clear; faith and not flesh relates us to Abraham! *(Grace rather than law is our true lineage. Ishmael represents so much more than the Muslim religion. Ishmael represents the clumsy effort of the flesh to compete with faith; the preaching of a mixed message of law and grace.)*

Gal 3:8 Scripture records prophetically that the mass of non-Jewish nations would be justified by faith and not by keeping moral laws. The origin of the gospel is found in this announcement by God over Abraham; he saw all the nations represented in the same principle of the faith that Abraham pioneered. "In you all the nations of the earth are equally represented in the blessing of faith." *([Gen 22:17] I will indeed bless you, and I will multiply your seed as the stars of heaven and as the sand which is on the seashore. And your seed shall possess the gate of their enemies, Gen 22:18 and by your seed shall all the nations of the earth bless themselves. Righteousness by faith is the revelation of the gospel; [Rom 1:17 and Hab 2:4] "the just shall live by his (God's) faith" Righteousness by faith defines your life!)*

Gal 3:9 As did Abraham so do we now find our source in the blessing of faith.

Gal 3:10 In clear contrast to faith, the law is the authority of the curse. As it is written, "Everyone who fails to perform the detailed requirements of the law, even in the least, is condemned." *(Deut 27:26)*

Gal 3:11 Habakkuk confirms conclusively that righteousness by God's faith is the only basis to life; this terminates any possible justification before God based on moral behavior. *(Hab 2:4, 3:17-19)*

Gal 3:12 Law and faith has nothing in common! Law measures man's doing and experience as defining his life. *(Faith measures God's doing in redeeming his design in us, as defining our lives.)*

Gal 3:13 Christ redeemed us from the curse as consequence of our failure to keep the law. In his cross he concentrated the total curse of the human race upon himself. In his abandoning himself to death, he absorbed and dissolved the horror of the curse in his own person. Scripture declares that anyone hanging on a tree embodies the curse. *(Deut 21:23)*

Gal 3:14 This act of Christ released [1]the blessing of Abraham upon the [2]Gentiles! Now we are free to receive [1]the blessing of the Spirit. *([1]Righteousness by God's faith in the achievement of Christ, and not as a reward to our behavior. In the obedience of Christ Deuteronomy 28 is out-dated! [Rom 5:19, Eph 1:3] [2]The mass of non-Jewish nations.)*

Gal 3:15 We are all familiar with the fact that in civil affairs a testament, once endorsed, is authoritative and cannot be tampered with at a later stage.

Gal 3:16 It is on record that the promise *(of the blessing of righteousness by faith)* was made to Abraham and to his seed, singular, *(thus excluding his effort to produce Ishmael.)* Isaac, the child of promise and not of the flesh mirrors the Messiah.

2 Cor 5:21 This is the divine exchange: he who knew no [1]sin embraced our distortion he appeared to be without form; this was the mystery of God's prophetic [2]poetry. He was disguised in our distorted image, marred with our iniquities; he took our sorrows, our pain, our shame to his grave and [3]birthed his righteousness in us. He took our sins and we [3]became his innocence. *(The word, [1]hamartia, comes from ha, without, and meros, form. The word, [2]poema, often translated "made" like in, "he was made to be sin." However, because of its context here I have translated poema to read prophetic poetry. As the scapegoat of the human race, he took on the distorted image of fallen man, he did not become a sinner, but the official representative of humanity's sin. Then Paul uses the word [3]ginomai, he birthed his righteousness in us; since we were born anew in his resurrection from the dead. Hos 6:2, Eph 2:5, 1 Pet 1:3.)*

Eph 4:7 The gift of Christ gives dimension to grace and defines our individual value. *(Grace was given to each one of us according to the measure of the gift of Christ. One measure, one worth! Our worth is defined by his gift not by a reward for our behavior.)*

Eph 4:8 Scripture confirms that he led us as trophies in his triumphant procession on high; he [1]repossessed his gift *(likeness)* in man. *(See Ephesians 2:6, We are also elevated in his ascension to be equally welcome in the throne room of the heavenly realm where we are now seated together with him in his authority. Quote from the Hebrew text, Ps 68:18, [1]lakachta mattanoth baadam, thou hast taken gifts in man, in Adam. [The gifts which Jesus Christ distributes to man he has received in man, in and by virtue of his incarnation. Commentary by Adam Clarke.] We were born anew in his resurrection. 1 Pet 1:3, Hos 6:2)*

Eph 4:9 The fact that he ascended confirms his victorious descent into the deepest pits of human despair. *(See John 3:13, "No one has ascended into heaven but he who [1]descended from heaven, even the son of man." All mankind originate from above; we are [1]anouthen, translated as from above [see Jas 1:17, 18].)*

Eph 4:10 He now occupies the ultimate rank of authority from the lowest regions where he stooped down to rescue us to the highest authority in the heavens, having executed his mission to the full. *(Fallen man is fully restored to the authority of the authentic life of his design. [Ps 139:8].)*

127

Eph 4:11 What God has in us is gift wrapped to the world.

1 Cor 1:22 The Jews crave signs *(to confirm their doubts)* while the Greeks revel in philosophical debate! *(Both groups are addicted to the same soul realm.)*

1 Cor 1:23 The crucified Christ is the message we publicly proclaim, to the disgust of the Jews while the Greeks think we are wacky!

1 Cor 1:24 The dynamic of God's wisdom is the fact that both Jew and Greek are equally included and defined in Christ.

1 Cor 1:25 It seems so foolish that God should die man's death on the cross; it seems so weak of God to suffer such insult; yet man's wisest schemes and most powerful display of genius cannot even begin to comprehend or compete with God in his weakest moment on the cross.

Heb 4:15 As High Priest he fully identifies with us in the context of our frail human lives. Having subjected it to close scrutiny, he proved that the human frame was master over sin. His sympathy with us is not to be seen as excusing weaknesses that are the result of a faulty design, but rather as a trophy to humanity. *(He is not an example for us but of us.)*

In conversation with Jesus this lady began to realize that Jesus was more than a Jew, and that mirrored in him, she was more than a Samaritan. Suddenly she understood that all people indeed share the same origin. The fountain of living water was not distant from her, beyond her reach, but waiting to awaken within her. Not any of her previous five marriages or even her religious tradition could quench her thirst. Not because she failed to meet 'Mr. Perfect' or the men in her life failed to meet her expectation, but simply because of the fact that a partner was never meant to define or complete her life. John 4

Many doctrines of men are based on isolated scripture references outside of the context of God's work of redemption as it is revealed in Christ. Any concept that excludes the good news of what God achieved on humanity's behalf in Christ is irrelevant, no matter how many scriptures can be quoted.

Jesus as the revealer and Redeemer of God's blueprint image and likeness in human form is the context of scripture. Not even the historic or traditional setting of Scripture can distract from the revelation of Christ in us. Luke 24:27,44, Col 1:27.

"Jesus who incarnated God 2,000 years ago is mystically present and waiting to be discovered in EVERY person you and I encounter" Tony Campolo

The law of perfect liberty is the image and likeness of God revealed in Christ, now redeemed in man as in a mirror. Look deep enough into that law of faith that you may see there in its perfection a portrait that so resembles the original that he becomes distinctly visible in the spirit of your mind and in the face of every man you behold. Mirror note Jam 1:25

God takes pleasure in mankind. His reference exceeds anything that could possibly disqualify man. In Christ he has broken down every wall of hostility and every excuse we have to feel distant from him.

The mystery that was hidden for ages and generations is now revealed! It is Christ in you! He is not hiding in history or in future, he is "I am" in you!

Thoughts on the New Birth

The moment of awakening to the truth of our redeemed identity and innocence can certainly be described as a 'new birth' experience! But that's not what Jesus said to Nicodemus, in John 3:3; he explained to Nico that we did not begin in our mother's womb, we *anouthen*, we are from above!

Paul didn't use the 'New Birth' message to get people to make a commitment to follow Jesus. He spoke the mystery of mankind's association in Christ's death and resurrection in such a clear way that many believed! Acts 14:1

Even Peter understands that the reference to our new birth is the resurrection of Jesus from the dead. 1 Pet 1:3

Paul says in Eph 2:5,6 that this happened "while we were still dead in our sins"! God made us alive together with Christ.

The days of window-shopping redemption realities are over! The mirror makes the Bible a new book! When I look into a mirror I can see the color of my eyes, they only reflect in the mirror, they are in reality in my face! Jesus is not hiding in the book! Christ only reflects in scripture to be revealed in reality in us!

A wrong perception of the "New Birth" was cause to a lot of confusion over the years. While the reference to the new birth experience leans on a mere decision one has to make for Jesus it carries with it every reason to disappoint and cause enough doubt to get one to wander away from God and go through the dreadful routine of backsliding and 'repentance' again and again. Many sincere believers thought that one needs to be born again and again. And that one has to dedicate and re-dedicate one's life frequently to stand the best possible chance to go to heaven one day! There must be more substance to faith than human willpower!

Some say that when a person comes to Christ he becomes a brand new species that never existed before! Now if that was the case then such a new species would certainly not be capable of doing the very same horific sins that eveybody else would be capable of.

Another popular perception in some Christian groups was the idea of "once saved always saved", suggesting that as long as you have made a commitment somewhere along the line, you can live like a devil for the rest of your life and you'll be okay in the final day! I mean, does Grace say, "It's all right for Christians to sin, they won't go to hell but if non Christians sin they gonna burn!" This doctrine carries the same error that many ideas about Universalism present. It is not the point of the gospel.

The gospel reveals how God succeeded to rescue mankind from the distorted mind-set we inherited from Adam; we have a new reference to live the life of our redeemed design now! What a waste to live an ignorant and inferior life in the meantime, regardless of whether or not you'll be okay one day!

Israel wasted forty years in the wilderness after being powerfully saved from Pharaoh. There was nothing inferior about their deliverance; there was just something inferior about their faith. They believed a lie about themselves! Num 13:33.

Neither Jesus nor Paul told people to "get born again"! You couldn't even get yourself born the first time, how are you going to get it right a second time?

Jesus did say to Nicodemus unless you're born from above (meaning unless you originate from above) you would have no interest or appetite for heavenly things! John 3:13

God is not man's idea; mankind is God's idea. Man began in God, not in his mother's womb. God says to Jeremiah, "I knew you before I formed you in your mother's womb" Jer 1:5 Mankind is by design the god-kind.

Religion and philosophy would endeavour to engage man in sincere pursuit in an effort to define the gods of their imagination by means of cleverly devised myths. Jesus did not come to compete with these, neither did he attempt to win doctrinal debates; he came to win our hearts with the most attractive and articulate unveiling of the invisible Creator in human form. He boldly declared, "If you have seen me you have seen the Father!" The Spirit of God bears witness with our spirits that we are born from God.

Rom 8:14 The original life of the Father revealed in his son is the life the Spirit now [1]conducts within us. *(The word, [1]agoo, means to conduct or to lead as a shepherd leads his sheep.)*

Rom 8:15 Slavery is such a poor substitute for sonship! They are opposites; the one leads forcefully through fear while sonship responds fondly to Abba Father.

Rom 8:16 His Spirit resonates within our spirit to confirm the fact that we originate in God.

Rom 8:29 He pre-designed and engineered us from the start to be jointly fashioned in the same mold and image of his son according to the exact blueprint of his thought. We see the original and intended pattern of our lives preserved in his Son. He is the firstborn from the same womb that reveals our genesis. He confirms that we are the invention of God. *(We were born anew when he was raised from the dead! [1 Peter 1:3] His resurrection co-reveals our common genesis as well as our redeemed innocence. [Rom 4:25 and Acts 17:31] No wonder then that he is not ashamed to call us his brethren! We share the same origin [Heb 2:11], and, "In him we live and move and have our being, we are indeed his offspring!" [Acts 17:28].)*

Rom 8:30 Jesus reveals that man [1]pre-existed in God; he defines us. He justified us and also glorified us. He redeemed our innocence and restored the glory we lost in Adam. *(As in Romans 3:23, 24; [1]prooritso, pre-defined, like when an architect draws up a detailed plan; kaleo, to surname, identify by name.)*

In Paul's understanding of our common genesis in God to begin with and then revealed again in the death and resurrection of Jesus Christ, he announces to the idol worshipping philosophers in Athens, that we are indeed God's offspring! Acts 17:28 and in verse 29 he says, "Being then God's offspring, we ought not to think that the Deity is like gold, or silver, or stone, a representation by the art and imagination of man."

Your new birth is not the result of a sincere decision you make to follow Jesus, but an awakening of your spirit to the truth of what already took place two thousand years ago when God raised Jesus from the dead. His resurrection from the dead included you! Hos 6:2, 1 Peter 1:3, Eph 2:5

Mankind share three births in common:

1/ Man began in God. Mal 2:10 Have we not all one father? Has not one God created us? See also Math 22:41-46 and Math 23:9

2/ The womb of a mother. Jer 1:5 "Before I formed you in the womb I knew you." The womb of a mother is everyone's passport to planet earth.

3/ The resurrection of Jesus from the dead. Eph 2:5 While we were still dead in our sins, he made us alive toghether with Christ and co-raised us together with Christ. 1Pet 1:3 We have been born anew through the resurrection of Jesus Christ from the dead. 2 Cor 5:15 Now if all were included in his death they were equally included in his resurrection.

Two births, first spirit, then flesh got us to where we are on planet earth; the new birth in our joint-resurrection with Jesus from the dead restored us to where we belong in heavenly places. Eph 2:5,6, 1 Pet 1:3

Consider your creation before your physical birth. Jer 1:5, Deut 32:18, Pr 8:22 - 25; Js 1:17,18; Isa 51:1; Ro 8:29,30; Ge 1:26; Jn 3:13; 2 Co 5:18,19; Gal 4:31; Mt 16:16-18.

To merely know ourselves according to the "flesh" is to underestimate ourselves! Paul says in Gal 1:15,16 "God separated me from my mother's womb and revealed his son in me." He discovered it was not his so-called "noble birth" as offspring of Jacob and Rachel's son Benjamin, that defined him, but Christ's resurrection giving mirror evidence of his original design.

When Paul preaches the resurrection in Acts 13, he quotes Psalm 2 as his text reference, "Today I have begotten you! Ask of me the nations and I will give you the ends of the earth as your inheritance!" He understands that the resurrection of Jesus represents the human race! Paul knows by revelation that what Hosea saw prophetically 800 BC was made a reality in the resurrection of Jesus from the dead. "After 2 days he will revive us, on the 3rd day he will raise us up!" In Eph 2:5 Paul draws the powerful conclusion that "while we were dead in our sins, God made us alive TOGETHER WITH CHRIST and raised us up together with Christ and seated us together with Christ in heavenly places!

Through the preaching of this gospel humanity is implored to awaken in their understanding to this reality: Paul urges us to relocate ourselves mentally; to see ourselves joint-seated with Christ in the throne room of God, in heavenly places! We have returned to where we originate from! Col 3:1-4.

The defeated Adam died in Jesus' death and the new (original) man was raised together with Christ in the resurrection. God knew man before he formed him in his mother's womb. Jer 1:5. See also James, the younger brother of Jesus who did not believe in Jesus until after the resurrection. John 7:5; "Then Jesus also appeared to James" (1 Cor 15:7) and suddenly James discovers that, without exception God's gifts are only good, its perfection cannot be improved upon. They come [1]from above, *(where we originate from)* proceeding like light rays from its source, the Father of lights. With whom there is no distortion or even a shadow of shifting to obstruct or intercept the light; no hint of a hidden agenda. *(The word, [1]anouthen, means, from above [Jn 3:3, 13]. Man is not the product of his mother's womb; man began in God.)* It was his delightful [1]resolve to give birth to us; we were conceived by the [2]unveiled logic of God. We lead the exhibition of his handiwork, like first fruits introducing the rest of the harvest he anticipates. *(The word, [1]boulomai, means the affectionate desire and deliberate resolve of God. Truth, [2]alethea, from a, negative + lanthano, meaning hidden; that which is unveiled; the word of truth.)* James 1:17,18.

Peter saw what Paul preached from Hos 6:2 and wrote in Eph 2:5, and then he wrote in 1 Pet 1:3, that we were born anew through the resurrection of Jesus from the dead! Like Paul and Hosea he realized that God made us alive together with Christ, and raised us up together with Christ!

What a wonderful clear reference the resurrection of Jesus is: the Trophy of man's true identity and innocence redeemed! What a glorious new birth is revealed; just like Isaac from Sarah's dead womb, we arose together with Christ from that rock-hewn tomb!

The incorruptible seed has been in the soil all along, even in the Sahara desert! It was just waiting for the rain! Isa 55:8-10 If the treasure was not already in the field, why would God be prepared to sell all he has to buy a piece of worthless field! Math 13:44 Paul says that we have this treasure in earthen vessels, but while the eyes of our understanding are veiled through our unbelief, we cannot see the truth about us.

2 Cor 4:2 We have renounced hidden agendas *(employing a little bit of the law in an attempt to "balance" out grace)*; we have distanced ourselves from any obscure craftiness to manipulate God's word to make it mean what it does not say! With truth on open display in us, we highly recommend our lives to every one's [1]conscience! Truth finds its most authentic and articulate expression in human life. This beats any doctrinal debate! *(It is our passion for all to see what is so completely obvious in the mirror of our redeemed likeness and innocence! [1]Conscience in Latin means to know together; in the Greek, [1]suneido, it translates as joint seeing; which is the opposite of hades, not to see.)*

2 Cor 4:3 If our message seems vague to anyone, it is not because we are withholding something from certain people! It is just because some are so stubborn in their efforts to uphold an outdated system that they don't see it! They are all equally found in Christ but they prefer to remain lost in the cul-de-sac language of the law!

2 Cor 4:4 The survival and self-improvement programs of the [1]religious systems of this world veil the minds of the unbelievers; exploiting their ignorance about their true origin and their redeemed innocence. The veil of unbelief obstructs a person's view and keeps one from seeing what the light of the gospel so clearly reveals: the [2]glory of God is the image and likeness of our Maker redeemed in human form;

this is what the gospel of Christ is all about. *(The god of this [1]aion, age, refers to the religious systems and governing structures of this world. The unbelief that neutralized Israel in the wilderness was the lie that they believed about themselves; "We are grasshoppers, and the 'enemy' is a giant beyond any proportion!" [Num 13:33, Josh 2:11, Heb 4:6] "They failed to possess the promise due to unbelief." The blueprint [2]doxa, glory of God, is what Adam lost on humanity's behalf. [See Eph 4:18])*

2 Cor 4:5 Even though we recommend ourselves with great confidence, it is not with arrogance; we do not preach ourselves! We preach Christ Jesus the Lord; we are salvation junkies; employed by Jesus for your sakes.

2 Cor 4:6 The light source is founded in the same God who said, "Light, be!" And light shone out of darkness! He lit the lamp in our understanding so that we may clearly recognize the features of his likeness in the face of Jesus Christ reflected within us. *(The same God who bade light shine out of darkness has kindled a light in our hearts, whose shining is to make known his glory as he has revealed it in the features of Jesus Christ. — Knox Translation)*

2 Cor 4:7 We have discovered this treasure where it was hidden all along, in these frail skin-suits made of clay. We take no credit for finding it there! It took the enormous power of God in the achievement of Christ to rescue our minds from the lies it believed. *("The kingdom of heaven is like treasure hidden in an agricultural field, which a man found and covered up; then in his joy he goes and sells all that he has and buys that field." [Mt 13:44] God invested all that he has in the redeeming of our original value! He rescued the life of our design. Our inner life hosts the treasure of the life of our design. Jesus said in John 7:37,38, "If you believe that I am what the scriptures are all about, you will know that you are what I am all about and rivers of living water will gush out of your innermost being!")*

Deu 32:18 You were unmindful of the Rock that begot you, and you forgot the God who gave you birth.

David declares the conclusion of the crucifixion revelation in Psalm 22:27 All the ends of the earth shall remember and turn to the LORD; and all the families of the nations shall worship before him.

In Eph 3:14 and 15 Paul prays: For this reason I bow my knees before the Father, from whom every family in heaven and on earth is named.

When Isaiah prophesies the birth of the Messiah he says in Isa 9:6,7 For to us a child is born, to us a son is given; and the government will be upon his shoulder, and his name will be called "Wonderful Counselor, Mighty God, Everlasting Father, Prince of Peace." Of the increase of his government and of peace there will be no end, upon the throne of David, and over his kingdom, to establish it, and to uphold it with justice and with righteousness from this time forth and for evermore. The zeal of the LORD of hosts will do this.

Mat 22:41-46 Now while the Pharisees were gathered together, Jesus asked them a question, saying, "What do you think of the Christ? Whose son is he?" They said to him, "The son of David." He said to them, "How is it then that David, inspired by the Spirit, calls him Lord, saying, 'The Lord said to my Lord, Sit at my right hand, till I put thy enemies under thy feet'? If David thus calls him Lord, how is he his son?" And no one was able to answer him a word, nor from that day did any one dare to ask him any more questions.

Mat 23:9 And call no man your father on earth, for you have one Father, who is in heaven.

Mat 16:15-18 He said to them, "But who do you say that I, the son of man am?" Simon replied, "You are the Christ, the Son of the living God." And Jesus answered him, "Blessed are you, Simon son of Jona! For flesh and blood has not revealed this to you, but my Father who is in heaven. And I tell you, you are Petros and on this rock I will build my ekklesia, and the gates of hades shall not prevail against it. (Notice the meaning of these Greek words, ekklesia from ek, origin or source and klesia from kaleo, to surname, to identify by name. The word hades has two components, ha, negative and ideis, to see, thus not to see.)

The revelation that the son of man is the son of God is the rock foundation that will free mankind from the lies they believed about themselves!

John 1:9 A new day for humanity has come. The authentic light of life that illuminates everyone was about to dawn in the world! *(This day would begin our calendar and record the fact that human history would forever be divided into before and after Christ. The incarnation would make the image of God visible in human form. In him who is the blueprint of our lives there is more than enough light to displace the darkness in every human life. He is the true light that enlightens every man! [Col 1:15; 2:9, 10; 2 Cor 4:6])*

John 1:10 Although no one took any notice of him, he was no stranger to the world; he always was there and is himself the author of all things.

John 1:11 It was not as though he arrived on a foreign planet; he came to his own, yet his own did not [1]recognize him. *(Ps 24:1, "The earth is the Lord's and the fullness thereof, the world and those who dwell in it [RSV]." The word, [1]paralambano, comes from para, a preposition indicating close proximity, a thing proceeding from a sphere of influence, with a suggestion of union of place of residence, to have sprung from its author and giver, originating from, denoting the point from which an action originates, intimate connection; and lambano, to comprehend, grasp, to identify with.)*

John 1:12 Everyone who [1]realizes their association in him, [6]convinced that he is their [2]original life and that [7]his name defines them, [5]in them he [3]endorses the fact that they are indeed his [4]offspring, [2]begotten of him; he [3]sanctions the legitimacy of their sonship. *(The word often translated, to receive, [1]lambano, means to comprehend, grasp, to identify with. This word suggests that even though he came to his own, there are those who do not [1]grasp their true [2]origin revealed in him, and like the many Pharisees they behave like children of a foreign father, the father of lies [Jn 8: 44].*

Neither God's legitimate fatherhood of man nor his ownership is in question; man's indifference to his true [2]origin is the problem. This is what the Gospel addresses with utmost clarity in the person of Jesus Christ. Jesus has come to introduce man to himself again; humanity has forgotten what manner of man he is by design! [Jas 1:24, Deut 32:18, Ps 22:27].

134

*The word, [2]**genesthai** [aorist tense] is like a snapshot taken of an event, from **ginomai**, to become [See 1:3]. The Logos is the source; everything commences in him. He remains the exclusive Parent reference to their genesis. There is nothing original, except the Word! Man began in God [see also Acts 17:28]. "He has come to give us understanding to know him who is true and to realize that we are in him who is true." [1 Jn 5:20].)*

*The word, [3]**exousia,** often translated "power;" as in, he gave "power" to [2]become children of God, is a compound word; from **ek**, always denoting origin or source and **eimi**, I am; thus, out of I am! This gives [3]legitimacy and authority to our sonship; [4]**teknon**, translated as offspring, child.*

*"He has given," [5]**didomi**, in this case to give something to someone that already belongs to them; thus, to return. The fact that they already are his own, born from above, they have their [2]beginning and their being in him is now confirmed in their realizing it! Convinced, [6]**pisteo**; [7]his name **onoma**, defines man [see Eph 3:15]. Mirror Bible*

"He made to be their true selves, their child-of-God selves." — The Message)

John 1:13 These are they who discover their genesis in God beyond their natural conception! Man began in God. We are not the invention of our parents!

John 1:14 Suddenly the invisible eternal Word takes on [1]visible form! The Incarnation! In him, and now confirmed in us! The most accurate tangible display of God's eternal thought finds expression in human life! The Word became a human being; we are his address; he resides in us! He [2]captivates our gaze! The glory we see there is not a religious replica; he is the [3]authentic begotten son. ([3]*monogenes begotten only by the Father and not by the flesh; in him we recognize our true beginning*). The [4]glory *(that Adam lost)* returns in fullness! Only [5]grace can communicate truth in such complete context!

*(In him we discover that we are not here by chance or accident or by the desire of an earthly parent, neither are we the product of a mere physical conception; we exist by the expression of God's desire to reveal himself in the flesh. His eternal invisible Word, his Spirit-thought, [1]became flesh, [1]**ginomai**, as in be born and [2]**theaomai**, meaning to gaze upon, to perceive. We saw his glory, [4]**doxa**, the display of his opinion, the glory as of the original, authentic begotten of the Father, full of grace and truth. He is both the "only begotten," [3]**monogenes**; as in the authentic original mold, as well as the first born from the dead [Col 1:18, 1 Pet 1:3]. He is the revelation of our completeness.*

*And of his fullness have we all received, grace against grace, [5]**garin anti garitos**, grace undeserved. For the law was given through Moses, grace and truth came through Jesus Christ. He who is in the bosom of the Father, the only original, authentic begotten of the Father; he is our guide who accurately declares and interprets the invisible God within us. Interesting that the revelation of the Incarnation in verse 14 doesn't follow verse 2 or 3, but verse 12 and 13! Genesis 1:26 is redeemed!*

The Great Awakening! The Metanoia-moment! *(See note on repentance p120)*

The Gospel holds the ingredient of the most powerful influence that the consciousness of man could ever encounter. Nothing known to man presents a greater wealth of wisdom and enrichment than the love of God realized. This great revelation is not only his love for us but also his love in us for others!

The awakening of the spirit of our understanding through the preaching of the gospel, is not something we do in order to "get saved" it's something that happens to us when we realize what Jesus has done for us! The "must do's" and "must become's" have all been replaced by a masterfully done deal through one brilliant move of God.

Faith is not a decision; faith is a discovery! The love of God realized awakens belief! Faith is not blind, neither is it unconscious; faith knows.

Rom 1:17 explains Rom 10:17; the "from faith to faith" only happens in the revelation of what God did right to put us right (this is totally superior to what Adam or we did wrong) Jesus is the source of faith; it is impossible for us to manufacture any valid faith outside of the revelation of grace.

While we are on the verse 17's, now Rom 4:17 suddenly makes sense! God called things (mankind's salvation) which were not as though they were!

If our point of departure is not God's faith in the finished work of Christ we have no valid gospel to preach! If our faith is not sourced and sustained in him as the mirror image of God revealed and redeemed in us we are deceiving ourselves with yet another religious disguise called christianity.

The days of window-shopping are over; now with unveiled faces we are gazing into the mirror of our revealed likeness and innocence. 2 Cor 3:18

Acts 14:1 The same thing happened in Iconium: Paul and Barnabas went to the synagogue and spoke in such a way that a great number of Jews and Gentiles became believers. GNB

Col 1:6, "So from the day that you heard and understood the grace of God in truth, you bore fruit!"

For Paul the understanding of mankind's joint inclusion in Christ's death and resurrection was his defining moment. He announced "From now on therefore I no longer know anyone after the flesh! (From a human point of view.) 2 Cor 5:16

The hearing of the gospel brings this "from now on moment" into the equation.

"Behold, everything has become new!" 2 Cor 5:17

James 1:18 It was his delightful [1]resolve to give birth to us; we were conceived by the [2]unveiled logic of God. We lead the exhibition of his handiwork, like first fruits introducing the rest of the harvest he anticipates. *(The word, [1]boulomai, means the affectionate desire and deliberate resolve of God. Truth, [2]alethea, from a, negative + lanthano, meaning hidden; that which is unveiled; the word of truth.)*

2 Cor 3:13 What we say is so unlike Moses who had to keep Israel in suspense with a veiled face; they did not realize that this arrangement would never suffice to secure their standing before God. In essence the letters on stone confirmed their death. All that they could see was the futility of the law of works; how entirely useless their best attempts would be to match the life of their design. *(In Adam all people alike stood condemned; they did not realize it until the law revealed it. In Christ all are declared innocent; yet they do not know it until the Gospel reveals it. [Rom 10:17 and Rom 7:4-25])*

136

2 Cor 3:14 Since the time of Moses until this very day their minds remain calloused and veiled. They are kept in suspense without realizing that there is no glory left in the law (whatever glory there was, carried merely a fading, prophetic glimmer); reading the Old Covenant without understanding that Christ is the fulfilment of Scripture is a complete waste of time. Only in discovering our union with Christ is the veil removed and do we realize that the old system is [1]rendered entirely useless. *(The word [1]katergeo comes from kata, meaning intensity, and argos, meaning labor, the law of works is rendered entirely useless; thus the new arrangement frees us from all self effort to attempt to improve what God has already perfected in Christ.)*

2 Cor 3:15 In the meantime, nothing seems to have changed; the same veil continues to blindfold the hearts of people whenever Moses is read. *(Moses symbolizes the futility of self righteousness as the universal blindfold of the religious world. [John 1:17] Against the stark backdrop of the law; with Moses representing the condemned state of mankind, Jesus Christ unveils grace and truth! He is the life of our design redeemed in human form.)*

2 Cor 3:16 The moment anyone [1]returns to the Lord the veil is gone! *(The word, [1]epistrepho means to return to where we've wandered from; "we all like sheep have gone astray." Jesus is God unveiled in human form. [Col 1:15] See also Hebrews 8:1, "The conclusion of all that has been said points us to an exceptional Person, who towers far above the rest in the highest office of heavenly greatness. He is the executive authority of the majesty of God. 8:2 The office he now occupies is the one which the Moses-model resembled prophetically. He ministers in the holiest place in God's true tabernacle of worship. Nothing of the old man-made structure can match its perfection. 8:10 Now, instead of documenting my laws on stone, I will chisel them into your mind and engrave them in your inner consciousness; it will no longer be a one-sided affair. I will be your God and you will be my people, not by compulsion but by mutual desire." See James 1:25, "Those who gaze into the mirror reflection of the face of their birth is captivated by the effect of a law that frees them from the obligation to the old written code that restricted them to their our own efforts and willpower. No distraction or contradiction can dim the impact of what they see in that mirror concerning the law of perfect liberty [the law of faith] that now frees them to get on with the act of living the life [of their original design]. They find a new spontaneous lifestyle; the poetry of practical living." [The law of perfect liberty is the image and likeness of God revealed in Christ, now redeemed in human life as in a mirror.])*

2 Cor 3:17 The Lord and the Spirit are one; his Lordship sanctions our freedom. A freedom from rules chiseled in stone to the voice of our redeemed design echoing in our hearts!

2 Cor 3:18 The days of window-shopping are over! In him every face is [1]unveiled. In [2]gazing with wonder at the [5]blueprint likeness of God displayed in human form we suddenly realize that we are looking at ourselves! Every feature of his [3]image is [2]mirrored in us! This is the most radical [4]transformation engineered by the Spirit of the Lord; we are led [6]from an inferior [5]mind-set to the revealed [5]endorsement of our authentic identity. Mankind is his [5]glory! *(The word, [1]anakekalumeno, is a perfect passive participle from anakalupto; ana, a preposition denoting upward, to return again, and kalupto, to uncover, unveil. The word, [2]katoptrizomenoi, is the present middle participle from katoptrizomai, meaning to gaze into a reflection, to mirror oneself. The word [4]metamorphumetha is a present passive indicative from metamorpho; meta, together*

with, and **meros**, *form. [The word commonly translated for sin,* **hamartia**, *is the opposite of this as* **ha**, *means without, and* **meros**, *form.] The word,* [3]**eikon**, *translates as exact resemblance, image and likeness;* **eikon** *always assumes a prototype, that which it not merely resembles, but from that which it is drawn;* [5]**doxa**, *glory, translates as mind-set, opinion from* **dokeo**, *authentic thought. Changed 'from glory to glory',* **apo doxes eis doxan; eis**, *a point reached in conclusion;* [6]**apo**, *away from, meaning away from the glory that previously defined us, i.e. our own achievements or disappointments, to the glory of our original design that now defines us. [Paul writes in Romans 1:17 about the unveiling of God's righteousness and then says it is* **from** *faith to faith. Here he does not use the word* **apo**, *but the preposition,* **ek**, *which always denotes source or origin.] Two glories are mentioned in this chapter; the glory of the flesh, and the unfading glory of God's image and likeness redeemed in us. The fading glory represented in the dispensation of the law of Moses is immediately superseded by the unveiling of Christ in us! Some translations of this scripture reads, "we are being changed from glory to glory." This would suggest that change is gradual and will more than likely take a lifetime, which was the typical thinking that trapped Israel for forty years in the wilderness of unbelief! We cannot become more than what we already are in Christ. We do not grow more complete; we simply grow in the knowledge of our completeness! [See Col 3:10] We are not changed "from one degree of glory to another," or step by step. How long does it take the beautiful swan to awaken to the truth of its design? The ugly duckling was an illusion! Whatever it was that endorsed the 'ugly duckling' mindset, co-died together with Christ!)*

Titus 3:2 Gossip is out! Never have anything bad to say about anyone! You do not have to win every argument; instead, avoid [1]quarrelling, be appropriate, always show perfect courtesy to one and all. *(The word,* [1]**mache**, *means controversial, striving. You don't have to wait for people to change before you are nice to them. There is a big difference between "fake politeness" and perfect courtesy!)*

Titus 3:3 Do not be harsh on others. Remember that we, too, were typically foolish; we were stubborn and indifferent to spiritual things, our addiction to the sensual and sexual kept us running around in circles, we were engaged in malice and spiteful jealousies, we were bored and lonely, often utterly disliking ourselves and hating one another!

Titus 3:4 But then, oh happy day! It was the generosity of God and his fondness for mankind that dawned on us like a shaft of light. Our days of darkness were over! Light shone everywhere and we became aware: God rescued the human race! *(See 2:11)*

Titus 3:5 Salvation is not a reward for good behavior. It has absolutely nothing to do with anything that we have done. God's mercy saved us. The Holy Spirit endorses in us what happened to us when Jesus Christ died and was raised! When we heard the glad announcement of salvation it was like taking a deep warm bath! We were thoroughly cleansed and resurrected in a new birth! It was a complete renovation that restored us to sparkling newness of life! *(We realized that we were indeed co-included, co-crucified, and co-raised and are now co-seated together with Christ in heavenly places! [See 2 Cor 5:14-21; Hosea 6:2; Eph 2:5, 6; and 1 Pet 1:3])*

Titus 3:6 The Holy Spirit is the extravagant Administrator of the salvation of Jesus Christ; he gushes forth in our midst like an artesian well. *(An artesian well is a well sunk through solid strata of sedimentary rock into strata from an area of a higher altitude*

138

than that of the well, so that there is sufficient pressure to force water to flow upwards. From the French word, artesian, referring to the old French province Artois, where such wells were common.

In John 7:37-39, John records how Jesus witnessed the eighth day, the great and final day of the Feast of Tabernacles, when, according to custom, the High Priest would draw water from the Pool of Siloam with a golden jar, mix the water with wine, and then pour it over the altar while the people would sing with great joy from Psalm 118:25-26, and also Isaiah 12:3; "Therefore with joy shall we draw water from the wells of salvation!" Then, Jesus, knowing that he is the completeness of every prophetic picture and promise, cried out with a loud voice: "If anyone is thirsty, let him come to me and drink! If you believe that I am what the scriptures are all about, you will discover that you are what I am all about, and rivers of living waters will gush from your innermost being!" See Rom 5:5)

Titus 2:11 The grace of God shines as bright as day making the salvation of humankind undeniably visible. *(For God's undeserved kindness has burst in upon us, bringing a new lease on life for all mankind. — Clarence Jordan)*

Titus 2:12 [1]The day and age we live in sets the stage for displaying the attraction of an [2]awe-inspired life; our [6]minds are rescued in the revelation of righteousness. We are in the [4]school of grace, instructed how to thoroughly [5]reverse the apathy and [3]indifference that erupts in a [5]wave of lust that would seek to dictate the day! *(The word, [1]aion, as in the day and age we live in; [2]eusebos, meaning godly, the attraction of devotion, awe; [3]asebeia, as in ungodliness, indifference; [4]paideou, training students; [5]arneomai, from a, negative, and rheo, pouring forth of utterance; [5]kosmikos epithumia, worldly lusts; [6]sophronos, saved minds; the revelation of righteousness shows how completely God redeemed mankind in Christ and empowers us to cultivate an innocence consciousness instead of a sin consciousness).*

Titus 2:13 Every one must [1]welcome with open arms the outrageously blessed expectation; Jesus is what the world was waiting for! He radiates the brilliant intent of God, engineered by his greatness to rescue the world in Jesus Christ. *(The word, [1]prosdechomenoi, means to receive to oneself, to welcome with open arms.)*

Titus 2:14 He gave himself as sacrifice in [1]exchange for our freedom. We are [1]redeemed from every obligation and accusation under the law and declared absolutely innocent. He defines who we are! [2]Our brand name is "I am." We are exclusively his. We are a [3]passionate people; we excel in doing everything we do beautifully. *(The word, [1]lutroo, means ransom, redemption price, to purchase from slavery; [2]periousios, comes from peri, for sphere, circuit, locality, pertaining to, and eimi, "I am;" [3]zelotes, translates as zealous, passionate; and [4]kalos, as beautiful.)*

Titus 2:15 Continue to communicate content in your every conversation; [1]inspire and entreat with conviction and assertiveness; you are not at the mercy of anyone's [2]suspicious scrutiny. *(Encourage everyone to become acquainted with their redeemed identity, [1]parakaleo; and the word, [2]periphroneo, translates as to think beyond what is obvious, suspicious scrutiny.)*

James 1:21 Get rid of any remaining residue of evil that polluted your life before *(if a quick temper was your problem then, don't make it your problem again.)* Welcome with sensitive embrace the word that powerfully conceives salvation in your soul. *(The inner man, your mind and emotion.)*

James 1:22 Give the word your [1]undivided attention; do not underestimate your-self. [3]Make the calculation. There can only be one logical conclusion: your authentic origin is mirrored in the word. You are God's poem; [2]let his voice make poetry of your life! *(The word, [1]akroate, means intent listening. James is not promoting the doing of the law of works; he is defining the law of perfect liberty. Doing the word begins with your undivided attention to the face of your birth. [2]A doer of the Word, poetes, means poet. Make the calculation, [3]paralogizomai, from para, a preposition indicating close proxim-ity, union, and logizomai, to reckon the logic in any calculation.)*

James 1:23 The difference between a mere spectator and a participator is that both of them hear the same voice and perceive in its message the face of their own gen-esis reflected as in a mirror;

James 1:24 they realize that they are looking at themselves, but for the one it seems just too good to be true, he departs (back to his old way of seeing himself) and im-mediately forgets what manner of person he is; never giving another thought to the one he saw there in the mirror.

James 1:25 The other one is [1]mesmerized by what he sees; he is [2]captivated by the effect of a law that frees man from the obligation to the old written code that restricted him to his own efforts and willpower. No distraction or contradiction can dim the impact of what he sees in that mirror concerning the law of perfect [3]liberty *(the law of faith)* that now frees him to get on with the act of living the life *(of his original design.)* He finds a new [3]spontaneous lifestyle; the poetry of practical living. *(The law of perfect liberty is the image and likeness of God revealed in Christ, now redeemed in man as in a mirror. Look deep enough into that law of faith that you may see there in its perfection a portrait that so resembles the original that he becomes distinctly visible in the spirit of your mind and in the face of every man you behold. I translated the word, [1]parakupto, with mesmerized from para, a preposition indicating close proximity, originating from, denoting the point from which an action originates, intimate connection, and kupto, to bend, stoop down to view at close scrutiny; [2]parameno, to remain captivated under the influence of; meno, to continue to be present. The word often translated as free-dom, [3]eleutheria, means without obligation; spontaneous.)*

Col 3:9 That old life was a lie, foreign to our design! Those garments of disguise are now thoroughly stripped off us in our understanding of our union with Christ in his death and resurrection. We are no longer obliged to live under the identity and rule of the robes we wore before, neither are we cheating anyone through false pretensions. *(The garments an actor would wear define his part in the play but cannot define him.)*

Col 3:10 We stand fully identified in the new creation renewed in knowledge ac-cording to the pattern of the exact image of our Creator.

Col 3:11 The revelation of Christ in us gives identity to the individual beyond anything anyone could ever be as a Greek or a Jew, American or African, foreigner or famous, male or female, king or pawn. From now on everyone is defined by Christ; everyone is represented in Christ. *(In seeing him not just recorded in history but revealed in us, we discover the face of our birth as in a mirror! [Jas 1:18])*

2 Cor 5:16 This is radical! No label that could possibly previously define someone carries any further significance! Even our pet doctrines of Christ are redefined.

Whatever we knew about him historically or sentimentally is challenged by this conclusion. *(By discovering Christ from God's point of view we discover ourselves and every other human life from God's point of view!)*

2 Cor 5:17 In the light of your co-inclusion in his death and resurrection, whoever you thought you were before, in Christ you are a brand new person! The old ways of seeing yourself and everyone else are over. Acquaint yourself with the new! *(Just imagine this! Whoever a person was as a Jew, Greek, slave or freeman, Boer, Zulu, Xhosa, British, Indian, Muslim or American, Chinese, Japanese or Congolese; is now dead and gone! They all died when Jesus died! Remember we are not talking law language here! The 'If' in, "If any man is in Christ" is not a condition, it is the conclusion of the revelation of the gospel! Man is in Christ by God's doing [1 Cor 1:30 and Eph 1:4]. The verses of 2 Corinthians 5:14-16 give context to verse 17! For so long we studied verse 17 on its own and interpreted the 'if' as a condition! Paul did not say, "If any man is in Christ," he said "THEREFORE if any man is in Christ ..." The "therefore" immediately includes verses 14 to 16! If God's faith sees every man in Christ in his death, then they were certainly also in Christ in his resurrection. Jesus did not reveal a "potential" you, he revealed the truth about you so that you may know the truth about yourself and be free indeed!)*

2 Cor 5:18 To now see everything as new is to simply see what God has always known in Christ; we are not debating man's experience, opinion, or his contribution; this is 100% God's belief and his doing. In Jesus Christ, God [1]exchanged equivalent value to redeem us to himself. This act of reconciliation is the mandate of our ministry. *(The word, [1]katalasso, translates as reconciliation; a mutual exchange of equal value.)*

2 Cor 5:19 Our ministry declares that Jesus did not act independent of God. Christ is proof that God reconciled the total kosmos to himself. Deity and humanity embraced in Christ; the fallen state of mankind was deleted; their trespasses would no longer count against them! God has placed this message within us. He now announces his friendship with every individual from within us!

2 Cor 5:20 The voice God has in Christ he now has in us; we are God's ambassadors. Our lives exhibit the urgency of God to [1]persuade everyone to realize the reconciliation of their redeemed identity. *(The word, [1]parakaleo, comes from para, a preposition indicating close proximity, a thing proceeding from a sphere of influence, with a suggestion of union of place of residence, to have sprung from its author and giver, originating from, denoting the point from which an action originates, intimate connection, and kaleo, to identify by name, to surname. In Luke 15:28, 31, His father pleaded with him, "My child, you are always with me, and all that I have is yours." "Be reconciled" could not be translated, "Become reconciled!" "Do in order to become" is the language of the Old Testament; the language of the New Testament is, "Be, because of what was done!"*

2 Tim 1:9 He rescued the [1]integrity of our original [2]identity and revealed that we have always been his own from the beginning, even [3]before time was. This has nothing to do with anything we did to qualify or disqualify ourselves. We are not talking religious good works or karma here. Jesus unveils grace to be the [4]eternal intent of God! Grace celebrates our pre-creation innocence and now declares our redeemed union with God in Christ Jesus. *([1]hagios, holiness, purity, integrity kaleo, often translated, holy calling; [2]kaleo means to identify by name, to surname; [3]pro xronos aionos; pro, before; xronos, a specific space or portion of time, season; aionios, without*

*beginning or end, timeless perpetuity, ages; this was before calendar time existed, before the creation of the galaxies and constellations. There exists a greater dimension to eternity than what we are capable of defining within the confines of space and time! God's faith antici-pated the exact moment of our redeemed union with him for all eternity! What happened to us in Christ is according to God's eternal purpose ([4]**prothesis**), which he has shown in every prophetic pointer and shadow; in the Hebrew tradition the showbread (**prothesis**) pointed to the true bread from heaven, the authentic word that proceeded from the mouth of God, Jesus the incarnate word sustaining the life of our design. See Heb 9:2 The first tented area was called the Holy Place; the only light here came from the lamp-stand illuminating the table upon which the showbread (**prosthesis**) was presented, (the lamp-stand was a beautifully crafted golden chandelier portraying budding and blossoming almond branches. Remember that this is also what Jeremiah saw in Jer 1:12, when God said, 'I am awake over my word to perform it.' The same Hebrew word is used here, **shaqad**, the almond was called the 'awake tree', because it blossomed first, while the other trees were still in their winter sleep. The show bread pointed towards the daily sustenance of life in the flesh as the ultimate tabernacle of God, realized in the account of Jesus with the two men from Emmaus; their hearts were burning with resonance and faith while he opened the scriptures to them, and then around the table their eyes were opened to recognize him as the fulfillment of scrip-ture, their true meal incarnated: Luke 24:27-31; Man shall not live by bread alone, but by the authentic thought of God, the Word proceeding from his mouth, the original intent, his image and likeness incarnated, revealed and redeemed in human life.)*

Titus 1:2 This is the life of the ages that was anticipated for generations; the life of our origi-nal design announced by the infallible resolve of God before time or space existed. (Man's union with God is the original thought that inspired creation. aionios, without beginning or end, timeless perpetuity, ages; xronos, a specific space or portion of time, season. This was before calendar time existed, before the creation of the galaxies and constellations. There ex-ists a greater dimension to eternity than what we are capable of defining within the confines of space and time! God's faith anticipated the exact moment of our redeemed union with him for all eternity!

This life was made certain before eternal time. (BBE 1949, Bible in Basic English)

2 Tim 1:10 Everything that grace pointed to is now realized in Jesus Christ and brought into clear view through the gospel: Jesus is what grace reveals. He took death out of the equation and re-defines life; this is good news indeed!

2 Tim 1:11 Grace is my commission; it is my job and joy to proclaim this message and guide the nations into a full understanding of the love initiative of God.

2 Tim 1:12 What I suffer because of this does not frighten me at all; faith has made him so [1]apparent. I am absolutely persuaded that I am safe in him. We are no longer looking for a future event, or another day, the day has come! Death is not dooms-day; nothing can interrupt what he has done! *(Greek, [1]eido, Latin, video, to see, to know)*

Heb 9:24 In Christ we have so much more than a type reflected in the tabernacle of holy places set up by human hands. He entered into the heavenly sphere itself, where he personally represents mankind before God.

Heb 9:25 Neither was it necessary for him to ever repeat his sacrifice. The High Priests under the old shadow system stood proxy with substitute animal sacrifices that had to be made once a year.

Heb 9:26 But Jesus did not have to suffer again and again since the [1]fall of the world; the [2]single sacrifice of himself in the fulfillment of history now reveals how he has brought sin to naught. *(The word, [1]katabole, means cast down. [2]God's Lamb took away the sins of the world!)*

Heb 9:27 The same goes for everyone: man dies only once, and then faces judgment.

Heb 9:28 Christ died once and faced the judgment of the entire human race! His second appearance has nothing to do with sin but to reveal salvation for all to lay a hold of him. *([See Heb 9:11] He appeared as High Priest before the Throne of Justice once, with his own blood to atone for the sins of the whole world. In his resurrection he appeared as Savior of the world! Sin is no longer on the agenda for the Lamb of God has taken away the sin of the world! The same High Priest who atoned for mankind is now also their Advocate! [1 Cor 15:3-5, Rom 4:25, Acts 17:30, 31, 1 Jn 2:1])*

Note: *(Even in his first coming, he did not come to condemn the world. The Father judges no one for he has handed over all judgment to the son, who judged the world in righteousness when he took their chastisement in his own body. Now in his appearance in us, his body, his mission is to unveil the consequence of redemption through the Holy Spirit.*

Many scriptures have been translated and interpreted with only a futuristic value and have consequently neutralized many to, like the Jews, diligently wait for the Messiah to still come. The Messiah has come once and for all as Messiah. Jesus appeared again after his resurrection and now his resurrection life in us as his body is the extension of his second appearance; God making his appeal to an already reconciled world to "be reconciled!" [Acts 3:26, 2 Cor 5:19, 20] The church continued to postpone the reality that God introduced in Christ. We are now already fully represented in his blamelessness! [See 1 Pet 1:10-13] The Aramaic word, maranatha, means our Lord has come!)

Joh 12:23 "The hour has come for the Son of man to be glorified. Joh 12:24 Truly, truly, I say to you, unless a grain of wheat falls into the earth and dies, it remains alone; but if it dies, it bears much fruit. What shall I say? 'Father, save me from this hour'? No, for this purpose I have come to this hour. Joh 12:28 Father, glorify thy name." Then a voice came from heaven, "I have glorified it, and I will glorify it again." Joh 12:31 Now is the judgment of this world, now shall the ruler of this world be cast out; Joh 12:32 and I, when I am lifted up from the earth, will draw all judgment to myself." Joh 12:33 He said this to show by what death he was to die. Isa 53:4,5; 1 Pet 1:10-12; Acts 17:31.

The most amazing thing about God's beautiful mind, is that he is mindful of us! Jesus is his mind made up about us!

The heavens declare his glory, night to night exhibits the giant solar testimony that is mathematically precise...revealing that God knew before time was the exact moment he would enter our history as a man, and the exact moment the Messiah would expire on the cross!

Within the vast context of this amazing setting, we find ourselves participate in choices beyond any definition of 'karma' where we are free to partake, delay or resist the love initiative of our Maker, beckoning us, I was ready to be found by those who did not seek me. I said, "Here am I, here am I," Isa 65:1

Our response is not a willpower driven decision to believe! We are wired by our Lover and Maker to spontaneously awaken to love's appeal! Love awakens faith! Gal 5:6

The attraction of the truth of the Gospel is such that to resist or reject it, or even to remain indifferent towards it demands a deliberate effort of the will.

To respond to the whooing of his love is as instinctive as falling head-over-heels in love! We don't need to go to kissing-school do we!

The mystery that was hidden for ages and generations is now revealed, it is Christ in us. To reject or suppress this truth causes one to deceive oneself just like so many millions of humans have done and still do; unredeemed time is a wasted life in terms of living the life of your design on planet earth.

Thank God for mercy and eternity and to know that sin was judged and dealt with once and for all. What remains is for the ambassadors of the kingdom to continue to be the voice of the spirit pleading with an already reconciled world to grab the advantage now!

Every contradiction becomes an opportunity for the reinforcement and confirmation of the truth, rather than a distraction from it.

Truth realized makes of faith a fortress!

If all God wanted was Jesus then why did he redeem you? We are not merely Christ-cloned; we are individually uniquely and awesomely designed to give display to the image and likeness of our Maker within our own person, our fingerprint, our touch, our smile, our voice, our countenance. God loves you as an individual; you matter to him! He is not looking for gigabyte or terabyte space in your mind; he has redeemed your original life, body soul and spirit in seamless harmony. Now you are free to be you as he always knew you!

1 Cor 13:12 There was a time of [1]suspense, when everything we saw was merely mirrored in the prophetic word, like in an enigma; but then *(when I became a man in the revelation of Christ)* I gaze face-to-face; behold, I am in him! Now I may know even as I have always been known! *(The word, [1]arti, comes from airo, meaning to keep in suspense. "I knew you before I formed you in your mother's womb!"[Jer 1:5])*

Confession

There is nothing wrong with saying sorry when you have done something wrong; but the essence of confession is a conversation inspired by the revelation of the love of God demonstrated in Christ. The content of this conversation is not about what you did wrong but what Jesus did right!

The Greek word, *homologeo*, means to speak the same thing, which means, to agree with God about you! To walk in the light as God is in the light! Ps 36:9 says , "In your light do we see the light, with you is the fountain of life!"

We are not qualified to be forgiven by the degree of our remorse or the acts of our restitution; God declares mankind forgiven and innocent based solely upon the obedience of Christ and his one act of righteousness.

Divine Embrace Chapter 9

Such a great salvation

A meaningful relationship with the Creator and our fellow humans, of tangible content and feedback was substituted for an airy-fairy philosophy of religious ritual, sentiment and dreams. Trapped in a spiritual vacuum of ignorance, we've latched on to worn-out and fading traditions of the past and vague future hopes.

A new day has dawned! Glad tidings of great joy that belongs to all people are proclaimed. This message includes all of mankind everywhere!

The Gospel reveals what God believes to be true about you.

Isa 55:10,11 "For as the rain comes down, and the snow from heaven, and do not return there, but water the earth, and make it bring forth and bud, that it may give seed to the sower and bread to the eater, so shall my word be that goes forth from my mouth; it shall not return to me void, but it shall accomplish what I please, and it shall prosper in the thing for which I sent it."

Jesus did not come to planet earth to begin the Christian religion, he came to reveal and redeem the image and likeness of God in human form! He did not fail in his mandate! He returned with the full harvest of mankind's salvation!

Eph 4:18 Mankind was darkened in their understanding, alienated from the life of God because of the ignorance that is in them, due to their hardness of heart;" RSV

Act 17:30 The times of ignorance God overlooked, but now he urgently implores all men everywhere to awaken in their understanding (metanoia). The Greek word metanoia, engages man's thoughts (about himself) with God's thoughts.

Jesus is God's thoughts packaged as it were in a human body, in human life. Not as an example for us but of us! The life of our design is on exhibition in him as in a mirror!

Good News

What makes the Gospel good tidings of great joy for all of mankind?

If what you hear does not fill you with great joy it's not good news. The best news is irrelevant if you are excluded.

This is the mystery of grace, God reveals us in Christ!

In the gift of Christ God fulfilled his dream and promise to redeem and restore fallen man to glory.
Jesus reveals that God is for you; his intention is only to greatly benefit you.

Through the law of association or the law of faith as Paul calls it in Rom 3:27, God associated man in Christ before the foundation of the world! Eph.1:4. Of God's doing are you in Christ...1 Cor.1:30.

This is the mystery that was hidden for ages and generations which none of the

145

rulers of this world understood otherwise they would never have crucified the Lord of glory!" 1 Cor.2:6,7. They thought that Jesus died as an individual, but in the mind of God mankind died when Jesus died! Jesus did not die as the second Adam but the last Adam; He brought an end to the Adamic race!

This statement defines the Gospel!

On the basis of its integrity Paul understands the love of Christ; and then makes the most powerful calculation recorded in Scripture, "if one has died for all then all have died!" Therefore from now on I no longer know anyone from a human point of view!

What God did in Christ more than 2000 years ago rescued the human race. His image and likeness in man was redeemed. In the Logos becoming flesh, the incarnation, Jesus proved that God did not make a mistake when he made man.

Paul wrote Rom 5:12-21 before any of us preached it; and at the risk of being misunderstood by the legalistic mind as he states in the next verse 6:1, shall we continue in sin so that grace may abound?

The mass of humanity deserves to hear this gospel, countless many are facing enormous crisis right now; let's live the living epistle to be known and read by all men now; uncluttered, unveiled and trust the design of the human spirit to grasp the true light that enlightens every man.

What happened to man in Adam is by far surpassed by what happened to man in Christ!

All of mankind is equally represented and included in Christ, before anyone but God believed it. "God was in Christ when he reconciled the world to himself." 2 Cor 5:18,19.

This is the essence of the good news we preach. Something doesn't become true by popular vote or when someone believes it! It is already true. When I get the correct answer in Maths, it was already the correct answer before I got it!

The next verse in 2 Cor 5 says, "now God pleads though us with an already reconciled world to be reconciled!" Note: not to "become reconciled", but "to be reconciled" because God already reconciled the world to himself in Christ!

Why would God plead with man?

This gospel mobilizes us to be the mirror voice of every person's true redeemed identity and the integrity of their innocence.

Paul says in 2 Cor 5:14, "The love of Christ constrains me!" Then he explains: "Because I am convinced that one has died for all, therefore all have died."

This simple calculation is the crux of the Gospel. In God's mind every human life is represented in Christ.

In Luke 15 Jesus tells how the Father pleaded with the other brother to persuade him: "My son you have always been with me and all that I have is yours!"

Rom 1:1 Paul, [5]passionately engaged by Jesus Christ, [1]identified in him to [2]represent him. My [3]mandate and [4]message is to announce the goodness of God to mankind. *(Mandate, the scope or horizon of my message, from [3]horitso, meaning marked out. The word, [2]apostelo, means an extension from him, a representative; [5]doulos, means slave from deo, to be bound or knitted together like a husband and wife; [1]kletos comes from kaleo, meaning called, to identify by name, to surname; and [4]eu + angellion, means well done announcement, good news, the official announcement of God's goodness.)*

Rom 1:2 This message is what the Scriptures are all about. It remains the central prophetic theme and content of inspired writing.

Rom 1:6 In Jesus Christ you individually discover [1]who you are. *(The word, [1]kaleo, means to call by name, to surname.)*

Rom 1:14 I am so convinced of everyone's inclusion; I am [2]indebted both to the Greeks as well as those many [1]foreigners whose languages we do not even understand. I owe this message to everyone, it is not a matter of how literate and educated people are; the illiterate are equally included in the benefit of the good news. *(The word, [1]barbaros, means one who speaks a strange and foreign language; [2]opheiletes, means to be indebted, obliges one to return something to someone that belongs to him or her in the first place.)*

Rom 1:15 Because of this compelling urgency I am so keen to preach to you Romans also.

Rom 1:16 I have no shame about sharing the good news of Christ with anyone; the powerful rescuing act of God persuades both Jew and Greek alike.

Rom 1:17 Herein lies the secret of the power of the Gospel; there is no good news in it until the [1]righteousness of God is revealed! The dynamic of the gospel is the revelation of God's faith as the only valid basis for our belief. The prophets wrote in advance about the fact that God believes that righteousness unveils the life that he always had in mind for us. "Righteousness by his *(God's)* faith defines life." *(The good news is the fact that the Cross of Christ was a success. God rescued [1]the life of our design; he redeemed our [1]innocence. Man would never again be judged righteous or unrighteous by his own ability to obey moral laws! It is not about what man must or must not do but about what Jesus has done! It is from faith to faith, and not man's good or bad behavior or circumstances interpreted as a blessing or a curse [Hab 2:4]. Instead of reading the curse when disaster strikes, Habakkuk realizes that the Promise out-dates performance as the basis to man's acquittal. Deuteronomy 28 would no longer be the motivation or the measure of right or wrong behavior! "Though the fig trees do not blossom, nor fruit be on the vines, the produce of the olive fail and the fields yield no food, the flock be cut off from the fold and there be no herd in the stalls, yet I will rejoice in the Lord, I will joy in the God of my salvation. God, the Lord, is my strength; he makes my feet like hinds' feet, he makes me tread upon my high places [Hab 3:17-19 RSV]. "Look away [from the law of works] unto Jesus; he is the Author and finisher of faith." [Heb 12:1].*

The gospel is the revelation of the righteousness of God; it declares how God succeeded to put mankind right with him. It is about what God did right, not what Adam did wrong. The word righteousness comes from the Anglo Saxon word, "rightwiseness;" wise in that which is right. In Greek the root word for righteousness is [1]dike, which means two parties finding likeness in each other. The Hebrew word for righteousness is [1]tzadok, which refers to the beam in a scale of balances. In Colossians 2:9-10, It is in Christ that God finds an accurate and complete expression of himself, in a human body! He mirrors our completeness and is the ultimate authority of our true identity.)

Ignorance is man's biggest enemy. Hos 4:6 My people are destroyed for lack of knowledge.

We ourselves were once foolishly ignorant...Titus 3:2-4.

The law reveals how exceedingly sinful man became in Adam; the gospel reveals how exceedingly righteous that same man became in Christ.

We didn't know sin until the law revealed it; in the same way we do not know righteousness until the gospel reveals it.

Rom 7:8 But the commandment triggered sin into action, suddenly an array of sinful appetites were awakened in me. The law broke sin's dormancy.

Rom 7:9 Without the law I was alive, the law was introduced, sin revived and I died.

Rom 7:10 Instead of being my guide to life, the commandment proved to be a death sentence.

Rom 7:11 Sin took advantage of the law, and employed the commandment to seduce and murder me.

In the light of the New Testament this would translate to "I was once dead apart from the gospel, but when the good news came to me, righteousness revived and now I live!

Rom 5:18 The conclusion is clear: it took just one offense to condemn mankind; one act of righteousness declares the same mankind innocent. *(Phillips translation: "We see then, that as one act of sin exposed the whole race of men to condemnation, so one act of perfect righteousness presents all men freely acquitted in the sight of God!")*

Rom 5:19 The disobedience of the one man [1]exhibits humanity as sinners; the obedience of another man exhibits humanity as righteous. *([1]kathistemi, to cause to be, to set up, to exhibit. We were not made sinners by our own disobedience; neither were we made righteous by our own obedience.)*

Rom 5:20 The presence of the law made no difference, instead it merely highlighted the offense; but where sin increased, grace superseded it.

So again, why does God plead through us with mankind?

Because "He desires to show more convincingly to the heirs of the promise the unchangeable character of his purpose." Heb.6:17 RSV

Heb 6:16 It is common practice in human affairs to evoke a higher authority under oath in order to add weight to any agreement between men, thereby silencing any possibility of quibbling. *(Putting an end to all dispute.)*

148

Heb 6:17 In the same context we are confronted with God's eagerness to go to the last extreme in his dealing with us as heirs of his promise, and to cancel out all possible grounds for doubt or dispute. In order to persuade us of the unalterable character and finality of his resolve, he confined himself to an oath. The promise which already belongs to us by heritage is now also confirmed under oath. *(The Promise is the oath; Jesus is the proof.)*

Effortless believing

So many sincere believers over the years have struggled to come to grips with the illusive victorious life and exhausted every altar call to dedicate and re-re dedicate their lives at every opportunity, struggling to get "assurance".

I am convinced that it has been the result not of a lack of sincerity on either the preacher or the convert's part, but very much a case of ignorance based wrong preaching bringing wrong believing.

Rom.3:23 was preached and taught and printed in every tract, while we failed to appreciate that verse 24 carried the main focus of the Gospel. The law revealed how sinful man was, while the Gospel proclaims how forgiven man is!

Unbelief, rooted in ignorance empowers an already defeated foe, "the god of this world blindfolds the minds of the **unbelievers** to keep them from seeing the light of the gospel which is the intent and blueprint opinion of God revealed in the face of a man!" 2Cor.4:4 Unbelief is to believe a lie about yourself! Num 13:33

Law encourages performance and guilt while love energizes spontaneity and life.

"Read your Bible pray every day", sounds like telling newlyweds to read the marriage documents and kiss every day!

So much of the typical Christian preaching and teaching reduced faith to just another set of rules and recipes demanding quality decisions, duty and discipline.

All willpower-driven energy remains trapped in a system of performance measured by success or failure, praise and guilt. It is a vicious circle.

Beginning with the sinner's prayer-formula, to the many discipleship disciplines diligently taught, we were introduced into a whirlpool of emotions that came and went with the next youth camp, seminar or visiting evangelist.

There is no record in scripture of any sinner's prayer formula used by Jesus or any of the Apostles. Yet much of the evangelistic emphasis adopted various methods to help introduce people to Christ in the popular "repeat after me" recipe. Followed by a bold, "and now you are born again!" remark, with all the forms and statistics filed for follow-up reference etc.

There is only one faith that matters, not what we believe about God, but what God believes about us! Jesus is what God believes!

Rom 3:23 Everyone is in the same boat; their [1]distorted behavior is proof of a [2]lost [3]blueprint. *(The word sin, is the word [1]hamartia, from ha, negative and meros, form,*

149

thus to be without form or identity; [2]hustereo, to fall short, to be inferior, [3]doxa, glory, blueprint, from dokeo, opinion, intent.)

Rom 3:24 Jesus Christ is proof of God's grace gift; he redeemed the glory of God in human life; mankind condemned is now mankind justified because of the ransom paid by Christ Jesus! *(He proved that God did not make a mistake when he made man in his image amd likeness! Sadly the evangelical world proclaimed verse 23 completely out of context! There is no good news in verse 23, the gospel is in verse 24! All fell short because of Adam; the same 'all' are equally declared innocent because of Christ! The law reveals what happened to man in Adam; grace reveals what happened to the same man in Christ.)*

Rom 3:25 Jesus exhibits God's mercy. His blood propitiation persuades humankind that God has dealt with the historic record of their sin. What he did vindicates God's righteousness.

Rom 3:26 All along God [1]refused to let go of man. At this very moment God's act of [2]righteousness is [3]pointing mankind to the evidence of their innocence, with Jesus as the [4]source of their faith. *(God's tolerance, [1]anoche, to echo upwards; God continued to hear the echo of his likeness in us. In both these verses [25+26] Paul uses the word, [3]endeixis, where we get the word indicate from. It is also part of the root for the word translated as righteousness, [2]dikaiosune. To point out, to show, to convince with proof. Then follows, [3]ek pisteos iesou, ek, source or origin and iesou is in the Genitive case, the owner of faith is Jesus! He is both the source and substance of faith! Heb 11:1, 12:2)*

Rom 3:27 The law of faith cancels the law of works; which means there is suddenly nothing left for man to boast in. No one is superior to another. *(Bragging only makes sense if there is someone to compete with or impress. "While we compete with one another and compare ourselves with one another we are without understanding. [2 Cor 10:12]. "Through the righteousness of God we have received a faith of equal standing." [See 2 Pet 1:1 RSV])*

Rom 3:28 This leaves us with only one logical conclusion, mankind is justified by faith and not by their ability to keep the law.

Rom 10:4 Christ is the conclusion of the law, everything the law required of man was fulfilled in him; he thus represents the righteousness of the human race, based upon faith *(and not personal performance).*

Rom 10:5 Moses is the voice of the law; he says that a man's life is only justified in his doing what the law requires.

Rom 10:6 But faith finds its voice in something much closer to man than his most disciplined effort to obey the law. Faith understands that Christ is no longer a distant promise; neither is he reduced to a mere historic hero. He is mankind's righteousness now! Christ is no longer hidden somewhere in the realm of heaven as a future hope. For the Jews to continue to ask God to send the Messiah is a waste of time! That is not the language of faith.

Rom 10:7 Faith knows that the Messiah is not roaming somewhere in the region of the dead. "Who will descend into the abyss to bring Christ back from the dead," is not the language of faith. *(Those who deny the resurrection of Christ would wish to send someone to go there and confirm their doubts, and bring back final proof that Jesus was not the Messiah. Faith announces a righteousness that reveals that humankind has indeed been co-raised together with Christ; the testimony of the risen Christ is confirmed in the heart and life of every believer.)*

Rom 10:8 Faith-righteousness announces that every definition of distance in time, space, or hostility has been cancelled. Faith says, "The Word is near you. It is as close to you as your voice and the conviction of your heart." We publicly announce this message *(because we are convinced that it belongs to every man).*

Rom 10:9 Now your salvation is realized! Your own [1]words echo God's voice. The unveiling of the masterful act of Jesus forms the words in your mouth, inspired by the conviction in your heart that God indeed raised him from the dead. *(In his resurrection, God co-raised us [Hos 6:2]. His resurrection declares our innocence [Rom 4:25]. Salvation is not reduced to a recipe or a "sinners prayer" formula; it is the spontaneous inevitable conversation of a persuaded heart! To confess, [1]homologeo, homo, the same thing + logeo, to say)*

Rom 10:10 Heart-faith confirms our redeemed righteousness and ignites the kind of conversation consistent with salvation. *(He restored us to blameless innocence! It is impossible not to boldly announce news of such global consequence [Isa 40:9].)*

Rom 10:11 Scripture declares that whosoever believes in Christ *(to be the fulfillment of the promise of God to redeem man)* will [1]not be ashamed *([2]hesitant)* to announce it. *([See Isa 28:16] These two Hebrew words, [2]cush, to make haste, and [Isa 49:23] [1]bush, to be ashamed, look very similar and were obviously confused in some translations — the Greek from Hebrew translation. The Septuagint was the Scriptures Paul was familiar with and there the word was translated from the word [1]bush.)*

Rom 10:12 Nothing distinguishes the Jew from the Greek when it comes to the generosity of God. He responds with equal benevolence to everyone who sees themselves identified in him *(they realize that God defines them and not their cultural identity.)*

Rom 10:13 Salvation is to understand that every person's [1]true identity is revealed in Christ. *(Whosoever shall [1]call upon the Name of the Lord shall be saved; [1]epikaleomai, to entitle; to identify by name, to surname.)*

Rom 10:14 How is it possible to convince people of [1]their identity in him while they do not believe that he represents them? How will they believe if they remain ignorant about who they really are? How will they understand if the Good News of their inclusion is not announced? *(The word, [1]epikaleomai, traditionally translates as "to call upon," from kaleo, which literary means to surname, or to identify by name. This is also the root word in ekklesia, with ek being a preposition that denotes origin, and kaleo. In the context of Matthew 16 where Jesus introduces this word, he reveals that the son of man is indeed the son of God, "I say to you Simon, son of Jonah, you are petros [Rock] and upon this petra I will build my ekklesia!" [See note on Rom 9:33].)*

Rom 10:15 What gives someone the urgency to declare these things? It is recorded in prophetic scripture, "How lovely on the mountains *(where the watchmen were stationed to witness the outcome of a war)* are the feet of them leaping with the exciting news of victory. Because of their eyewitness encounter they are qualified to run with the Gospel of peace and announce the consequent glad tidings of good things that will benefit everyone."

Rom 10:16 It is hard to imagine that there can yet be a people who struggle to hear and understand the good news. Isaiah says, "Lord, who has believed our report?"

Rom 10:17 It is clear then that faith's [1]source is found in the content of the message heard; the message is Christ. *(We are God's audience; Jesus is God's language! The Greek, [1]ek, is a preposition that denotes source or origin; thus, faith comes out of the word that reveals Christ. The word "Christ" appears in the best manuscripts. Herein lies the secret of the power of the gospel; there is no good news in it until the righteousness of God is revealed! [See Rom 1:17] The good news is the fact that the cross of Christ was a success. God rescued the life of our design; he redeemed our innocence. Man would never again be judged righteous or unrighteous by his own ability to obey moral laws! It is not about what man must or must not do but about what Jesus has done! God now persuades everyone to believe what he knows to be true about them. [It is from faith to faith.] The prophets wrote in advance about the fact that God believes that righteousness unveils the life that he always had in mind for us. "Righteousness by his (God's) faith defines life." [Hab 2:4].)*

In Christ God has overlooked the times of ignorance, as Paul says to the Greek philosophers, "God now urges all men everywhere to 'repent', to metanous, to discover his mind made up about man!

Because God has appointed a day and a person, and on that day in that person God would judge the world in righteousness! And of this righteous judgement he has given proof by raising Jesus from the dead! The resurrection of Jesus from the dead is God's testimony of mankind's innocence!

His body on the cross was the document of our guilt; his body raised from the dead is the receipt of our acquittal!

Rom 4:25 Our sins [1]resulted in his death; his resurrection is [1]proof of our righteousness. *(His resurrection is the receipt to our acquittal. This is one of the most important statements in the entire Bible. Why was Jesus handed over to die? Because of [1]dia, our sins. Why was he raised from the dead? Because of dia, we were justified! His resurrection reveals our righteousness!*

Here is the equation: his cross = our sins; his resurrection = our innocence!

If we were still guilty after Jesus died, his resurrection would neither be possible nor relevant! This explains Acts 10:28 and 2 Cor 5:14 and 16. And in Acts 17:31, "because God had fixed a day on which he would judge the world in righteousness by a man whom he has appointed, and of this he has given assurance to all men by raising him from the dead.")

How does this gospel translate into a transformed life?

God's work of redeeming mankind was not a desperate effort to engage man in a lifelong struggle to gradually improve or upgrade his behavior; he rescued his image and likeness in man. The "life more abundantly" that Jesus restored man to, can only be measured by the original blueprint. John 10:10, Gen.1:26, Col 1:13,15,2:9,10.

The 'ugly duckling' did not see a potential swan reflected in the mirror! The swan saw the swan!

We have a brand new point of departure! Instead of wasting time in the wilderness of survival and striving playing snakes and ladders and memorizing

Deut 28, we awaken to throne room realities! We are seated in Christ in heavenly places to begin with!

The truth does not set people free; Jesus said, "You will KNOW the truth and the truth will set you free!" What does he mean by this, to know the truth; the truth about what? The truth about you! Jesus is the truth about you!

Eph 4:21 It is not possible to study Christ in any other context; he is the incarnation, hear him resonate within you! The truth about you has its ultimate reference in Jesus. *("The truth as it is in Christ." He did not come to introduce a new compromised set of rules; he is not an example for us but of us!)*

Eph 4:22 Now you are free to strip off that old identity like a filthy worn-out garment. Lust corrupted you and cheated you into wearing it. *(Just like an actor who wore a cloak for a specific role he had to interpret; the fake identity is no longer appropriate!)*

Eph 4:23 Be renewed in your innermost mind! *(Pondering the truth about you as it is displayed in Christ)* will cause you to be completely reprogrammed in the way you think about yourself! *(Notice that Paul does not say, "Renew your minds!" This transformation happens in the spirit of your mind, awakened by truth on a much deeper level than a mere intellectual and academic consent.)*

Eph 4:24 Immerse yourself fully into this God-shaped new man from above! You are created in the image and likeness of God. This is what righteousness and true holiness are all about.

Eph 4:25 Faking it and lying to one another was part of the old life; now truth remains the constant inspiration in your every conversation. We are related to one another like different parts in the same body. *(Which means that cheating one another would be cheating yourself! Truth only finds context in Christ [v 21])*

Eph 4:26 Even if you think you have a valid excuse, do not let anger dominate your day! If you don't deal with it immediately (in the light of the likeness of Christ in you) the sun sets for you and your day becomes one of lost opportunity where darkness employs anger to snare you into sin.

Eph 4:27 Any sin that you tolerate is an open invitation to the devil. Do not give him a platform to operate from.

Eph 4:28 If you were a thief before, you are one no more. Find an honest job where the fruit of your labor can be a blessing to others!

Eph 4:29 Instead of cheap talk, your mouth is now a fountain of grace, giving encouragement and inspiration to everyone within earshot.

John writes, It is not a new message, it is the word that was from the beginning; yet it is new when you discover that what is true in Jesus is equally true in you! 1 John 2:7, 8. As he is so are we in this world! 1 John 4:17. "We know that the son of God has come, and he has given us UNDERSTANDING to know him who is true, and WE ARE IN HIM WHO IS TRUE!" 1 John 5:20

Col 3:1 You are in fact raised together with Christ! Now ponder with persuasion the consequence of your co-inclusion in him. Relocate yourselves mentally! Engage your thoughts with throne room realities where you are co-seated with Christ in the executive authority of God's right hand.

Col 3:2 Becoming affectionately acquainted with these thoughts will keep you from being distracted again by the earthly *(soul-ruled)* realm. *(A renewed mind conquers the space that was previously occupied by worthless pursuits and habits.)*

Col 3:3 Your union with his death broke the association with that world; see yourselves located in a fortress where your life is hidden with Christ in God! *("In that day you will know that I am in my father, and you in me and I in you." [Jn 14:20] Occupy your mind with this new order of life; you died when Jesus died, whatever defined you before defines you no more. Christ, in whom the fullness of deity dwells, defines you now! The secret of your life is your union with Christ in God! [See Col 2:9, 10])*

"Risen, then, with Christ you must lift your thoughts above where Christ now sits at the right hand of God, you must be heavenly minded; not earthly minded, you have undergone death, and your life is hidden away now with Christ in God. Christ is your life, when he is made manifest you are made manifest in his glory." — Knox Translation)

Col 3:4 The exact life on exhibit in Christ is now repeated in us. We are being [1]co-revealed in the same bliss; we are joined in oneness with him, just as his life reveals you, your life reveals him! *(This verse was often translated to again delay the revelation of Christ to a future event! The word, [1]otan, often translated as "when" is better translated as "every time." Thus, "Every time Christ is revealed we are being co-revealed in his glory." According to Walter Bauer Lexicon, otan is often used of an action that is repeated. Paul declares our joint-glorification in Christ! We are co-revealed in the same bliss. [See 1 Cor 2:7-8, Rom 3:23-24, Rom 8:30, 2 Pet 1:3.] In him we live and move and have our being; in us he lives and moves and has his being! [Acts 17:28])*

Col 3:5 Consider the members of your body as dead and buried towards everything related to the porn industry, sensual uncleanness, longing for forbidden things, lust and greed, which are just another form of idol worship. *(Idol worship is worshipping a distorted image of yourself!)*

Col 3:6 These distorted expressions are in total contradiction to God's design and desire for your life. *(The sentence, "upon the sons of unbelief" was added later in some manuscripts.)*

Col 3:7 We were all once swept along into a lifestyle of lust and greed.

Col 3:8 But now, because you realize that you co-died and were co-raised together with Christ, you can flush your thoughts with truth! Permanently put these things behind you: things such as violent outbursts of rage, depression, all manner of wickedness, slander *(any attempt to belittle someone else and to cause someone to receive a bad reputation, **blasphemos**)*, and every form of irregular conversation. *(The lifelong association with sin is broken; the dominion of the character of God is revealed again in ordinary life.)*

Col 3:9 That old life was a lie, foreign to our design! Those garments of disguise are now thoroughly stripped off us in our understanding of our union with Christ in his death and resurrection. We are no longer obliged to live under the identity and rule of the robes we wore before, neither are we cheating anyone through false pretensions. *(The garments an actor would wear define his part in the play but cannot define him.)*

Col 3:10 We stand fully identified in the new creation renewed in knowledge according to the pattern of the exact image of our Creator.

Rom 6:6 We perceive that our old lifestyle was co-crucified together with him; this concludes that the vehicle that accommodated sin in us, was scrapped and rendered entirely useless. Our slavery to sin has come to an end.

Rom 6:7 If nothing else stops you from doing something wrong, death certainly does.

Rom 6:8 Faith sees us joined in his death and alive with him in his resurrection.

Rom 6:9 It is plain for all to see that death lost its dominion over Christ in his resurrection; he need not ever die again to prove a further point.

Rom 6:10 His appointment with death was [1]once-off. As far as sin is concerned, he is dead. The reason for his death was to take away the sin of the world; his life now exhibits our union with the life of God. *(The Lamb of God took away the sin of the world; [1]efapax, once and for all, a final testimony, used of what is so done to be of perpetual validity and never needs repetition. This is the final testimony of the fact that sin's power over us is destroyed. In Hebrews 9:26, "But Jesus did not have to suffer again and again since the fall (or since the foundation) of the world; the single sacrifice of himself in the fulfillment of history now reveals how he has brought sin to naught." "Christ died once, and faced our judgment! His second appearance (in his resurrection) has nothing to do with sin, but to reveal salvation unto all who eagerly embrace him [Heb 9:28].")*

Rom 6:11 This reasoning is equally relevant to you. [1]Calculate the cross; there can only be one logical conclusion: he died your death; that means you died unto sin, and are now alive unto God. Sin-consciousness can never again feature in your future! You are in Christ Jesus; his Lordship is the authority of this union. *(We are not being presumptuous to reason that we are in Christ! "[1]Reckon yourselves therefore dead unto sin" The word, [1]logitsomai, means to make a calculation to which there can only be one logical conclusion. [See Eph 1:4 and 1 Cor 1:30].*

"From now on, think of it this way: Sin speaks a dead language that means nothing to you; God speaks your mother tongue, and you hang on every word. You are dead to sin and alive to God. That's what Jesus did." — The Message)

Rom 6:12 You are under no obligation to sin; it has no further rights to dominate your dead declared body. Therefore let it not entice you to obey its lusts. *(Your union with his death broke the association with sin [Col 3:3].)*

Rom 6:13 Do not let the members of your body lie around loose and unguarded in the vicinity of unrighteousness, where sin can seize it and use it as a destructive weapon against you; rather place yourself in [1]readiness unto God, like someone resurrected from the dead, present your whole person as a weapon of righteousness. *(Thus you are reinforcing God's grace claim on mankind in Christ; [1]paristemi, to place in readiness in the vicinity of).*

Rom 6:14 Sin was your master while the law was your measure; now grace rules. *(The law revealed your slavery to sin, now grace reveals your freedom from it.)*

Rom 6:15 Being under grace and not under the law most certainly does not mean that you now have a license to sin.

Rom 6:16 As much as you once gave permission to sin to trap you in its spiral of spiritual death and enslave you to its dictates, the obedience that faith ignites now, introduces a new rule, rightness with God; to this we willingly yield ourselves. *(Righteousness represents everything that God restored us to—in Christ.)*

Rom 6:17 The content of teaching that your heart embraced has set a new [1]standard to become the [1]pattern of your life; the grace of God ended sin's dominance. *(The word, [1]tupos, means form, mold. The Doddrich translation translates it as, "the model of doctrine instructs you as in a mold.")*

Rom 6:18 Sin once called the shots; now righteousness rules.

2 Pet 1:1 I am Simon the Rock, bondman and ambassador of Jesus Christ. The righteousness of God *(what God accomplished in Christ in order to redeem his image and likeness in us)* is what gives our faith its valid reference. God's faith [1]sees everyone equally justified in Jesus Christ. *(If righteousness had anything to do with personal merit or performance, then only the good enough amongst us would qualify. The word, [1]lanchano, means to be measured out beforehand, to be allocated something by allotment. This emphasizes the fact that nothing we did or determined to achieve had any influence upon God to qualify us. Faith is not a reward for personal diligence; it is everyone's portion. No one's faith is inferior to another's because God sees all equally justified in Jesus Christ. Salvation belongs to everyone based on exactly the same merit. God's righteousness is responsible for our faith [Rom 1:17].)*

2 Pet 1:2 With a faith of equal value as our reference, we may now increasingly know ourselves the way God has always known us *(the knowledge of God)*, realized in Jesus our leader, and be engulfed with grace and peace fully amplified within us. *(In this context no one can ever feel ignored or neglected again.)*

2 Pet 1:3 God's powerful intervention gifted us with all that it takes to live life to the full. He has always known us. *(Jer 1:5, 1 Cor 13:12)* He introduced us as it were to ourselves again *(kaleo, to surname)* through a glorious display of his efficiency. *(Through his own glory and virtue, or "through a glorious display of his efficiency" as Dr. Robinson (Lexicon) renders it.)*

2 Pet 1:4 This is exactly what God always had in mind for us; every one of his abundant and priceless promises pointed to our restored participation in our godly origin! This is his gift to us! *(Had it been a reward for good behavior, we would never have qualified!)* In this fellowship we have escaped the distorted influence of the corrupt cosmic virus of greed. *(Our godly origin: his image and likeness redeemed in us. The factory settings are restored. Every compatible program is again installed in our hard-drive to facilitate the life of our design.)*

2 Pet 1:5 Now *(in the light of what we are gifted with in Christ)* the stage is set to display life's excellence. Imagine the extreme devotion and focus of a [1]conductor of music, how he would [2]diligently [3]acquaint himself with every individual voice in the choir, as well as the contribution of every specific instrument, to follow the precise sound represented in every note in order to give maximum credit to the original composition. This is exactly what it means to exhibit the divine character. You are the choir conductor of your own life. Study the full content of faith; you will find virtue there, and within virtue, faith-inspired enlightenment will voice its contribution. *(There is a level of understanding that can only be accessed by faith. In*

*Hebrews 11:3, "by faith we understand that the ages were framed by the Word of God." The word, ¹**epichoregeo**, comes from **epi**, a preposition of position, over, in charge, + **chorus**, choir, orchestra, or dance + **ago**, meaning to lead as a shepherd leads his sheep; thus, the director of music. "Giving all diligence, extreme devotion." The word, ²**spoude**, means to interest one's self immediately and most earnestly. The word, ³**pareisenengkantes**, comes from **pareisphero: para**, a preposition indicating close proximity, a thing proceeding from a sphere of influence, with a suggestion of union of place of residence, to have sprung from its author and giver, originating from, denoting the point from which an action originates, intimate connection, + **eisphero**, to reach inward. Before a performance, the first violinist will give the exact key of the piece to be played; now every instrument can be finely tuned to that note, in the same way the faith of God gives that exact pitch.)*

2 Pet 1:6 The one attribute reveals the other, strength of character emerges out of faith-knowledge, in its strength follows the ability to prevail in patient perseverance; these are the ingredients that constitute your devotion,

2 Pet 1:7 out of such devotion and worship flow true friendship. Brotherly affection is founded in agape. ¹The agape-love of God is at the heart of every virtue that faith reveals. *(Worship and devotion to God includes esteeming and honoring friendship with people [Jas 3:9]; the same voice that magnifies God cannot insult a man made in God's image. The word, ¹**agape**, is from **ago**, meaning to lead as a shepherd leads his sheep, and **pao**, to rest; as in Psalm 23, "he leads me besides still waters, he restores my soul; by waters of reflection, my soul remembers who I am!"*

See The Message translation, " ... each dimension fitting into and developing the other.")

2 Pet 1:8 While you diligently ¹rehearse the exact qualities of every divine attribute within you; the volume will rise with ever increasing gusto, guarding you from being ineffective and barren in your knowledge of the Christ-life displayed with such authority and eloquence in Jesus. *("These things being in you." The word, ¹**uparcho**, translates as to begin under, from **upo** + **archomai**, to commence or rehearse from the beginning.)*

2 Pet 1:9 If anyone feels that these things are absent in his life, they are not; spiritual blindness and short-sightedness only veil them from you. This happens when one loses sight of one's innocence. *(The moment one forgets the tremendous consequence of the fact that we were cleansed from our past sins, one seems to become pre-occupied again with the immediate sense-ruled horizon, which is what short-sightedness is all about; this makes one blind to his blessings. Spiritual realities suddenly seem vague and distant. Practice your innocence!)*

2 Pet 1:10 Therefore I would encourage you, my Brothers, to make every immediate effort to become cemented in the knowledge of your ¹original identity ²revealed and confirmed in the logic of God. Fully engage these realities in your lifestyle; if you do this you will never ³fail. *(Your original identity, ¹**kaleo**, often translated as calling, to surname, to identify by name; ²**eklogen**, often translated as election; yet the two parts of this word, **ek**, a preposition denoting origin or source, and **lego**, from **logos**, suggests the original word (the logic of God) as our source [Jn 1:1,14]. The word, ³**ptaio**, means to fail, falter, or get out of tune again in the context of verse 5, literally to fall, lose height, to stop flying.)*

2 Pet 1:11 Thus the great ¹Conductor of music will draw your life into the full

volume of the harmony of the ages; the *2royal song of our Savior Jesus Christ. (In Colossians 2:19, "You are directly connected to Christ who like a choir conductor draws out the music in everyone like a tapestry of art that intertwines in harmony to reveal the full stature of divine inspiration," which is Christ in you. Again the word 2epichoregeo is used, the choir conductor; this time, God is doing the conducting and is leading us into his harmony; 2eis + odos, meaning access into the road. Yet, in this context I prefer the thought that we are led into a song, an ode; a ceremonious lyric poem. The form is usually marked by exalted feeling and style. The term ode derives from a Greek word alluding to a choric song, usually accompanied by a dance; also a poem to be sung composed for royal occasions.)*

2 Pet 1:12 Having said all this I am sure that you can appreciate why I feel so urgent in my commitment to you to repeatedly bring these things to your attention; as indeed you have already taken your stand for the truth as it is now revealed *(in the Gospel).*

2 Pet 1:13 So while I am still in this body-suit, I take my lead from the revelation of righteousness and make it my business to thoroughly stir you until these truths become permanently molded in your memory.

2 Pet 1:14 All the more since I know that my time in this tabernacle is almost done; our Lord Jesus Christ has prepared me for this.

2 Pet 1:15 In the meantime, I will do whatever it takes to make it possible for you to always be able to easily recall these realities even in my absence.

2 Pet 1:16 We are not con-artists, fabricating fictions and fables to add weight to our account of his majestic appearance; with our own eyes we witnessed the powerful display of the illuminate presence of Jesus the Master of the Christ-life. *(His face shone like the sun, even his raiment were radiant white [Mt 17].)*

2 Pet 1:17 He was spectacularly endorsed by God the Father in the highest honor and glory. God's majestic voice announced, "This is the son of my delight; he has my total approval."

2 Pet 1:18 For John, James, and I the prophetic word is fulfilled beyond doubt; we heard this voice loud and clear from the heavenly realm while we were with Jesus in that sacred moment on the mountain.

2 Pet 1:19 For us the appearing of the Messiah is no longer a future promise but a fulfilled reality. Now it is your turn to have more than a second-hand, hearsay testimony. Take my word as one would take a lamp at night; the day is about to dawn for you in your own understanding. When the morning star appears, you no longer need the lamp; this will happen shortly on the horizon of your own hearts.

2 Pet 1:20 It is most important to understand that the prophetic word recorded in scripture does not need our interpretation or opinion to make it valid.

2 Pet 1:21 The holy men who first spoke these words of old did not invent these thoughts, they simply voiced God's oracles as they were individually inspired by the Holy Spirit.

Thoughts on hell

It is so sad that for many years the church had to reduce its message to a heaven or hell theme in order to persuade people into making a decision for Christ.

Any fear-based relationship has to be sustained by fear and removes all possibility for romance.

The Gospel reveals the love initiative of God and how he loves his creation not as a reward for their good behavior but because he knows the integrity of their design. It declares what God believes and what God achieved on humanity's behalf in the death and resurrection of Jesus Christ. If the Gospel has the power to get people to fall head over heels in love with God and to love their neighbor as much as they love themselves, then this Gospel demands our total attention and emphasis.

This automatically frees anyone anyway from the dread of hell or any sense of pending or possible punishment. 1 Jn 4:18 There is no fear in love, but perfect love casts out fear. For fear has to do with punishment. 1Jn 4:19 We love, because he first loved us.

There is no law against the free expression of the fruit of the spirit. No one can exaggerate love, peace, joy, endurance, kindness, goodness, faith, gentleness, self control. Legalism can neither match nor contradict this. There is no law against love! Galatians 5:22,23. The Spirit finds expression in love, joy, peace, endurance, kindness *(usefulness, obliging)*, goodness, faith, gentleness, self control *(spirit strength)*.

In total contrast to the tree of the knowledge of good and evil *(poneros, harships labors and annoyances)*, the tree of life bears fruit effortlessly consistent with the life of our original design!

Love does not compete with law; love is extravagant in its exhibition of the Christ-life.

The urgency to tell everyone the good news of their redeemed innocence because of the success of the cross and God's act of kindness in Christ to rescue mankind from an inferior expression of life into the most attractive life possible can never be matched by a fear motive! Paul gives context to the motivation of ministry when he declares that "the love of Christ constrains us, because we are convinced that one has died for all, therefore all have died!"

Our message is powerful enough to stop people in their tracks with the best news ever! Sin in its every disguise doesn't have what it takes to even remotely match the attraction and total contentment and appeal of the Christ-life!

The truth of our original identity revealed and redeemed in Christ, sets us totally free from every distortion that we could possibly accommodate in our minds about the life of our design.

We declare the intimate resolve of God and his intent to engage with the individual in the most personal tangible way possible.

The biggest waste is to miss out on one day of fellowship with your Creator.

I am often overwhelmed with the thought of the ultimate extent of the great work of redemption and act of reconciliation that God undertook to rescue the human race. Underestimating this great salvation has always been the biggest sin of the church.

The greatest safeguard we can ever give someone against a wasted life is in our message that reveals truth in such a way that every possible excuse we could have to experience distance from God or to continue in any form of sin, guilt, fear or an inferior lifestyle is done away with. In its stead there remains only the wide open arms of Father longing to embrace the individual and the world into unrestricted friendship.

There is enough content in the positive revelation of Christ in you to rid you of a sin consciousness and its dreadful consequence of even a moment's sense of separation.

Our message is not to persuade people that there is no hell, but rather to convince them that Christ suffered the horror of it to liberate us from its dread both in this life and the next. To influence people into making a decision for Christ based on hell is to distract from the truth. The focus and central theme of the Gospel is the revelation of the mystery of man's inclusion in the death Jesus died and our co-resurrection and joint-position in the father's right hand. The liberating truth of the forgiveness of sins awakens an understanding of the integrity of our innocence; this naturally leads to a tangible intimacy with the living God and a spontaneous love for people. God pleads through us to bring people to realize their full inclusion in the Gospel.

Let his love in you reveal him to your neighbors and the nations. His love is unthreatened and needs no defense!

Col.4:4 This is my prayer request, that I may be able to present this message in the most effective way possible.

Col. 4:5 Do not spoil your chance to touch others with the word through a lack of wisdom. Redeem the time by making the most of every opportunity. (Time only finds its relevance in redemption-realities)

Col. 4:6 Season your conversation with the revelation of grace. This remains the most attractive and appropriate option to respond in every situation.

The object of New Testament ministry is not in the first place to get people to go to heaven one day! It is the unveiling of the most attractive life possible, the life of our design redeemed again. Now to be enjoyed in an immediate, intimate, daily, constant, conscious feedback encounter with the Living God in Spirit and in truth and undiluted friendship with our fellow man!

He overlooked the times of ignorance and now urges all men everywhere to discover his eternal thoughts about mankind, revealed in Christ, when we were judged in righteousness in one man's death, and raised in his resurrection as the trophy of justice redeemed! Acts 17:30,31. Having made purification for sins he sat down! His throne authority is established upon our redeemed innocence

The more we declare the integrity of God's persuasion concerning us demonstrated in his son's obedience in our favor, the less we have to prompt people to believe, their believing will be most spontaneous!

Even our faith is from him! Eph 2:8 Your salvation was a grace thing from start to finish, you had no hand in it; because it is all God's gift to you, because he believes in you. (Mirror Bible)

Eph 2:8 For by grace you have been saved through faith; and this is not your own doing, it is the gift of God-- (RSV)

Eph 2:8 Your salvation is not a reward for good behavior! It was a grace thing from start to finish; you had no hand in it. Even the gift to believe simply reflects his faith! *(You did not invent faith; it was God's faith to begin with! It is from faith to faith, [Rom 1:17] He is both the source and conclusion of faith. [Heb 12:2])*

Paul preached in such a way that many believed! Acts 14:1 Yet he never asked for a show of hands to indicate their 'decision' to believe!

The more we make an issue of "Now do you believe this? Because if you don't you're going to hell!" the more we disguise the very message we've just proclaimed!

God's work of redemption is valid with immediate effect. "The hour all creation was waiting for has come. The son of man is glorified! The single grain of wheat did not abide alone; it fell into the earth and died and bore much fruit!" John 12:23,24. Mankind died in his death and was made alive together with him and raised together with him and is now seated together with him in heavenly places. Every human life is fully and equally represented and justified in one man's act of righteousness. 2 Cor 5:14,16; Acts 10:28. "Jesus reveals that man pre-existed in God; he defines us. He justified us and also glorified us. He redeemed our innocence and restored the glory we lost in Adam. (Rom 3:23,24; prohoritso, pre defined, like when an architect draws up a detailed plan; kaleo, to surname, identify by name) What further ground can there possibly be to condemn man? In his death he faced our judgment; in his resurrection he declares our innocence; the implications cannot be undone! He now occupies the highest seat of authority as the executive of our redemption in the throne room of God. (See verse 1, also Rom 4:25) Rom 8:30,34

Jesus is what God believes. If every human life is equally included in God's economy of grace then man deserves to hear this Gospel more than what any man deserves to be judged.

Our influence in society, regardless of our profession, is determined by our faith and not our job-description; our faith is sourced in Christ, in his perfect work of reconciling a hostile world to himself. While we proclaim the sinful state of humanity we are not proclaiming the gospel, and life changing faith cannot come to the people! This conviction is critical, if we are serious about impacting our world with the proclamation of the Gospel

It is so sad that we allow the deception of a Christless "universalism" to hijack words like 'inclusion' and 'universal.'

These words powerfully and significantly describe the masterful genius of God when Jesus died humanity's death! This is the mystery that none of the rulers of this world understood, otherwise they would never have crucified the Lord of glory!

The point is that the gospel is good news for all people because the gospel reveals how fully included they are in Christ by God's doing; truth is already true before anyone believes it; a diamond doesn't become a diamond when you discover it, obviously God hid the diamonds and treasures in the earth for man and not from man! That is why we preach with passion, urgency and persuasion in order to awaken every mans mind and instruct every man and present (prove) every man perfect in Christ Col 1:28, because the mystery that was hidden for ages and generations is now revealed

We have underestimated the Gospel of Jesus Christ for centuries, because we have adopted an interpretation that robbed us of the true impact of salvation in its relation to life in the here & now on planet earth. We have felt more comfortable with a faith that refers us to a place in heaven one day rather than to see faith as the now & relevant substance of things we always longed for & the evidence of unseen realities around us & within our grasp; the life of our design is redeemed!

Jesus didn't die 99% or for 99%

He died humanity's death one hundred percent! If Paul had to compromise the last part of verse 14 of 2 Cor 5, to read: "one died for all therefore only those who follow the prescriptions to qualify, have also died," then he would have had to change the first half of the verse as well!

Only the love of Christ can make a calculation of such enormous proportion!

The same all who died in his death were raised together with him! According to the only scripture in the entire OT that refers to the 3rd day resurrection, we are included! "After 2 days God will revive us, on the 3rd day he will raise us up!!" Hos 6:2 When Paul ponders this scripture (he also quotes it in 1 Cor 15:4) he makes one of his most radical discoveries in his gospel; he writes "While we were dead in our sins (before we knew or believed the gospel) God made us alive together with Christ, and raised us (mankind) together with Christ and seated us together with Christ in heavenly places! Eph 2:5,6 This is the point of the gospel; what happened to Christ happened to us before anyone but God believed it! We're not window-shopping here, we are gazing into the mirror!

For so many years we've read 2 Cor 5 verse 17 out of its context! Paul does not say, "If any man be in Christ", he says 'Therefore, if any man be in Christ!' Verse 14 and 16 gives context to verse 17. Therefore the IF cannot be a condition it must be a conclusion otherwise verse 14 also becomes 'iffy'!!

162

The gates of hades will not prevail against the testimony of truth; the weapons of our already won warfare tears down every argument and resistance to the knowledge of God; love wins. I can see even the 'other brother' tapping his foot and awakening to the festive sound!

I suppose I would still have questions if I think about all the contradictions and issues that theology presents us with; but for years now I have determined to go with what I know by revelation concerning his perfect work of redeeming his image in us: to live daily in the full benefit of that and to unveil him in every person I have the privilege to meet; that keeps one pretty busy enjoying him and sharing him!

I am addicted to the Philemon 1:6 kind of koinonia! The koinonia (communication) of our faith is ignited by the acknowledging of every good thing that is in us in Christ!

Exploring the extent of his love initiative and where it leads us truly exceeds any limitation or dimension! And we are all in it together! Wow what eternal bliss and glory we participate in!

The hubble telescope surely increases our horizon daily, only to realize again and again that we are dealing with measureless dimensions in outer space that reflect in us! That we may be filled with all the fulness of God is a thought that breaks all boundaries; we are fearfully and wonderfully made and equally fearfully and wonderfully redeemed!

The whole earth is full of his glory, "and as truly as I live", says the Lord, "all the earth shall be filled with the knowledge of my glory, even as the waters cover the sea!" Jesus said: if you believe that I am what the scriptures are all about, then you will discover that you are what I am all about and rivers of living waters will gush out of your innermost being! John 7:37

The good news unveils the love of God spectacularly! The dimensions of his love exceed any concept we could possibly have of height, length, breadth or depth!

The gospel can be underestimated, but never exaggerated! The half could not be told of Solomon's wisdom and wealth and in Luke 11 Jesus says, "A greater than Solomon is here"!

Rev 5:13 And I heard every creature in heaven and on earth and under the earth and in the sea, and all therein, saying, "To him who sits upon the throne and to the Lamb be blessing and honor and glory and might forever and ever!"

While we argue that all would be okay regardless, we still miss the point! The urgency to communicate this gospel is not compromised thru speculations about the future, but constrained by the revelation of how God's faith included hostile indifferent mankind in the sacrificial death of Christ, and his triumphant resurrection, when he represented the entire human race; multitudes are living in torment right now because they have never heard the truth of their redemption; what a waste to postpone redemption to life hereafter if it can happen now! How all will eventually discover what they have missed and how they will be 'judged' is none of our business anyway; it is our business to live the living epistle to be known and read by all men! And to give everyone within earshot on this planet the opportunity to hear truth that ignites life-changing faith!

The greatest hell anyone can face in any age is the torment of the ignorance of their true redeemed identity revealed in Christ as in a mirror.

Before we assume the right to condemn anyone to hell lets discover the height and length and breadth and depth of the love of Christ that surpasses knowledge and declare the gospel that reveals that something bigger has happened to man in Christ than what happened to man in Adam!

"On this mountain the Lord will swallow up that veil that shrouds all the peoples, the pall thrown over all the nations; he will swallow up death forever. Then the Lord God will wipe away the tears from every face and remove the reproach of his people from the whole earth." Isaiah 25:7-8, The New English Bible

BEGOTTEN

Does the rain have a Father?

Who begot the drops of dew?

Who birthed the morning?

Caused the dawn to know its place?

Have you comprehended the expanses of the earth?

Have you comprehended their origin?

He knows you by name

His design is his claim

He boldly declares, "Measure me"

Have you measured your heart?

Have you measured the volume of your being?

He has chosen you to accommodate the fullness of his dream

Have you comprehended? He is at home within your heart,

A dwelling built within you without walls.

Take my love to its conclusion.

Take my love to every man,

Count the stars, count the sand

Measure the nations in my Hand,

Come on now, measure me

I fulfill your eternity.

(This song was written by Anthea, she was part of our ministry called, the Acts Team in the eighties and only 19 years old then.)

Francois grew up in a home where Jesus was loved and lived. His parents were in fulltime ministry in an interdenominational mission. His eldest brother Leon, is a missionary in the Ukraine and Russia for many years.

Lydia and Francois met on the 25th of August 1974, while he was working with Youth For Christ. She was sixteen and he nineteen! The following year he studied Greek and Hebrew at the University of Pretoria for three years while Lydia completed her nursing training. In 1978 Francois also spent a year with Youth with a Mission.

They married in January 1979 and are blessed with four amazing children, Renaldo, Tehilla, Christo and Stefan. They worked in fulltime mission for fourteen years, during which time they also pastored a church and led a training facility for more than 700 students over a five-year period.

They then left the ministry and for ten years did business mainly in the tourism industry. They built and managed a Safari Lodge in the Sabi Sand Game Reserve and eventually relocated to Hermanus where they started Southern Right boat-based whale watching.

In December 2000 Francois began to write the book, "God believes in You" which led to him being invited to speak at various Christian camps and churches.

They are now back in fulltime ministry since February 2004, and travel at least once a year abroad and almost every month into Africa and around South Africa.

Francois has written several books in both English and Afrikaans, including God Believes in You, Divine Embrace, Done! and The Mystery Revealed. He is currently passionately engaged in continuing with *The Mirror Translation.*

His work is being translated into several African languages as well as Chinese, Russian, Hungarian, German, French, Spanish, Polish, Portugese, Dutch and Slovakian.

They reach thousands of people daily on facebook and bulk email. You can also subscribe to his daily devotionals.

REFERENCES & RESOURCES

Referred to by the author's name or by some abridgment of the title.

BBE (1949, Bible in Basic English)

Andre Rabe (www.hearhim.net)

Clarence Jordan (Cotton Patch Gospel - Paul's Epistles by Clarence Jordan - Smyth & Helwys Pub. 2004)

J.B. Phillips Translation (Geoffrey Bles London 1960)

KJV (King James Version - In 1604, King James I of England authorized that a new translation of the Bible into English. It was finished in 1611)

Knox Translation (Translated from the Vulgate Latin by Ronald Knox Published in London by Burns Oates and Washbourne Ltd. 1945)

NEB (New English Bible New Testament - Oxford & Cambridge University Press 1961)

RSV (The Revised Standard Version is an authorized revision of the American Standard Version, published in 1901, which was a revision of the King James Version, published in 1611.)

The Message (Eugene H. Peterson Nav Press Publishing Group)

Weymouth New Testament *(M.A., D.Lit. 1822-1902)*

CPSIA information can be obtained at www.ICGtesting.com
Printed in the USA
LVOW011719291112

309398LV00022B/1082/P